THE POLITICS OF THE NEAR

THE POLITICS OF THE NEAR

On the Edges of Protest in South Africa

JÉRÔME TOURNADRE

Translated by Andrew Brown

FORDHAM UNIVERSITY PRESS NEW YORK 2022

Frontispiece: RDP House. District of Vukani. Grahamstown.

Fordham University Press gratefully acknowledges financial assistance and support provided for the publication of this book by the Institut des sciences sociales du politique (CNRS, Univ. Paris Nanterre, ENS Paris Saclay, Univ. Paris Lumières).

Library of Congress Cataloging-in-Publication Data available online at https://catalog.loc.gov.

Library of Congress Cataloging-in-Publication Data

Names: Tournadre, Jérôme, author. | Brown, Andrew (Literary translator), translator.
Title: The politics of the near : on the edges of protest in South Africa / Jérôme Tournadre ; translated by Andrew Brown.
Description: New York : Fordham University Press, 2022. | Series: Thinking from elsewhere | Includes bibliographical references and index.
Identifiers: LCCN 2022010493 | ISBN 9780823299966 (hardback) | ISBN 9780823299959 (paperback) | ISBN 9780823299973 (epub)
Subjects: LCSH: Protest movements—South Africa. | Social movements—South Africa. | Social change—South Africa. | South Africa—Social conditions—1994–
Classification: LCC HN801.A8 T6913 2022 | DDC 303.48/40968—dc23/eng/20220307
LC record available at https://lccn.loc.gov/2022010493

Printed in the United States of America

24 23 22   5 4 3 2 1

First edition

For my eldest son, Ulysse

CONTENTS

THE POLITICS OF THE NEAR

INTRODUCTION

To begin with, there was a rumor: women's bodies found in the veld, the grassy and shrubby savannah surrounding the town. It was being claimed in particular that these bodies had been dismembered to be used in traditional medicine. Word of mouth quickly spread that a man had been arrested, a Muslim trader from Pakistan. In October 2015, Grahamstown was soon awash with the muddy waters of xenophobia. Over just a few days, nearly a hundred businesses run by Pakistanis, Bengalis, and Chinese people, but also by Zimbabweans, Nigerians, and Ethiopians, were looted, destroyed, or burned down by crowds of often young Black women and men. In the early hours of the second day, with no letup in clashes between looters and police, three military helicopters crisscrossed the sky. And yet, as the mayor and police officials tried to convince the public in the following days, no bodies had been profaned, and there was no foreigner suspected of black magic in the recent records of the Grahamstown police station.

Early accounts of these xenophobic attacks, including those published in the daily press, established that the violence had first swept through small shops in the town center owned by Pakistani traders before spreading east into the township.[1] It all seemed to have started with a demonstration of taxi owners and drivers. These taxis are private minivans that make up for the lack of public transport in a more or less formal context. Gathered under the windows of the town hall, these drivers wished to protest against the bad maintenance of the streets and roads within the conurbation. This rally was illegal, not anticipated by the authorities, and not supervised by the police. Very quickly, it seems, corporatist chants gave way to slogans hostile to the "foreigners," accused of criminal activities in the township.

These collective acts of violence in the spring of 2015 were not without precedent in the history of the young South African democracy. While there were no deaths in Grahamstown, the lynchings that had taken place in Johannesburg six months earlier had claimed about a dozen victims. Long before that, in May 2008, a wave of aggressions prompted several thousand families from Zimbabwe, Malawi, Somalia, the Democratic Republic of Congo, and Burundi to take refuge in the country's police stations and churches to seek some semblance of protection. Ten days of rioting followed, which left more than sixty dead.

The many analyses generated by this "dark side" of South African democracy (see Crush 2000; Neocosmos 2006; Crush, Chikanda, and Skinner 2015) have brought to light some of the political and socioeconomic roots of the hatred of foreigners. The fact that this is sometimes tinged with beliefs in supernatural phenomena such as witchcraft and zombification (Comaroff and Comaroff 2003) should not deceive us. This surprising coupling actually masks more trivial realities such as anxieties about unemployment and poverty, considerations on the "immorality" of foreigners, and a more general crisis of social reproduction (Hickel 2014, 106–107). It also attests to the success of a discourse on national identity that reduces the world to an opposition between "autochthons" and "aliens" (Comaroff and Comaroff 2012).

Looters, rioters, police officers, soldiers, and victims figured in an initially convincing picture of those troubled days in Grahamstown. But this picture would be incomplete if one particular group of women and men were omitted from it. In the early hours, a few dozen people made their way through the Black and poor neighborhoods in the grip of violence to help foreign traders and their families to find shelter. For several days they attempted to bring the violence to an end by talking with community leaders in the most severely affected neighborhoods and trying to reason with looters they sometimes knew personally, since they frequently ran into them in their neighborhoods. They also organized meetings in the hope of restoring calm. It was these same people who, one month later, joined a vigil in front of the town hall held by a hundred or so people badly affected by the disturbances, requesting the necessary help from the authorities to return to a normal life. These residents were members of, or linked to, a relatively visible organization in the Grahamstown social landscape, an organization that usually militates against poor living conditions in the local township and informal settlements, where the unrest was most intense: the Unemployed People's Movement (UPM).

The UPM is one of those protest groups that have contributed to the emergence of a social movement representing the poor in postapartheid South Africa (Ballard, Habib, and Valodia 2006; Pithouse 2006; Beinart and Dawson 2010; Dawson and Sinwell 2012; Brown 2015; Paret, Runciman, and Sinwell 2017; Tournadre 2018; Chance 2018). These structures, which include the Anti-Privatisation Forum (Johannesburg), the Concerned Citizens' Group (Durban), the Anti-Eviction Campaign (Cape Town), the Soweto Electricity Crisis Committee (Johannesburg), the Landless People's Movement (Johannesburg), and Abahlali baseMjondolo ("those who live in shacks," Cape Town and Durban) often gave voices and faces to the discontent that, at the dawn of the twenty-first century, spread through the poorest areas in the country. The reasons for this anger were quite simple: lack of housing; poor, nonexistent, or unaffordable access to basic services (water, electricity, health); the economic inability of the youngest people to gain independence from their families; domestic violence and crime in the township; unemployment. All these problems pointed to the failure of the promises of "a better life for all"[2] that had accompanied the establishment of a liberal democracy from the mid-1990s onward. It was therefore largely the question of the building and proper functioning of the home, raised by these processions of women and young and middle-aged men that directly challenged the legitimacy of the democratic political elites.

While the anger did not subside in the course of the 2010s, the main organizations that until then had embodied it gradually melted away (see Runciman 2015). This was not the case for the UPM, founded in 2009 in Grahamstown. Its members have regularly addressed their concerns to the authorities of this midsized town in the Eastern Cape, one of the poorest provinces in the country. They have demonstrated against the delays in the development of the lower-class neighborhoods, participated in the construction of barricades on the roads that run past the many local shantytowns, organized sit-ins against the corruption of local elected officials, gone on marches to denounce the sexual violence gnawing away at the township, and dumped buckets of excrement in the atrium of the town hall to remind the mayor that, just a few miles away from the comfort of his office, the system that is supposed to overcome the lack of toilet facilities by using simple plastic buckets—the bucket system—remains a reality for hundreds of those in his town.[3] To put it more concisely, the UPM *claims* and *protests*.[4]

Before going any further, it may be necessary to point out the extent to which the history of South African society has helped to make protest a fairly commonplace means of participation in the eyes of many inhabitants, even though it is often viewed with suspicion in Western liberal democracies. As the institutional political space was forbidden to nonwhites, it was into demonstrations and protest marches that a large part of the socio-political expression of these populations was directed in the apartheid years. At first glance, the start of the democratic era seems not to have completely reversed this order of things. Between 15 percent and 25 percent of Black South Africans claimed to have taken part in this "contentious politics" in one way or another (signing petitions, marches, participating in rallies, painting slogans on the walls, etc.) between 1994 and 2000 (Klandermans, Roefs, and Olivier 2001, 215). However, the repression and criminalization that befell any challenge to government policies from the late 1990s onward (see Chapter 10; see also McKinley and Veriava 2005) strongly invite us to put such figures into perspective. More generally, the "normalization" that its new leaders wanted to impose on South Africa very quickly called into question the status of protest within the spectrum of legitimate forms of participation. Emblematic of the struggle in the 1980s, the figure of the young Black activist organizing an uprising in his community was doomed to embody extremism and disorder (Barchiesi 2011, 66), since it was necessary to reassure people (both within and outside national borders) that the new elites were able to govern the country. The last decade of apartheid, however, had seen thousands of young people locally challenging white power and thereby experiencing a certain form of politics in their very own flesh. Pamela Reynolds (2013) surveyed about fifteen of them as the country entered the democratic era. She recounted their young years, ravaged by the war that the apartheid regime had waged against them a few years earlier. They were just teenagers and had been exposed in their daily lives to betrayal, humiliation, suffering and state violence. After 1994, however, little support or reparation "for opportunities lost" (103) were conceded by a democratic society to which they could well feel they had contributed. As Reynolds suggests, it was perhaps not "in the interests of those in authority" to recognize the "experiences of youth in conflict" (107). It is an anger often imbued with this same lack of recognition and consideration that will be encountered in this book.

It sometimes happens, however, that UPM militants depart from their primary object, namely protest. This was the case in the short narrative with which I began. With the exception of the evening vigil, the attention of these women and men was only rarely directed to the representatives of political authority over those days of violence. There are also other moments, less dramatic, when those individuals undertake actions where banners and demands are not appropriate either; actions far removed from those sometimes noisy confrontations with the spokespersons of politico-administrative power that so often serve as a starting point for defining collective protest movements. *This*, to a large extent, is what this text will focus on: all those moments, those interactions, those actions, those utterances where *protest is no longer just protest.*[5]

One could, by forcing things a bit, consider that the following pages draw mainly on scraps. Like the pieces of cloth or wood that the tailor or carpenter discards after making a cut, the material of this text comes from observations and reflections that the sociology and anthropology of social movements might be tempted to ignore, so remote do they seem from social protest.[6] These fragments were often collected during days imbued with boredom, spent without any real purpose on the premises of the organizations in question, gradually coming to realize the obvious: militant time, even protest time, largely consists of waiting. I was witness to innocuous conversations between activists and people from the outside, mostly neighbors. I was also present in situations seemingly disconnected from the heroic deeds and logic of protest—situations that might include neighborhood conflicts or family disputes for which the mediation of activists was desired. At other times, these same individuals were working, among other things, to convince poor people in Grahamstown to plant a vegetable garden alongside their modest homes. In these different frameworks, the state, the ruling party—the African National Congress (ANC)—and the municipal authorities were no longer in the firing line of the women and men who, in spite of everything, continued to act on behalf of the protest collective. The main difference from what I could observe the rest of the time was that these activists were then entirely turned toward the neighborhood, caught up in its social mesh. The repetition of these moments has therefore led me to develop a first hypothesis: we cannot see and understand any protest movement as a whole if we focus only on "those moments in which people gathered to make vigorous, visible, public claims, acted on those claims in one way or another, then turned to other business" (Tilly 1995, 32). Attention should also be brought to bear on some of this "other business" that appears on *the edges of protest*, away from banners, barricades, marches, and other clashes with the police that give substance to contentious politics.[7] This hypothesis lies behind the *parti pris* that my book is based on. In my view, trying to avoid a certain political bias justified an attempt to *(re)embed* protest in the realm of the *social*, or at least in one of its various forms. To begin with, it is one of the most obvious forms, the one that shapes the immediate environment of the agents of protest, that I will here focus on: the mesh of relations, institutions, and configurations that make up the social life in the lower-class districts in which the rumbles of anger can be heard.[8] So I will let myself be guided by an obvious fact that the noise of demonstrations sometimes makes us forget: far from being a free-floating object, protest is rooted in frequently regular and repeated relations—relations that are sometimes described as "normal" (Auyero 2005, 128). Such an approach is obviously not entirely new. It partly forms the heart of the very fine book in which Roger Gould (1995) compared the 1848 French revolution with the Commune. In particular, he showed the importance of forms of sociability at district level and neighborhood solidarities in the emergence of the latter. The following pages obviously owe much to his research, even if the ordinary aspects of local life will here be more central. The attention paid to the normal and usual order of things in the township will lead me to dive into the living conditions of activists and their contemporaries, to explore the multiple social regulations of their neighborhood, to understand the place and the role they occupy in it, and so on. Adopting an approach that stands at something of an angle to more traditional forms of the analysis of collective movements will, however, justify taking things a little further. In fact, it will also be a matter of catching a glimpse through the doors of the private worlds of the individuals who lie at the center of this book, so as to apprehend those repeated experiences which help to shape what is habitually called subjectivity: "the felt interior experience of the person that includes his or her positions in a field of relational power" (Das and Kleinman 2000, 1).

Because it is most often adorned with habits and repetitions, the ordinary is what goes without saying for individuals. It is what is *already there*; what they can on principle take for granted. The ordinary therefore has marked affinities with everyday life, that temporality where what is instituted is produced and maintained (Buton et al. 2016). Such a presumption of regularity obviously does not make ordinary life a smooth and uniform thing, without any relief. Often seen as involving a certain banality, it is also characterized "by ambivalences, perils, puzzles, contradictions, accommodations and transformative possibilities" (Neal and Murji 2015, 812). As Veena Das notes, the everyday is both the site of "routines, habits, and conventions" and of "disorders, doubts, and despair" (2014, 285). At the end of an ethnographic study that took some fifteen years, Fiona Ross (2010) convincingly brought out the terms of this complexity. She achieved this by observing, day by day, the lives of poor people living on the outskirts of Cape Town, in places that are altogether similar to some of those that will be depicted in the course of the following pages. In a context where the fragility of people's lives was the dominant factor, Ross emphasized how "disruption was part of everyday life" (71). The same imperative imposed itself continually on these women and these men: they had to show enough "social dexterity" (i.e., a mixture of "social skills and networks of relations to make ends meet in times of need," 123–124) if they were to endow the everyday with a minimum of stability and predictability. The development and maintenance over time of daily rhythms and routines thus became an objective in itself. However, these efforts were constantly under threat from an environment in which incomes were unreliable, jobs scarce, and bodies exposed to violence and disease. Much of what I observed over the 2010s fell into the continuity of the reality described by Fiona Ross in the two previous decades. It is largely this continuity—in other words, the persistence of "raw life" for millions of South Africans—which, in my view, helps us understand the sense of abandonment and social relegation often expressed by the individuals at the center of this book. A work such as that of Ross also shows how the ordinary is not a site to be overlooked when one thinks about the forms and localizations of the political. Daily life in this poor community was indeed shaped by multiple relationships of dependence and domination, whether they were racial, sexual, domestic, or bureaucratic, related to generation or social class. More generally, it was also in the very midst of the ordinary that individuals assumed, and made their own, certain norms and social forms by trying to conform to them. Ross shows this very clearly when she dissects the ideal of "respectability" that poor households set for themselves, an ideal that also underlined how much these women and men had incorporated their marginality vis-à-vis the "South African miracle." These contradictions and discrepancies, which in part reflect the state of a society, are undoubtedly political.

Ordinary and everyday life are no strangers to the analysis of protest. The studies that deal with this relationship try, more often than not, to understand how a questioning of authority dresses itself in the clothes of the ordinary, in particular in the form of more or less silent, more or less explicitly endorsed resistances, rebellions, or struggles. The work of theorization undertaken by James Scott (1985, 1990) provides a perfect illustration of this. The author of *Weapons of the Weak* has shown how subordinate groups can daily challenge the domination of the powerful through discrete, hidden, or anonymous gestures and behaviors. These resistances are "infrapolitical" forms of protest that develop away from the control of the dominant groups. They are, according to Scott, the most common way of criticizing the social order in societies where subaltern groups do not have any opportunity to publicly express their disagreement.

In what, this time, is an explicitly different perspective from the "literature of resistance," Asef Bayat has focused on what he calls the "quiet encroachment of the ordinary" (1998). This may include the illegal constructions built by some of the disenfranchised or the activities of street vendors and the like. In fact, under this concept Bayat brings together "non-collective but prolonged direct action[s] by individuals and families to acquire the basic necessities of their lives (land for shelter, urban collective consumption, informal jobs, business opportunities and public space) in a quiet and unassuming illegal fashion" (Bayat 2000, 536). In Bayat's view, this type of action cannot be analyzed as a "politics of protest" (549). Illegally tapping into a water or electricity network, for example, is not in itself a resistance to some form of oppression. It is, more simply, a necessity for millions of women and men throughout the world, particularly in what is often referred to as the Global South.[9] These acts nonetheless lie at the root of "significant social changes" (Bayat 1998, 5). The "immediate outcomes" to which they lead help these urban poor to improve their material existences. Above all, even if they are not imagined as deliberately political acts by those who carry them out, such encroachments are a direct test of state domination. This pragmatic, day-to-day playing with norms raises questions about state prerogatives, such as "the meaning of order, control of public space, of public and private goods and the relevance of modernity" (Bayat 2000, 546).

We could thus give many more examples attesting to the interest of the social sciences in the marriage between the ordinary, the everyday, and more or less explicit forms of protest, resistance to an oppressor, and autonomization vis-à-vis the rules set by the state.[10] In the early 1990s, Arturo Escobar (1992, 420) even called for an anthropology of social movements that focused on the "micro-level of everyday practices and their imbrication with larger processes of development, patriarchy, capital and the state." Some of these practices, indeed, can be found in the "ethnographic study of domestic worlds" that Anne-Maria Makhulu (2015, 1) has carried out in squatter camps on the outskirts of Cape Town. More often than not, however, these contributions concentrate on actions whose horizon does not exclude a relation (of power) with those in authority. Of course, this is explicitly at the heart of the demonstrations of Scott, whose ideas are based on an oppressor/oppressed model. This relationship is also latent in the work of Bayat: the urban poor need to ensure that they do not pass a certain "tolerable point" (1998, 14) when they seek to get round the regulations and disciplines fixed by the state. If they go any further, the state will resort to repressive measures and will threaten the gains they have patiently obtained, which will then lead to those conflicts characteristic of what Bayat designates as "street politics."[11]

I have no intention of arguing against these models, which have made possible a nuanced way of apprehending subaltern agency, especially in nondemocratic regimes. It is simply that the heart of my book lies on another level. Oversimplifying somewhat, we might say that it is not the reflection of protest or rebellion in the daily routine of life that will be most important here, but its exact opposite. I will be examining what, in the uneventful character of both the *social* and the *personal* lives of the poor residents in a township, sheds light on certain aspects of their protest. This approach will therefore sometimes intersect with Alpa Shah's invitation to enter the "intimacy of insurgency" by going "beyond grievance" (2013). Shah has shown how much the spread of Maoist guerrilla warfare in the Indian state of Jharkhand was encouraged not only by the anger of people condemned to poverty but also by the development of intimate relations between these people and the revolutionaries. The Maoists could even be perceived by the villagers "as part of an extended family." Sian Lazar's anthropology of Argentinian trade union *militancia* (2017) adopts a different approach to intimacy. It explores some of the "intimate spaces of political activism within a social movement" (9), emphasizing activists' family lives, friendships, and daily existences. However, the trade union, its history, its mode of operation and the activism associated with it remain at the center of Lazar's analysis. Conversely, my aim is to seek the ordinary and the intimate *beyond* the political struggle and the borders of the collective (even if, as we shall see, the organizational boundaries of a poor people's movement are difficult to define).

In short, the bias of this text is to start from what makes the existence of South Africa's poor populations in order to better understand the shaping and expression of their discontent, and not to apprehend the latter when it is already built and inscribed within the binding framework of its relationship to political power.

It is thus a decentering of analysis that this book will set out. It will propose that we leave the space of protest as such, so as better to explore the apparently more ordinary territory on its periphery. More precisely, it will try to see what is *also* happening *in parallel with* what usually attracts the specialists' attention, moving away from questions of political socialization and activist experience (preexisting or not) of individuals. Such a shifting of attention is not a mere piece of coquetry. The ambition of the pages that follow is, on the contrary, to emphasize how much this shift can refine our understanding of movements similar to that of the unemployed in Grahamstown. Beyond its peculiarities, the UPM can indeed be linked to the extended family of poor people's movements (see Zorn 2013), these collective and concerted mobilizations of women and men whose lives seem to be mainly shaped away from the processes that organize production, consumption, and, very often, official political representation in a society. While it may nurture a sense of collective isolation (which reinforces identification with the group), this apparent life on the sidelines does not amount to total exclusion, however. Things are always more complex and changing. Thus, the informal economy, regularly associated with poor populations, is far from constituting an insular set of activities. Even if they are found on the fringes of societies, these individuals and their friends and relatives are regularly in contact with some of the central axes of state activity (see Das and Poole 2004). From the point of view of activism alone, they are also not prohibited, as we will see, from directly competing with local representatives of the "official" political world. The following pages, however, will focus on how poverty can be more than a statistical reality. It also involves the shared experience of forms of discrimination that reflect being assigned to a social category (the fact, for example, of being denied in one's subjectivity by those in a dominant position, as we will see regularly in this book). It is in large part this phenomenon that contributes to the formation of a group apart in a society, prompting some of its members to mobilize in a collective such as the one at the center of *The Politics of the Near*.

The study of poor people's movements has occupied an important place in the social sciences, and has done so for several decades (Piven and Cloward, 1977; Gamson and Schmeidler 1984). However, the notion is not exempt from criticism. Like another flagship category in anthropology and sociology, namely that of the "urban poor" (Das and Walton 2015), it can in fact be accused of reducing local particularities and, consequently, of standardizing what it is supposed to describe. The warning should particularly be heeded in this present case. The fact that the poor at the center of this book are Black is obviously no accident and must, more precisely, be understood in the light of the postcoloniality of South African society. Even in a country free from apartheid, poverty still has a certain color: in 2015, 93 percent of South Africans living below the poverty line were Black (Statistics South Africa 2017, 57). The reasons for this intertwining of race and class lie mainly in the way the economic order has been constructed and reproduced since the early days of colonization. The concept of "racial capitalism," although debated and controversial, certainly helps to encapsulate this genesis with some precision. As sociologist John Rex has emphasized, unlike a more conventional capitalism, based on the expansion of market relations and on a production system using "free labor," the South African model profited from the conquest of the Bantu peoples, the grabbing of their land, and their integration into a system based on "unfree labor" (Rex 1973; Hall 1980). The systematization of segregation from the end of the nineteenth century institutionalized and hierarchized races, thus enshrining white supremacy (Terreblanche 2002). The end of apartheid and the efforts of democratic governments to promote a Black capitalist elite, sometimes in the name of "racial nationalism" (MacDonald 2004), have not, however, undermined the foundations of South African capitalism. Mainly owned by white interests, the capitalist system continues to rely largely on the exploitation of "cheap black labor" and a "highly unequal and racialized partition of land."[12] Now, however, its needs no longer justify the absorption of all the low-skilled or unskilled Black workforce on which its expansion has depended for decades. Over the years, large segments of the Black working population have consequently been relegated to a "wageless life" (Denning 2010), which has, without difficulty, convinced these women and men that blackness continued to define "a condition of marginality" (Posel 2013, 73). Social protest activists operate with this conviction on a daily basis, which in turn feeds the belief that they have been betrayed by the ANC elites. Claiming, in the early 2010s, that apartheid "was only abolished on paper," one of the leaders of the unemployed in Grahamstown summed it up pretty well: "we Blacks are tired of standing at the touchlines to witness a game that we should be playing."[13] In sum, if entry into liberal democracy has allowed a large aspect of citizenship to be detached from race, by granting the same political and civil rights to all the population, the movement seems—to put it mildly—unfinished. I will come back to this.

These sociohistorical peculiarities, which are regularly found in other postcolonial contexts, do not preclude identifying a set of shared features that make it possible to use this category of "poor people's movement," a kind of common and minimal base that can be observed in a large number of mobilizations of the poor and that is well reflected in a rapid analysis by the UPM.

At first glance, the cause defended by this South African collective appears to be a national one, since it is supposed to merge with the interests of all those who have not benefited from the development promised in 1994. The organization, via its press releases (but in other ways too), turns its fight into a component of the "Rebellion of the Poor"[14] that swept through the country in the first decade of the twenty-first century. Parallels are also frequently drawn with international protest movements such as the Occupy movement or the movement denouncing the situation of Palestinians in the West Bank. However, this same cause is mainly dominated by exclusively local expectations of concrete results, as reflected by the almost systematic way that demands are addressed to the municipality and rarely to the state. In addition, if more sophisticated slogans, such as those of the fight against "patriarchy" or for LGBTI rights in the township, can find their way into some of the protests of the movement, they never take precedence over demands for jobs, access to housing, sanitation, and so on. This focus on very tangible things, arising from the demands of the immediate, is found outside South Africa and is one of the characteristics of many poor people's movements around the world. It can be found, among other places, in Asef Bayat's conclusions from his study of politics and "ordinary people" in the Middle East:

> "Low-politics," or localized struggles for concrete concerns, are the stuff of the urban dispossessed. For the dispossessed, it is largely the localized struggles, unlike the abstract and distant notions of "revolution" or "reform," that are both meaningful and manageable—meaningful in that they can make sense of the purpose and have an idea of the consequences of those actions, and manageable in that *they,* rather than some remote national . . . leaders, set the agenda, project the aims, and control the outcome. (Bayat 2010, 201)

Behind these "concrete concerns," we can sense everything that ought to comprise a proper life in the eyes of those who live in an informal settlement, a township, a slum, or a favela, and in particular the hope of a home offering the possibility of a "normal" existence, without depending on the sun's cycle for one's light and heat. (However, as we will see, these materialistic claims are not devoid of moral and symbolic foundations, as the quest for dignity or recognition.) The demarcation between the extraordinary nature of revolt and the ordinary nature of everyday life therefore tends to diminish. Perhaps it would be more accurate to say that there are in fact a multitude of connections, links, and interpenetrations between the two. There is nothing very surprising about this. Wherever they occur in the world, the struggles of poor people's movements generally reflect the condition of those who comprise them and those they seek to mobilize. The reason is quite simple: "Most people in the world have very little money; so, most people depend on spatially situated sociality for child care, for security, for caring of the sick, for fire fighting, and for burying their dead" (Pithouse 2013, 105). And we could add to this list: "for activism." Among these populations, those who become politically committed do so in a very specific relationship to the world, "rooted" in a familiar and habitual environment. This obviously does not preclude some of them, more specifically their leaders, from traveling into and even out of their country, like the "rooted cosmopolitans" described by Sidney Tarrow,[15] in order to share their experience. The sense of rootedness, however, remains fundamental and consubstantial. It does explicitly lie at the heart of this notion of "community-based organization" that UPM activists regularly brandish with pride so as to define their collective. This relationship with the local sphere is obviously not specific to the poor people's movements. We find it in other types of collective mobilizations. It is, of course, the case with NIMBY movements, which "resist the siting of some unwanted land use in a particular neighborhood, community, or region" (Driscoll 2013, 852). These movements can also be led by rich people determined to fight against what they perceive as a threat to their private property. Even more generally, it is in any case not an overstatement to conclude that there is "an embodiment and emplacement to human life that cannot be denied" (Escobar 2008, 7). However, this seems to me even truer in the case of poor people. The link between these groups and the local sphere is thus part of an order of things from which their members can hardly be separated. (I am aware, however, of the case of individuals forced to emigrate for economic reasons.) As a result, the space in which their mobilizations are organized merges quite perfectly with their places of life, where the worlds of experience that shape their subjectivities unfold. On the basis of this postulate, I intend, throughout this book, to demonstrate that the social relations characterizing one space (the space of the struggle) overlap or regularly intersect with those that define the other (the space of everyday life, the familiar, and the ordinary), and vice versa. This justifies continually reexamining and reworking what constitutes the backbone of the book: the multiple links that activists of a movement of the poor weave *with* and *in* their places of life (especially as residents, interacting with other residents) and some of the moral and socioeconomic experiences that they have to live out on a daily basis (in a personal capacity or as members of one of the poor communities of the city, for example). It is therefore important to understand the nature of these relationships and experiences and to determine their points of attachment to the cause. I believe the study of the Unemployed People's Movement makes this possible. In 2009, responding to journalists, one of the main leaders highlighted his status as a "casual worker"[16] to justify his presence at the head of the first major demonstration held by the young organization in the streets of his city. The collective cause and the personal history of the activist thus echoed one another: *I am demonstrating because what I am experiencing here and now, what provides the raw material for my commitment and the cause I support, justifies it.*

Such a formula synthesizes quite perfectly some of the most basic characteristics of poor people's mobilizations. Above all, it makes it possible to include the commitment of these women and men in the "regime of the near" ("*régime du proche*"): sociologist Laurent Thévenot sees it as connected to the way in which "personal and local ties increasingly form the basis of social movements: these may be proximity to an endangered environment, one's own body being affected by a harmful substance or a disease, or a deficient habitat" (Thévenot 2006, 220). Thévenot supports his argument with reference to the movements of unemployed French people, in which "the expression of distress is often validated by the authenticity of a personal violation" (220).

Nothing suggests that this "regime of the near"[17] is particularly recent or peculiar to contemporary social movements. We *rarely* find any trace of it in the antinuclear movement or in protests against animal experiments. Unlike poor people's movements, these are not always "tied to specific populations" and sometimes even mobilize socially very diverse groups. Their members most often criticize and contest "what they perceive as undesirable conditions or future human catastrophes affecting humanity in general" (Morris and Braine 2001, 33). Finally, and perhaps most important, they do not *systematically* have a "personal history, directly related to the movement" (Mansbridge 2001b, 9) and its cause. On the other hand, this latter is one of the main characteristics of individuals participating in the mobilizations of the poor. This is why it is, in my opinion, justified to speak of "regime of the near" when we are interested in the commitment of the women and men who join these movements: what is affected and justifies commitment lies literally at the heart of the symbolic and material worlds in which these individuals move daily. Perhaps it is for this reason that commitment is most often presented as obvious by those it has taken hold of. After a first, somewhat stereotypical discourse, the reasons given for what has prompted people to mobilize are often the same and betray an emotion that, to my mind, is quite unfeigned: "because we're suffering."

Resorting to the regime of the near does not mean conceptualizing for the sole, vain pleasure of playing with abstractions. "Concepts plunder but never exhaust the wealth of experience," as Michael D. Jackson points out (1995, 5). These intellectual constructions also often tend to crush anything that does not fit into the reality they claim to portray. There is also the risk of decking out the fragile lives I am studying in abstractions and thus playing into the hands of a certain aestheticization of poverty. Concepts are in fact useful only when they allow themselves to be "observed walking on dry land, in a given empirical context" (Scott 2008, 4). The interest of the regime of the near is that it both accounts for an empirical reality and operates as an analytical category closely tied to a process in itself.

The first task of the following pages will therefore be to describe this reality by going back to the origins of the aforementioned "ties," whether in the lives of activists, in their subjectivity, or in the social landscape of Grahamstown. In particular, such an approach reveals in depth what claims owe to ordinary phenomena of domination, be they based on race, gender, or class. Anchored in proximity, the familiar and the usual, and even in the intimate, the regime of the near should therefore encourage us not to try and understand the dynamics of mobilization solely by the yardstick of protest activity in the strict sense of the term. One example, which will be discussed at greater length throughout this text, will be enough to convince the reader: that of the legitimacy of the UPM when it claims, with some success, to speak on behalf of the poor of the city. This legitimacy, essential to the early stages of any mobilization, draws on different sources, all of which reflect the rootedness of the movement and its practices in the everyday environment of the people of Grahamstown. It relies in particular on the private and intimate activity of activists (when they render services to their neighbors, for example), but also on the social positions some of them occupy in their neighborhood (I am here thinking of those who claim to be community leaders, though there are other examples). However, these various social relations are external to those in which the heart of protest activity lies. They do not appear systematically when one is interested solely in demonstrations.

Writing this, I am not suggesting that the analysis of social movements in general is limited to the moment and the gesture of protest. The almost constant interest shown by such analysis in the trajectories of activists and their previous socialization would prove me wrong. Similarly, my attempt to reembed the protest and its agents in the social networks of poor South

African neighborhoods sometimes borrows from the "spatial turn" on which part of the sociology of protest movements has been engaged since the end of the twentieth century (Tilly 2000; Sewell 2001). As Javier Auyero notes, some of this work has shown that "space determines everyday life as well as acts of contestation, without, therefore, there being a break between the two" (2005, 126). However, the near, as I conceive it, cannot be reduced to any spatiality, to any relationship with the local or a "place attachment" (Scannell and Robert 2010; Lewicka 2011). Admittedly, in the case of the poor people's movements, the constrained mobility of individuals gives them a "lived sense of place" (Pithouse 2013, 105) doubtless central in the architecture of their worlds. But the near is not just a matter of GPS coordinates. *It is what makes the daily life of an individual.* As such, it is the sum of the places involved, of course, but also of the people and interactions that make up the material and sensitive worlds in which individuals operate and with which they identify. It bears repeating: these worlds are woven from the social and moral experiences to which the women and men involved in the mobilization are exposed; through these experiences are shaped some of their activist subjectivities. They are, more generally, worlds of habits, attachments and memories, repetitions and belongings; worlds, too, where *what we care about* can be found. Finally, familiar worlds are, in large part, *common worlds.* Those of the UPM activists are thus largely shaped by the poverty that haunts the physical, symbolic, and intimate landscapes in which these people operate on a daily basis. It is on this common experience that the movement and its cause are built. The fact that everyone claims to be "poor" does not, however, imply that there is only one and the same way of living this condition. Poverty is undeniably a racial phenomenon, but it is also linked to gender. Statistically, to begin with, it impacts more heavily on women, whose access "to resources, opportunities and education, as well as their access to the growth and wealth of the country is severely limited" (Kehler 2001, 41). One of the main reasons for South Africa's poverty—a lack of jobs accentuated by the deindustrialization that began at the end of the twentieth century—is also not experienced uniformly in the poor districts. Women living in kinships and communities ravaged by unemployment and AIDS have thus seen their domestic burdens and responsibilities increase, while their status has not improved (Mosoetsa 2011, 59). "Being a woman is everyday activism," a young activist told me one day. Furthermore, patriarchalism has declined less than expected, as men, whose role as breadwinners was shaken by the economic crisis, have withdrawn into their homes.[18] Wounded in their masculinity because they are now unable to provide financially, they have sought to exercise a power presented as "traditional" and often entailing violence. The macabre episode with which this book opens illustrates this reality very well: most of the women living in the township "experience poverty not only as a struggle with scarce resources, inadequate assets and ill health, but also as a battle against domestic violence and abuse" (Mosoetsa 2011, 59).

If they lead the women and men of the UPM to fight side by side for a "decent life," these different aspects of life in poor and working-class neighborhoods obviously tend to singularize the *near* and part of the meaning that everyone gives to their commitment. Being sensitive to this multiplicity of experiences allows us, for example, to better understand the strong presence of female pensioners within the movement and in the processions that it organizes (Chapter 6), and the fact that some young women *also* perceive their activist commitment as an emancipation from assignments of gender and generation (Chapter 8). Getting as close as possible to familiar worlds, as ethnography enables one to do, is therefore essential.

The regime of the near therefore insists on both the lived experience and the present experience of these women and men. It thus allows us to consider the overlaps and continuities between collective protest and ordinary life and to connect the shaping of discontent on the one hand with activist subjectivity and living conditions and everyday life on the other. In so doing, it somewhat dilutes the often arbitrarily drawn boundaries between the political, social, and economic dimensions of human activities and experiences. The near thus brings together things that traditionally tend to be kept at a distance. As such, the use of this concept may represent the beginnings of a response to David Snow's call for "a more inclusive and elastic conceptualization" of social movements (Snow 2004, 10):

> We need to broaden our conceptualization of social movements beyond contentious politics. I have not recommended that we throw aside the idea of contentious politics. Rather, I am suggesting that since not all social movements fall within the political domain of social life, we need to broaden our conceptualization of movements to include collective challenges to systems or structures or authority beyond the government and state. . . . The most obvious analytic benefit is that it forces us to consider

more carefully social movement activity in other institutional and cultural spheres of social life. (Snow 2004, 19)[19]

The decentering of the gaze brought about by the regime of the near helps us not to be obsessed by the "political" tropism that permeates the analysis of social movements. It does contribute, however, to a widening of horizons that differs somewhat from the one imagined by Snow. In fact, the movement at the center of this book is still relatively recognizable by the most classic criteria of the analysis of mobilizations: it is a collective and concerted action in favor of a cause. Nevertheless, by studying this object when it goes outside this framework and reveals its attachments to the ordinary and to what is not immediately given as *political* or *protest*, the near makes it possible to highlight facets of activist work and organization that do not appear so explicitly when we simply stay within the eye of the storm of protest. It helps us understand, among other things, that in some ways activism is not just a set of activities and practices. It is also a social relation in itself. Being aware of this can help, for example, to determine the extent to which forms of commitment and, more important, which *activist styles* are related to the way individuals fit into the local space (Mischi 2016).

To sum up: The idea at the heart of this book is that it is necessary to broaden the field of study of a mobilization when the latter arises from a poor people's movement. Why? Because, more than in other categories of movement, this is often intimately linked to the physical, social, and symbolic environment around the people taking part. These individuals move in a *spatially situated sociality*, their demands reflect needs that reveal the relationship to the world imposed on them, and we can, more generally, conclude that what is affected, what justifies (at least in their view) their commitment, dwells in the most central and sometimes the most vital and intimate aspects of their lives. It is in this respect that their commitment is deployed in a "regime of the near."

From the foregoing, two hypotheses emerge, which are interwoven at the heart of this book and could almost summarize its ambition. The first one is that the exploration of the edges and peripheries of social protest (where the aforementioned familiar and near worlds take shape) highlights elements that are often neglected but illuminate certain aspects of mobilization. The second one is that this same approach sheds new light on things that have traditionally been at the heart of the analysis of social movements. We will see to what extent it helps, for example, to understand how, despite failures and lack of resources, a collective such as the Unemployed People's Movement (in other words, a movement with deep local roots) and the individual commitments on which it relies can be maintained over time. It allows, among other things, a better understanding of the springs of attachment to the movement.

Verification of these assumptions is not an end in itself, however. This text must also allow us to go a little further. At first glance, most of the elements of this book align it with what appears to have been the main trend in the anthropology of and from South Africa since the beginnings of the postapartheid era. In an incisive article, Andrew Spiegel and Heike Becker thus described a "reconceptualization" of the discipline around a strong focus on "social suffering" (2015, 758)—at least in the work produced by South Africa–based anthropologists. This trend has been criticized for underestimating wider and macrostructural issues, and, because it is said to have concentrated on social problems alone, for ruling out the possibility of any "in-depth analysis of the full range of human experience" (758). However, one of my wagers in *The Politics of the Near* is to believe that an approach centered on the near will avoid being monopolized by "social suffering" alone, even when an interest is taken in lives marked by poverty. This can provide an opportunity for reflecting on the different ways—even the most unsophisticated—of producing the political. As Veena Das and Shalini Randeria have pointed out, a certain type of analysis, influenced by the thought of Hannah Arendt, has often tended to consider that the poorest "are not capable of politics" (Das and Randeria 2015, S4). Overburdened by problems linked to their subsistence, they are deprived of the freedom indispensable for deliberation and collective action, two categories which are deemed to define what is political. Such a reading of things is obviously questionable, at least for two reasons.

On the one hand, the management of concrete problems and the most urgent needs is not devoid of political dimensions: far from it. In the case of South Africa (though the same would be true for the poor inhabitants of India, Brazil, Nigeria, and elsewhere), the struggle to get a roof, a job, or access to water reflects as much a desire to lead a "normal life" as the critique of being excluded from full citizenship. Moreover, what is the regime of the near in a movement of the poor if not the matrix of a mobilization that essentially seeks to turn questions traditionally confined to the private sphere—as they involve life, survival, care, and need—into elements of public interest, requiring the attention of the politico-legal institutions?[20]

On the other hand, as Daniel Cefaï notes, "something like 'the political' arises as such each time that collectives form, raise questions or engage around issues where there is a common/public good to be attained or a common/public evil to be averted" (2011, 546). The movements of the poor, such as the UPM, are certainly no exception to this principle. Even on the edges of protest, even far from the rulers and official institutions, a political form emerges through the actions of its activists: a politics of the near. Consubstantial with the commitment of this poor people's movement, it will appear in the course of these pages, most often quite transparently, without necessarily being perceived or announced as such. Its presence can certainly be guessed at in the way activists' daily practices are imbued with autochthony, with proximity (social and spatial), with legitimacy, and with a "lived sense of place." Its very existence will further suggest how, beyond certain theoretical impulses, it does not make much sense to set a priori limits to what is political. On the contrary, ethnography helps to show how this delimitation can evolve over the course of the action. In such contexts, this also helps us to get beyond the highly institutionalized definition of the political that has spread across the world, in the wake of the liberal-democratic model. South African society offers, perhaps, a particularly propitious terrain for such an approach. Antina von Schnitzler (2016) has emphasized this, demonstrating the "political salience" of technological devices apparently as harmless as the prepaid water meters installed in Soweto, one of Johannesburg's black townships. It is through these that, every day, individuals experience the material dimension of the state and their own citizenship, far from the channels on which political analysis usually focuses. The aim of the present work is clearly different. However, here too I will be seeking "a politics that takes shape in less visible locations" (von Schnitzler 2016, 5). Just as much as the "techno-politics" that von Schnitzler has outlined, the politics of the near shows that more often than people believe, "the political is not delimited in a sphere beyond the private concerns of daily life, nor does it necessarily take the form of public deliberation or demonstration" (9). It appears in more sensitive arenas, where the possibilities of arrangements with social and legal norms are being tested, and in direct contact with ordinary but vital needs.

Because it partly borrows from a localized ethnography, the approach at the heart of this book is inevitably exposed to the requirement of the *higher level of generality* regularly imposed on the social sciences as a pledge of their seriousness. In a previous survey, I tried to paint a picture of postapartheid discontent (Tournadre 2018). The point was then to vary the scales of analysis (from international militant spheres to the streets of the neighborhood), so as to bring this discontent within historical and sociopolitical trends that were both singular and more global. Attempting today to grasp this phenomenon *at ground level*, however, does not mean writing the same story only *smaller*. We do not systematically see things better, but otherwise. This approach first allows us to rediscover a certain human depth by bringing out stories at the crossroads of the individual and the collective, even the psychic and the social. It also reveals other logics and other types of interaction, anchoring the analysis of behaviors in social spaces where they concretely take on shape and meaning. It is then a question of bringing this cloud of scattered information (Revel 1996, 12) into a coherent whole and thus creating a *case*. A case certainly involves singularities (is this not the main feature of a case?) but cannot be reduced to an anecdote or a mere example. This is a finding that has been perfectly well established in microhistory (see Levi 1988 and Ginzburg 1992). Nor is it a question of telling a particular story but of "constructing [this narration] from a question" (Haegel and Lavabre 2010, 84) with a more global inflection. It is a question of intermingling and interpenetration that is gradually formulated in this text—intermingling and interpenetration of ordinary life and protest of course, but also of private life and activism.

Finally, as isolated as it may seem, a case is embedded in contexts, dynamic processes and chains of relationships that transcend it at one time or another, transform it to varying degrees and, in so doing, give it meaning. To put it another way, the group of individuals studied here moves against the backdrop of much broader sociopolitical phenomena and processes than the revolt of a handful of the poor in a medium-sized town in South Africa. Through it we can glimpse the outline of the democratic disenchantment and the closing of the political field characteristic of so many contemporary liberal democracies. We can also see how it reflects the universal propensity of capitalism to sort out individuals by category, and the declining centrality, in much of the world, of livelihoods based in stable waged labor. Finally, we can see the silhouette of that indisputable anthropological fact, the need for recognition (Bourdieu 2000, 313). In short, the challenge is always to capture "the great world in the little" (Geertz 1973, 22).

My approach could have been tried out in many places other than Grahamstown. The essential thing was that it should be part of a circumscribed field of observation making it possible to reconstruct everything that shapes the behaviors, interactions, and decisions of individuals. Some might object, however, that this Eastern Cape town is neither Johannesburg nor Cape Town, and that what is observed in it cannot claim to be at all representative. This would be to forget that neither Johannesburg nor Cape Town is South Africa. In addition, some of the essential social features of Grahamstown, such as its poverty rate (55 percent in 2015), place it precisely in the national average.[21] The surveys I have conducted in Johannesburg, Durban, and Cape Town since 2009 and the reading of other specialists' studies have mainly taught me that the people I meet in Grahamstown are similar to those in Soweto, Thembelihle, and Khayelitsha.[22] They are exposed to the same difficult living conditions, feel disillusioned when they remember the hopes of 1994, and have the same sense that their citizenship is still incomplete.

Finally, if it turned out to be so easy for me to choose this middle-sized city as my field of study, this was also in my view because Grahamstown offers an almost stripped-down sample of some of the contradictions and polarizations characterizing the "postcolonial city" in its ideal-typical form. I remain convinced (and this is the subject of the first chapter of my book) that it is in these contradictions and polarizations that lies one of the main keys to understanding the subjectivities of the women and men that I have observed and accompanied over the years. The spatially divided appearance of the city, where the east seems to be continually opposed to the west,[23] gives, for example, a particular salience to the feelings of relegation and abandonment that many of the poorest residents in the townships express, including the members of postapartheid protest organizations.

I also hope to avoid giving in to a certain "magnifying effect" that consists of overestimating the presence and the importance of the UPM and protest in the daily life of the residents of Grahamstown. Perhaps this is one of the risks with close observation of such objects. The simplest solution is therefore to remember that this organization is based on relatively small numbers: a few dozen individuals, albeit sufficiently committed to be able to gather one hundred, two hundred, or even three hundred people on protest marches. This may seem rather trivial—but only if we forget that the virtual absence of transport from which a proportion of the population suffers can prevent some people from getting to the starting point of an event that is supposed to disperse in front of the City Hall.

Let us now clarify the social and spatial landscape of this survey. To put it in a nutshell, the spaces we are interested in here are neighborhoods in which the Black populations of Grahamstown live: the township and the informal housing areas. If social differentiation is less pronounced in a town such as Grahamstown than in conurbations such as Johannesburg or Cape Town (Seekings and Nattrass 2015, 106–132), where the townships most often have very contrasting social faces, the places where the Black populations of this locality of Eastern Cape live do not form a single block. Every day, an unemployed person living in a tin shack in one of the most remote areas of Grahamstown, a young woman living at her parents' home and employed packing goods in one of the town center's supermarkets, and a female town hall employee about to become a homeowner may cross each other's paths. It is obvious that these three individuals do not have the same life chances, to use Weberian terminology. These varied realities are interconnected, however: while not all the residents in these neighborhoods are poor, they usually (but neither systematically nor uniformly) occupy dominated social positions, which expose them (to very varying degrees, of course) to a certain economic fragility. In a report published in March 2018, the World Bank estimated that poverty affected not only the 50 to 55 percent of South Africans officially considered poor. At times, it could catch those who were "transient poor," but also a part of this lower-middle class that its access to "precarious ownership" has not made less "vulnerable." A "constant threat" (World Bank 2018, xviii) therefore hovers over the daily lives of more than 75 percent of South African citizens, the vast majority of whom are Black.[24]

In addition to this socioeconomic aspect, there are specificities or forms of cultural separation that are quite evident in the case of a South African township. The neighborhoods that make it up are indeed embedded in a common lifeworld: they thus share the history of a segregation that is not such a distant memory. These spaces together give shape to an urban form that appears as a coherent "anthropological place"[25] and exists through a set of relationships, stories, and memories that allow those who inhabit it to identify with this place, irrespective of their differences.

Before going any further and taking a look at the edges and peripheries of social protest, I should perhaps mention, however briefly, my concern for embodiment, which justifies the presence of photographs. The relationship between the social sciences and this visual technology is relatively old. In the nineteenth century, it was an essential element in the imperial enterprise of the ethnographic classification of colonized bodies (Ryan 1997). Such a heritage has long since led to a heavy weight of suspicion hanging over photography: the suspicion that it is "a technology that is productive of racial ideas and orders" (Poole 2005, 160). In a different register, sociological inquiry also won some of its first spurs at the sides of photography. The origin of this alliance can be sought in the snapshots of Parisian hovels taken by Maurice Halbwachs in 1908, fifteen years before certain members of the Chicago School made their own contribution. Photography then appeared, notably in the context of Nels Anderson's investigation of the hobo (1923), as a means of representing the routine lives of the subjects studied. No real theoretical reflection accompanied such a practice, however (Harper 2003). A detailed history of this relation—which is not the object of the present few lines—would also need a reference to the work of Bronisław Malinowski (Young 1998), Isaac Schapera's sober snapshots of the daily life of the Tswana in the 1930s (Comaroff, Comaroff, and James 2007), the three thousand pictures taken in the same period by Claude Lévi-Strauss in Brazil, the initial sketches of a theoretical approach based on fieldwork by Margaret Mead and Gregory Bateson in Bali a decade later, and then the emergence, in the 1960s and 1970s, of a proper reflection on "visual sociology" (Becker 1974; Becker 1981; Harper 1982) and "visual anthropology." A chronological narrative of this kind would definitely conclude with some remarks on recent, productive experiments with "photo-ethnography."[26]

Such developments, however, failed to overcome a certain mistrust. The marriage of the social sciences and photography has often been accused of overemphasizing the aesthetic dimension and thus pandering to a certain lie. The objectivity of photography is obviously an illusion (Ihl 2016, 121–122): the composition, the choice of angle and depth of field fully express what the photographer wanted to highlight, isolate, or minimize. Nevertheless, the images that punctuate my text are as immediate as possible. The captions accompanying them are also minimal. I'm not convinced that captioning is systematically the most important part of photography, the "foundation of meaning."[27] Such a statement is certainly valid in the context of a documentary logic, which was precisely not mine. Furthermore, captioning tends to objectify images, to give them a way of detaching themselves from the text. Taken between interviews or during my odysseys across the township, these snapshots show the ordinary aspects of militant lives and the worlds of which these existences are part. Their sole ambition is thus to supplement my words in their description of the daily life of South African lower-class neighborhoods. They are illustrations, in the strongest sense, and thus show what a text fully equipped with the imperatives of the social sciences often finds it difficult to make perceptible.

1

A SOUTH AFRICAN CITY

Grahamstown is located in the middle of nothing. Almost 130 kilometers of a monotonous road, set in a continuous landscape of thorns and bald hills, separate it from Port Elizabeth, the provincial capital. At regular intervals along the roadside, a gate opening onto a dusty track reminds the passerby that many landowners have come round to the idea that land in South Africa is now essentially meant to be used for animal reserves.

After landing at the Port Elizabeth airport and driving for two hours, you turn off National Highway 2, leaving it to continue to Durban, eight hundred kilometers away. The visitor then takes a short stretch of sloping road. Grahamstown is in a slight depression accentuated by its surrounding range of hills. The first thing you see is the monumental beige brick building overlooking the city: the 1820 Settlers National Monument, a real affirmation, at the time of its conception, of a South African Englishness as opposed to Afrikaner nationalism. It was from its forecourt that, in the 1980s, the apartheid police monitored the protests brewing in the township. The building is located on the axis of Beaufort Street, the long artery that crosses Grahamstown from west to east and connects the old "white" city to the first homes in the Black neighborhoods. A successful exercise in the charmless architecture of the 1970s, both massive and angular, the building now seems to taunt an era where streets too explicitly evocative of the old days of white power are given new names, while the statues of its historical representatives are torn down.[1]

Everything in this place, both its name and its presence at the gates of the city, remind us that the "city is born of conquest."[2] The visitor's intuition is confirmed when he or she ventures into the garden of the monument, a large rectangle of stones and yellowed grass, barely distinct from the semiarid landscape that surrounds the city. In this garden a statue has been erected—more precisely, three figures united in the same bronze: a woman, a man, and a child, all dressed in the middle-class clothes of the first years of the nineteenth century. The child's face is turned toward the mother. She, meanwhile, like her husband, resolutely gazes toward the horizon in a posture that the sculptor seems to have designed to express great determination (the features of the adults are filled with serenity and confidence) and sobriety (their gestures and their clothes are imbued by austerity). They are the perfect incarnation of the arrival, two centuries ago, of families and merchants determined to turn this outpost of British troops in Xhosa lands into a new beacon for the Cape Colony.[3] Describing the birth of another city surrounded by the veld, Bloemfontein, the novelist Karel Schoeman (1991) perfectly portrayed these members of the European bourgeoisie who, in the second half of the nineteenth century, endeavored to revive their memories of Germany, England, or Holland in the supposed virgin lands of "another country."

Not far from the monument stands the university, another symbol of the "white" history of Grahamstown. Ranked among the most elite universities in Africa, it bears the name of Cecil Rhodes. In addition to being the prime minister of the Cape Colony in the late nineteenth century, Rhodes was one of the prime figures in South African capitalism. He played a part, for example, in the foundation of the diamond company De Beers. Convinced of the colonial vocation of the United Kingdom, he also gave his name to Rhodesia, now Zimbabwe, while fantasizing about the improbable route of a railway line between Cape Town and Cairo. On the opposite pavement there stretch the white facades of sober Cape Victorian-style cottages, partially hidden by a regular line of trees. The almost austere appearance of the city center streets and the reputation of rectitude associated with Grahamstown certainly owe much to the early generations of Methodist, Presbyterian, Catholic, Pentecostal, and Baptist pioneers who built this "City of Saints" with its sixty spires. Nowadays, this severity has been diluted by the steady and somewhat noisy flow of students going to and fro between the university buildings and coffee shops, bars, and businesses on the main streets. Until late into the night, these young people share the pavements of the city center with women and men from the townships who, in return for a few coins, keep an eye on parked vehicles. Black children and teenagers are also gathered at street corners, busy getting a couple of coins off passers-by who are obviously too used to their presence to even pay them much attention.

Now, after crossing the city center, you should join Beaufort Street and follow it eastward. This wide artery, which leads to the Black districts of Grahamstown, helps to make you aware that apartheid was first and foremost a "geographical policy in the sense that space [was] used to shape society and impose identities on everyone" (Gervais-Lambony 2001a, 121). At the end of a few score meters, the impression of leaving the city becomes obvious, though in fact you are only moving away from its center, its shops, bars, churches, university, and affluent residential areas. Along the way, Black women and men walk, alone or in groups, on increasingly irregular pavements as we get closer to the township; this group of buildings was erected in the time of racial segregation to accommodate a population which, in the regime's view, was not fit to stay in the city.[4]

The road changes its name to become Jacob Zuma Drive just as it comes to a small white bridge crossed by hundreds of people each day. The older residents can certainly remember that under apartheid, at dusk, this structure became a border that Blacks could not cross. Four or five meters long, the bridge overlooks a narrow river whose official name is Matyana but which is still known by some as "The River of Blood," in memory of the Xhosa warriors killed in clashes with British troops in the early nineteenth century.

The various streets starting from the Beaufort Street/Jacob Zuma Drive axis are riddled with wide, deep potholes that force cars to weave erratically between them. One of these roads leads to a seemingly anonymous place on the edge of the city: a football field whose lines have been drawn out across somewhat broken ground. At one end of what is ultimately just a wasteland, a strange brick building has been erected. It resembles a bandstand with its roof removed, or the broad pedestal of an invisible statue. A few meters high, the structure also seems to act as a promontory or a place for observing the surrounding hills. It is actually a memorial built in 2001 to remind passers-by that here, on April 22, 1819, on the eGazini (literally, "the place of blood") Plateau, the artillery of a British regiment of 450 men bloodily defeated nearly 10,000 Xhosa warriors led by the prophet Makhanda. The price paid by the Europeans was minimal: the loss of three soldiers, one of them an officer, and two horses. Captured a few weeks later,

Makhanda was imprisoned several hundred kilometers away on Robben Island off Cape Town (see Mostert 1992, 472–481). A century and a half later, this same island was to "welcome" Nelson Mandela and many of ANC leaders. A cast iron plaque affixed to the memorial seeks to provide reassurance, saying that this tribute to "warriors" and "soldiers" marks above all a desire for "peace and reconciliation." The monument is part of a larger government program that, at the dawn of the twenty-first century, was intended to deliver South African "memory" from its "dark areas" and its "silences" (Wells 2003, 80), the last obstacles to the birth of a nation. It is hard to imagine that this building, which its geographical location alone renders virtually anonymous, could act as a counterbalance to the imposing Settlers Monument overlooking the city. The comparison between them, however, provides a perfect synthesis of what Grahamstown is. At the end of apartheid, the city was seen by many as the most segregated in South Africa (O'Meara and Greaves 1995).

Liberal democracy does not seem to have fully remedied this. Nowadays, if the big cities like Cape Town or Johannesburg are highly segmented, Grahamstown is a divide in itself, squeezed into a few dozen square kilometers. In the west we find the heart of the colonial city, with its mixture of businesses,

eGazini Memorial

Cape Dutch houses, Elizabethan buildings and more modern and functional blocks; in the east lies the "African" part.[5] Beyond its topographical dimension, this split is also confirmed by the Gini coefficient, a fairly clear measure of inequalities.[6] The Gini coefficient for Grahamstown was 0.615 in 2016 (Eastern Cape Socio Economic Consultative Council 2017, 59). It is certainly a little lower than the national reference level (0.628), but far higher than what a Western observer may be used to.[7] Thanks to one of those ruses of history and the political management of memory, this urban confrontation was given a certain administrative cachet at the beginning of the twenty-first century. The city, founded by Lieutenant Colonel John Graham, was administratively amalgamated with several small neighboring communities to form a new municipality, Makana.[8] The name of this new entity owed nothing to chance. It was a tribute to the man who had defied British troops two centuries earlier.[9]

Grahamstown suffers from many ailments. Among the phenomena that imbue and affect it, we find in particular the survival of a racialized compartmentalization of space or, as we have just seen, the existence of memorial conflicts embodied in infrastructures and monuments. This reminds us, sometimes without any nuance, that Grahamstown is quite simply a "postcolonial city," a complex urban form that is often difficult to grasp (see Yeoh 2001). These characteristics produce ways of experiencing the city and perceiving one's life in it that are not foreign to the feelings of exclusion and isolation expressed by its poorest residents and their self-appointed spokespersons.

The first stratum of the "African" part of Grahamstown took shape during the 1840s, when the authorities, anxious to control the arrival of Black squatters on the outskirts of the city, established the first Black "location."[10] Mfengus, allies of the British against the Xhosa, were among the first to settle here. This Bantu people also gave their name to the land which, a few decades later, became Fingo Village, an assemblage of small brick houses and huts. A little further on are the first houses of Joza, a Black location built in the 1950s after the coming to power of the National Party and the establishment of its program of apartheid (Afrikaans for "separateness"). Although this is obviously due to the situation of Grahamstown, a middle-sized town surrounded by the veld, the physiognomy of these neighborhoods rests, as in so many other parts of the developing world (Davis 2006, 9–11), on a hesitation between the urban and the rural. The dirt roads, plains, and weeds are a permanent challenge to the influence of cement and asphalt. If we wanted to wax folkloric about it, we would need only mention the presence of hundreds of stray dogs, but also of cows and donkeys: no one seems to be very clear about whether the latter once belonged to somebody or not.

The public authorities provided the township with a dozen extensions in the 1980s and 1990s. The whole township, with nearly 80 percent of the population, is composed of spaces sometimes separated from each other by roads or undeveloped areas. It is mainly here, east of the city, that the poverty which affects the lives of 55 percent of the residents is concentrated.[11] Poverty continues to have a color in South Africa. In 2016, in Grahamstown, it affected more than 60 percent of the Black population, which, moreover, constitutes nearly 80 percent of the city's residents. The descendants of Europeans make up about 10 percent of the total population of the municipality, and only 1 percent of whites were considered poor (Eastern Cape Socio Economic Consultative Council 2017, 61). Such data are all the more understandable when we realize the extent to which poverty, inequality, and unemployment are linked in this country. At the national level, and throughout the first two decades of the twenty-first century, official figures regularly established that 25–30 percent of working-age people were unemployed. These statistics, however, have often been accused of involving a very narrow definition of a phenomenon that some experts thought actually affected 35–40 percent of this population. Whatever the method used to isolate it, the social evil of joblessness is in any case more devastating and more widespread in the Black townships than elsewhere. This fact has regularly led activists of the Unemployed People's Movement to claim that 70 percent of adults in Grahamstown Township were unemployed—a figure often slipped into the movement's press releases from the beginning of 2010 onward. It is difficult to know its origin and just as difficult to check its accuracy. We can obviously decide that it might well be exaggerated or, perhaps more cautiously, see it as a way of expressing a reality that is more felt than proven. Such a figure nevertheless has the merit of drawing attention to the gray area surrounding employment in a context of high job insecurity.[12] The importance of the "informal" economy,[13] the number of casual workers, temporary workers, day laborers, and other working poor (Rogan and Reynolds 2015) make the boundaries between employment and unemployment both porous and questionable.[14] Perhaps this 70 percent also includes a statistically rather vague social group that provides a strong contingent of the jobless, namely the group of individuals who, discouraged, do not seek work or have stopped looking for work. This eventuality seems to find an echo in some of the official data: more than 63 percent of the "potential labor force" did not work in 2016 (Makana Municipality 2016, 73).

As Jeremy Seekings remarks, "South Africa's poverty and unemployment crises are clearly rooted in a long history of dispossession and disadvantage . . . but they also have immediate roots in the collapse of formal un- and even semi-skilled employment" (2014, 138). Until the 1980s, most of South Africa's low-skilled labor force was largely absorbed by the needs of mining and agriculture. The situation deteriorated during the following decade, as a result of liberalization of the economy and the end of the protectionist measures taken by the apartheid governments (Barchiesi 2011, 75). However, the manufacturing sector was not able to fill the gap, since it failed to be sufficiently competitive in "global manufacturing export markets" (Bhorat et al. 2016, 3). The narrowness of the domestic market and the lowering of tariff barriers, a decision made by the first democratic governments in the interests of moving into international trade, further contributed to the weakness of the country. Policies encouraging high-wage, high-productivity sectors and activities rather than labor-intensive ones completed the picture (Seekings and Nattrass 2005). These guidelines most likely cost more than one million jobs in South Africa between 1994 and 1997 (Altman 2003, 169), a decade before the 2008 global crisis destroyed another 800,000 jobs, mostly among unskilled workers. The "informal" economy partly took over, but to a lesser extent than in most developing countries.

Grahamstown does not have an industrial history. As elsewhere in the Eastern Cape, however, many of its male residents went to work in other provinces during apartheid and the 1990s, particularly in mining areas. They were inevitably directly affected by the changes mentioned earlier. The Grahamstown area was also hit by the collapse of agricultural employment. At the same time, many farms in the area were converted into game reserves, which are less demanding on labor. Families that until then had access to milk and sometimes meat had no choice but to leave these farms and move to the informal settlements of Grahamstown in the 2000s. It is in the light of these different changes that we can understand the huge presence, both in the township and in the ranks of the UPM, of thirty-year-olds who had never had formal employment and of men in the prime of life for whom it is now a memory going back more than a decade. Like millions of poor people in the world, these women and men seem to be getting drawn into this vast "surplus" that no longer meets the needs of capitalism (Li 2009). The agents of the latter, who took advantage of these populations when they formed a "reserve army," especially under apartheid, no longer seem to pay them any attention. Momentum has now migrated to the service sector, which demands a skilled labor force that still comprises only a minority of workers (World Bank 2018, 84). The implications of such a mismatch between part of the Black population and the economic system inspire a certain resignation among several South African poverty specialists, as James Ferguson reports: "The fact is that there are at least ten million people who could drop dead tomorrow and the JSE [Johannesburg Stock Exchange] wouldn't register so much as a ripple" (Ferguson 2015, 11). This finding, whether provocative or in line with reality, finds a certain echo in the feelings of relegation expressed by many poor South Africans and running through this book from beginning to end.

In the early 2000s, several maps of major South African cities were dotted with large blank areas. These voids were obviously where they were for a reason. Even the most distracted observer soon understood that they were appearing in specific parts of the townships, leading to the belief that these were fleeting and unstable places. Current technology can take this experiment further. Just enter the name of Grahamstown in the collection of maps that one famous digital search engine provides and observe the unambiguous result that appears on the computer screen. Poor Black and working-class neighborhoods have certainly not been replaced by virgin areas. Roads and streets can be clearly seen, drawn in white on a gray background— except in informal settlements. Strangely, however, *putting them on the map* seems to have regularly led to their names being omitted. This treatment could lead one to believe that these places are completely homogeneous, but there is nothing to verify this. It would indeed be mistaken to apprehend Black neighborhoods as totally uniform ensembles in Grahamstown, Cape Town, or Johannesburg. Eluxolweni, Vukani, Hlalani, Joza, and Phaphamani display landscapes with a certain variety. Some of these neighborhoods are the living places of very poor workers or households, while others are home to a Black petite bourgeoisie that remains one of the most visible achievements of the postapartheid era. In Grahamstown as elsewhere, this Black lower-middle class is overwhelmingly rooted in public and local government sectors (Southall 2016). It consists of municipal employees, nurses, police officers, and schoolteachers, but also modest wage-earners and entrepreneurs. Even though they have remained in the township, these households have distinguished themselves by becoming the owners of slightly larger than average houses financed by bank loans, that is, the "bond houses."

Crossing the township, the visitor thus passes from these seemingly comfortable three-, four-, or five-room houses to more modest "matchbox houses" built under apartheid and sometimes recently extended (an extra room made of cinderblocks, for example), all a short distance from shacks and mud houses. These latter are (to put it mildly) rudimentary houses whose walls are made of earth reinforced by branches of acacia or a few handfuls of cement. Since the mid-1990s, the township has also seen the emergence of spartan standardized houses that need a bit of historical explanation. In April 1994, the government that emerged from the first democratic elections had the difficult task of healing the wounds of apartheid. It therefore set about implementing "catch-up" policies for the poorest "non-white" populations. The Reconstruction and Development Programme (RDP), initially the electoral manifesto of the ANC and then the roadmap for the first governments, aimed to improve the standard of living in South Africa by promoting employment, health, access to basic services such as water and electricity, education, and, perhaps most important, giving everyone a roof over their heads. This last objective was indeed enshrined in the constitution adopted in 1996. Article 26 states that "everyone has the right to have access to adequate housing." The state "must take reasonable legislative and other measures, within its available resources, to achieve the progressive realisation of this right." A system of public subsidies, with a particularly low threshold of access, was set up to ensure the diffusion of private property among a Black and poor population to which apartheid had refused this right.[15] Nearly 3.3 million "RDP houses" were built between 1994 and 2013 (Palmer, Moodley, and Parnell 2017, 237). The urban landscape inevitably changed as a result, gradually being filled with glum new estates with small standardized houses of between 30 and 40 square meters, when even the "matchboxes" built under apartheid had an area of about 50 square meters. In addition, these houses were built on the outskirts of cities, where land is certainly cheaper but the dwellings lie far from the urban labor market.

There were a number of these construction programs in Grahamstown.[16] They took the form of veritable fields of well-aligned houses—identical dwellings, separated from each other by a few meters. Here and elsewhere, RDP houses have been in the headlines from the late 1990s onward. These homes often suffer from shoddy workmanship that has led to cracks, recurrent leaks, and sometimes collapsing walls. In the Sun City district, which for a long time was a transit camp, the first houses experienced recurring plumbing problems in the months following their construction in 2010. Some have never even been connected to running water.[17] The time of construction of each unit (less than three weeks) and its cost (R70,000, about US$6,000 at the time) are perhaps the main reason for this accelerated dilapidation. Here, as elsewhere, the blame lay mainly with the various entrepreneurs, who, often because of their supposed proximity to the governing party, felt they could get away with building houses with planned obsolescence. This "tenderpreneurship" (i.e., the allocation of public tenders by public servants and politicians to benefit those close to the party in power) has been one of the most controversial evils of the postapartheid era. In 2009–10, 1,135 public officials were suspended by the Public Service Commission because of their involvement in the wrongful allocation of tenders (Southall 2016, 93). These peculiarities were certainly the results of a particularly complex economic environment for small- and medium-sized businesses, one that forced them to place themselves in a relationship of dependence on political power. To put it more simply, it was above all an "outcome of the rent-seeking, cronyism and corruption that have increasingly become central to the reproduction of the ANC's party-state bourgeoisie" (94).

RDP dwellings have also been at the heart of another type of problem. Since the beginning of the 2000s, many ward councilors have been caught making money out of the right to acquire these houses, regardless of the waiting lists that some households had been on since the second half of the 1990s.[18] Grahamstown was not immune from these fraudulent allocations, which were denounced by the members of the Unemployed People's Movement. In June 2016, in Mayfield, in the northern part of the township, more than 150 people—activists and residents who felt they had been cheated—gathered in the middle of an area of newly built RDP houses. The organizers then showed the journalists who were present seven buildings that had been illegally allocated to municipal officials, to relatives of councilors, and, more generally, to households whose income far exceeded the regulatory

District of RDP houses

ceiling of R3,500. In the following hours, one of the leaders of the movement posted on his Facebook profile the names of the officials who, he alleged, were involved in this financial impropriety. In other neighborhoods, the cross-referencing of information gleaned from residents sometimes allowed UPM activists to prove that some councilors had, via front men, obtained ownership of several houses before reselling them. In 2013, the mayor of Grahamstown was forced to acknowledge flagrant cases of fraud. Carried away by his zeal, or forced to take action by the revelations, he promised to set up an investigation. It never saw the light of day.

Adopting a purely moral point of view of these arrangements of cronyism and nepotism would certainly be of little use to anyone trying to understand how they are experienced by the women and men of the UPM. As we will see in Chapter 5, in the eyes of many of these activists, who of course live outside the circles in which these jobs or houses are handed out, such practices are above all signs of their distance from a "normal life" and from fully belonging to the "new" South Africa.

In the late 1990s, while discovering the great township of Soweto, Michel Agier described his impression of being in a "big city in Black Africa" where there was "a part" missing. This missing piece was actually visible in the distance: Johannesburg, "the city itself" (1999, 74). Such an observation is no longer entirely appropriate two decades later. The iconic township of Johannesburg has opened itself up to some extent, especially to market and consumer institutions. It now hosts several malls and has covered itself with billboards, and tourists can explore some of its sites of memory by bicycle or enjoy its popular "wine and lifestyle festival." In sum, Soweto "is being sold as hip and as a place to be. . . . If you can have it in Sandton,[19] then you can have it in the township, too" (Mbembe, Dlamini, and Khunou 2008, 243). In Grahamstown, on the other hand, the link between the former colonial city and the township does not seem to have undergone the same evolution. The (albeit relative) heterogeneity of the Black districts does not mitigate the sense that these ensembles are a "non-city" (Agier 1999). In addition to the monotony, there is a virtual absence of apparent activity. There are many public buildings (mainly schools and libraries) and churches, but shops are scarce. There are taverns and pubs called shebeens, places of sociability specific to the townships, but also a number of spaza shops, small informal shops providing factory-produced bread, milk, sweets, sodas, and other goods. In addition, there are some grocery stores, often run by foreigners—Pakistani, Somali, or Bangladeshi. The destruction of these stores in the xenophobic violence of 2015 left in a state of utmost destitution those who are entirely reliant on these convenience stores for food. While residents of middle-class neighborhoods have cars, which allow them to travel to the city center or work there, most of those living in the poorest areas of the township may feel that they live in collective isolation. The latter has, very concretely, the objectivity of the many kilometers separating these spaces from the city center, with its jobs, businesses, and infrastructures. In everyday life, the situation can be experienced as a way of keeping these residents at a distance (which was, after all, the whole point of apartheid), especially insofar as a majority of them obviously do not own a vehicle. The absence of public transport in Grahamstown therefore leaves no option but to turn to shared taxis, the price of which can be offputtingly high. Just to get to the very central High Street from the easternmost point of the city costs nearly R10 when more than half of the residents live on less than R25 per day (US $2). These distances are implacably reminiscent of how "the lack of capital intensifies the experience of finitude: it chains one to a place" (Bourdieu 1999, 127). They creep into people's minds, too: Even if there were more means of leaving the township, what would the poorest find to do in this "white city" where they do not work and where they often find that the things on sale are unaffordable? This situation is perhaps even more significant in the informal settlements which have come into being over the years as land has been illegally occupied. For example, eThembeni is a plot of veld and marshland on which have been built dozens of tin shacks and an equal number of those mud houses that the municipal administration modestly classifies in the category "traditional housing."

If they appear—quite justifiably—to be pockets of misery in the eyes of outside observers, informal settlements can also be spaces of welcome for new urbanites in search of a place allowing them to build a home and to claim their "right to the city" (Ferguson and Li 2018, 3). The fact that the first arrivals in the early 1990s called this piece of land eThembeni (Xhosa for "hope") obviously tends to confirm as much. Since 2004, the national government has officially planned to upgrade the informal settlements instead of eradicating them. However, eThembeni only began to develop in this way at the end of the 2010s, with the electrification of the three hundred shacks. Until then, as soon as night fell, most of the residents remained cloistered for fear of crime; and they relied on paraffin to provide light and heat, even though this caused many fires and cases of poisoning. Access to water is only made possible by four outdoor public taps installed by the municipality. There has however been no dearth of commitments made by successive ward councilors. The construction of houses has been regularly announced, then postponed or denied. The repetition of these "unfulfilled promises" obviously betrays a certain cynicism. They can also be seen as the result of very prosaic budgetary questions and of the defective management that led the municipality to be placed "under administration" in the middle of the 2010s.[20] So it is difficult to indulge in "pessimistic functionalism,"[21] which would only view this situation as resulting from a deliberate desire to expose the poorest to a typical "politics of waiting" (Auyero 2012a) whose goal is to keep them under the domination of political and administrative power. However, these false promises, which get repeated for mainly electoral reasons, undeniably have the effect of keeping the residents in a state of uncertainty while preserving a semblance of hope. The situation thus created is wearying and inevitably produces an impression of abandonment, stronger perhaps than in other parts of the city.[22]

Such an experience of being relegated to *the margins of the margins* also creates a sense of indignity. The latter feeds effortlessly on the prejudices that regularly affect these residents and which, for example, focus on their hygiene. This lies behind some of the features of the "territorial stigmatization" that Loïc Wacquant dissected in his study on "urban outcasts" (Wacquant 2007, chapter 6). Because it is fully incorporated by those who are its victims, this symbolic stigma sometimes comes to shape the "mental structures of marginality" (197) and to give birth to feelings of self-hatred and self-defeat. This seems to confirm the difficulty one young resident of eThembeni finds in even walking peacefully through the city center: "When we walk in the streets, we can't say anything because others will [tease us and] say that we are from the "chocolate houses" [i.e., mud houses]. Even if you had to take a girlfriend home, she would be shocked, saying, 'I didn't know that you were living in a place like this.'"[23]

This perception of the world can, logically enough, lead to the temptation to withdraw that we find far beyond eThembeni and Grahamstown. It also happens that the feeling of shame associated with it can work its way into the very heart of families. Witness the words of this man who joined a squatter camp in Cape Town on his release from prison for murder:

> It's very tragic. I actually grew up on a farm, and if my father and sisters have to find out that I'm living in a squatter camp. . . . I don't know if I'll be able to invite them for a visit. . . . The rest of my family will be too scared to visit me because I live in a squatter camp. They don't know anything about a squatter camp. They don't know anyone. . . . I mean, they don't know about building a house with zinc sheets. They wouldn't consider my place to be a home. (Ross 2010, 24)

The frequency of such experiences inspired one of the young activists of the Unemployed People's Movement to write a piece that the local newspaper published in the series "Tales of a Divided City." Thanks to a government loan, Siyanda had just left the shack that he shared with his mother and sister in Extension 8 to settle in a university residence and study philosophy and Xhosa. In a few lines, he described this new life on the campus of Rhodes University. He revealed how much his poverty was daily reflected in the eyes of other students, giving him the feeling of being "alien, inferior, despised . . . like an untouchable."[24] A year earlier, the same series of articles had publicized the dialogue that had been going on for several months between a philosopher at Rhodes University and students from one of those secondary schools in the township that the middle classes were now trying to avoid by sending their children to city center schools.[25] The teenagers spoke of their desire to leave a place that prevented them from succeeding ("the township is no place for humans to thrive") and kept them "in a state of perpetual depression." The township appeared as "a place of dread" marked by violence, especially that of petty criminals, the *tsotsis*. Conversely, the western part of the city, "cruelly teasing," symbolized material success and reminded these teenagers of their own condition.

Reading these words, it is difficult not to have in mind those which Frantz Fanon used in the 1960s to express the gulf separating the "settler's town" from the "native town" in the colonial world:

> The colonial world is a world cut in two. . . . The settlers' town is a strongly built town. . . . It is a brightly lit town; the streets are covered with asphalt, and the garbage cans swallow all the leavings, unseen, unknown and hardly thought about. . . . The settler's town is a well-fed town, an easy going town. . . . The town belonging to the colonized people, or at least the native town, the Negro village, the Medina, the reservation, is a place of ill fame. . . . The native town is a hungry town. . . . The native town is a crouching village, a town on its knees, a town wallowing in the mire. (Fanon 1963, 38)

Many historians have since shown how the cuts and divisions were far from being as marked between the worlds of the colonizers and those of the colonized. It can be assumed that they are even less so in postapartheid Grahamstown. But that is actually not the point. It is not so much a matter of confirming or denying the objective reality of this urban Manichaeism as of considering how the ways of experiencing the city on a daily basis can influence representations of the world and shape subjectivities. We must therefore take seriously the words of the schoolchildren and those of Siyanda. They are an opportunity to capture, albeit surreptitiously, some of the intimate subjective experience that may fuel social discontent. This obviously does not make it any easier to describe the township and the lives that give it its vitality. For the outside observer, there is still a fear of making the picture seem too dark or of giving way to exaggeration. Life in the township most often reveals itself in the guise of suffering. "We're suffering," my interlocutors regularly tell me, as if they wanted me to bear witness to the social and physical violence that is prevalent in their environment. The fact is that most of those living in these neighborhoods form a set of fragile lives whose silhouettes stand out against a landscape of precarity and precariousness. The lives of those women and men who engage in protest are no exception.

Other outside observers, such as Fiona Ross, who wrote an ethnography of the "raw life" of the residents of an informal settlement in the Western Cape, have merely confirmed this aspect of reality:

> Nowhere have I seen this exposure [to the terror and fragility of life] more visibly manifest than among those with whom I worked, where attempts to create predictability and routine in everyday lives are punctured by violence and lack, where stability is limited and even the most strenuous efforts often secure only temporary well-being, and where interpersonal and structural violence sometimes intercept to render life in its crudest terms. (Ross 2010, 3)

However, it is not a question of incautiously engaging on the "dark turn" that, since the end of the twentieth century and as a result of the omnipresence of "neoliberalism" in our lives, would lead part of the social sciences, in particular anthropology and sociology, to focus only on the "suffering subject": pain, poverty, violence, oppression, and so forth (see Ortner 2016 and, in counterpoint to this, Robbins 2013). In Grahamstown, as in many parts of the world, there is obviously unemployment, bad housing, sexual and domestic violence, and crime, as well as illness, which I sometimes learn has taken the life of an activist during my absence. It may be AIDS or something else.[26] Among the ills that plague it, Grahamstown has the unhappy distinction of the highest tuberculosis rate in the Eastern Cape. The marshy areas, as in eThembeni, and the many cases of illegal dumpsites in the township certainly make a large contribution to this. As Javier Auyero has pointed out, the analysis of poverty must include that of the often degraded environments in which the poorest live, insofar as, quite obviously, they "do not breathe the same air, drink the same water or play on the same playground as others" (Auyero 2021, 177).

But there is more than this to life in these neighborhoods. The streets of the township are relatively peaceful during the day. Children play there. Approaching taverns, as night falls, you can often hear laughter. Everyday life is therefore not just about suffering and frustration—not even in the deprived neighborhoods. In his study of Brazil, James Holston has also shown that living in the peripheries of contemporary societies, or at least on the outskirts of cities, does not prevent individuals from innovating or showing an ingenuity that allows them to escape, to some degree, from the models imagined for them by external forces, whether local or international, economic, legal, or environmental (Holston 2007). More generally, as Du Toit and Neves point out, "even within the 'margin' there are 'winners' and 'losers,' power holders and disempowered people—and everyone in between" (Du Toit and Neves 2007, 30).

Moreover, without fundamentally questioning it, the following chapters will bring some nuances to the idea of "collective isolation" that I mentioned in the previous pages. The first of these nuances are the opportunities, however modest, that the so-called "informal" economy can offer in the poor neighborhoods of the township. This includes such disparate things as spaza shops, small hairdressing salons run from home, small builder businesses, and repairers of all kinds. But it can also encompass such innocuous things as simply watching neighbors' children or renting space in fridges or freezers (Du Toit and Neves 2007, 23). Most often elusive and unprofitable, these activities still allow the townships not to be totally the "dead economic zones"[27] that might be suspected at first glance. Many parts of this "informal economy" are also connected to "formal economy." Shebeen owners, for example, buy their supplies in medium and large shops (Valodia and Devey 2010). In the opposite direction, some craft goods often end up in formal retail stores. The isolation of some people in poor areas can also be mitigated by political clientelism in the township. Whatever we may think, this type of relationship can be a way for the poorest to access certain goods, such as food parcels, or certain state resources, such as social grants. Finally, the social assistance system that has gradually been set up with democracy remains one of the most redistributive "in the world in terms of cash transfers" (Seekings and Natrass 2015, 15). It focuses on children, old people, and the disabled. Even in very poor areas, these populations therefore maintain contact with the State.

Finally, if there are nuances in poverty—statistics are clear about this, as they distinguish extreme poverty from other kinds—there are just as many ways of living it. The words of the young resident of eThembeni who said he

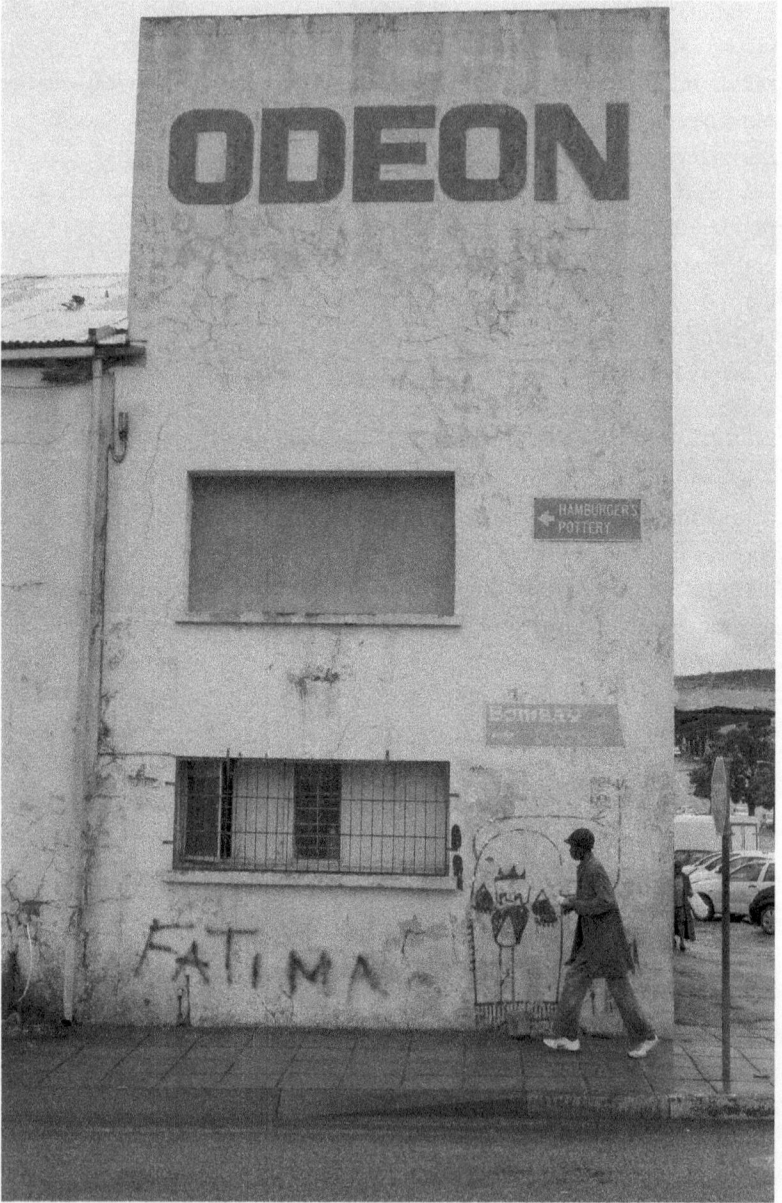

Downtown Grahamstown

did not feel at home in the streets of the city center certainly do not sum up the attitudes of all the disadvantaged households in the township. Access to a house, even one as rudimentary as those built as part of the RDP programs, is experienced as gaining a form of comfort but also as a sign of respectability, however much the social condition of the new owner, categorized as a jobless person, fails to develop in tandem. In the mid-2010s, two economists sought to compare objective and subjective poverty rates in South Africa. Their results brought to light a certain shift: "three-fifths of all households which [were] identified as poor in terms of per capita household expenditure [were] also self-assessed as poor" (Posel and Rogan 2014, 13). The other two-fifths therefore took a quite different view of things and of their own condition.

Provided, of course, that a means of transport to get there can be found, UPM activists move freely in what was once the "white city." In fact, they had premises there throughout the 2010s. For a while, one of them even considered leaving the township to settle with his family in a house in the city center. The household's economic situation had improved greatly over the decade. After a few months spent looking, however, he explained to me that the many "obstacles" intended to deter Blacks from carrying out such plans had defeated him. A few days later, as I reported this to her, a white academic close to the UPM ascribed the situation rather to a limited supply of real estate, for which there was great demand. Anyway, for this activist as for his comrades and, I imagine, most of his neighbors, friends, and relatives, the "city" remains an impregnable space, which is opposed to what many refer to as "Grahamstown East": the township. We must not only see this as due to the weight of representations. What could be more concrete, for example, than those kilometers which place the poorest at a distance from what they may perceive as "normal life"? The social reality that emerges from these various elements inevitably influences the subjectivities of the poorest residents and, *a fortiori*, those of activists. It is all the more important to be sensitive to this fact, since it is on these same subjectivities that the "bases" of agency are formed (Ortner 2005), at least in part.

2

THE SENSE OF COMMUNITY

It was an October morning in 2009, and dozens of women and men had gathered in front of a community building in Joza, one of Grahamstown's oldest Black neighborhoods.[1] There were young and old, women and men, a handful of activists from Jubilee South Africa, a collective that agitates for the cancelling of the debts of developing countries, and several members of the Rural People's Movement. The day before, in Johannesburg, the Anti-Privatisation Forum and the Landless People's Movement, two of the main postapartheid protest organizations, had publicly expressed their support for the march.

Under the close supervision of UPM activists, the procession gradually set off to the rhythm of songs expressing the desire to continue the fight for a better life. It crossed several districts of the Black part of the city, attracting several onlookers who joined it as it wended its way toward the town hall, seven kilometers away from its starting point. The objective assigned to this action was simple, and would serve as a model for most of the following marches: to present the representatives of the municipality with the four memoranda written by the organizers of the demonstration, denouncing the problems affecting housing, water, and electricity, as well as unemployment, violence against women and children, and the increasing practice among city employers of using casual workers. These demands were the mirror image of a major aspect of everyday life in neighborhoods where water and electricity cuts are legion, where families are crowded into often dilapidated and cramped shacks and houses, where the proliferation of sexual aggression has led some NGO leaders to talk of a "rape culture," and where a majority of residents are unemployed.[2] But the most important feature was the slogan painted on the main banner of the procession: "Demanding, not requesting"—an assertion of how legitimate these women and these men felt that their expectations of development really are.

The Unemployed People's Movement was formed only a few weeks before this demonstration, in the middle of an election year that was marked by an upsurge of protest across the whole country.[3] The birth of a protest organization in this town in the Eastern Cape, one of the poorest provinces in South Africa, was somewhat belated given what had happened elsewhere, in other localities in the country. In Johannesburg, the Soweto Electricity Crisis Committee and the Anti-Privatisation Forum had been founded at the very start of the twenty-first century. The same was true of the Anti-Eviction Campaign in Cape Town. In Durban, the Concerned Citizens Forum had brought together different mobilizations in Black and Indian townships since 1999. In the same conurbation, the squatters' movement Abahlali baseMjondolo ("those who live in shacks") was launched in 2005 and regularly brought together several hundred women and men, despite the political and police violence regularly directed at its members. However, it was not until the end of the first decade of the new century that, as a UPM press release put it, "The Rebellion of the Poor Comes to Grahamstown." The previous years had, of course, not been unaffected by expressions of anger. In January 2006, the local press reported on the "uprising" of nearly three hundred residents in Zolani and Phaphamani neighborhoods. In reaction to the mayor's refusal to come and see for himself the insalubrious conditions in this part of the city, dozens of people had erected barricades of burning tires to disrupt traffic. This discontent, however, lacked a more organized, less sporadic shape. It needed to be embodied in some form that would not simply collapse with the last barricade.

Preceded by many discussions between just a handful of residents, a movement capable of embodying this anger really started to take shape in July 2009. This came about at the end of a meeting organized as part of the Integrated Development Plan (IDP), a tool of municipal governance designed to repair the urban fragmentation caused by apartheid; it actually consists of a public document providing different municipal projects with their allocated budgets. It needs to be informed by neighborhood participation and consultation initiatives, but within a relatively controlled framework. The IDP's procedure is limited to a statement of objectives by the representatives of the municipality and a few minutes for oral or written questions from the audience. What happened on that particular day had been related to me several times since my first stay in Grahamstown, and by various activists present in the community hall where the meeting was held. I was told about the stormy discussions on the problems of housing, water, and electricity, and then about the frustration and annoyance that overcame some of the participants and led them to gather informally at the end of the meeting:

> "I attended some few IDP meetings. People said that something needed to be done . . . I stood up to make a point. A number of people knew my activism, so after the meeting . . ." Ayanda said.
> *"They knew you?" I asked.*
> "Yes, some people knew me because of my activism at school. I have always been an activist in my community. So people recognized me. And I was a member of AZASM [Azanian Students' Movement] at high school. . . . I have always been controversial [*laughs*]. After the meeting, people came and we had a discussion: 'We have to do something because these people are taking us for granted.' We decided to form a movement. It made sense to me. The community needed a watchdog. I agreed immediately."

These women and men came from different neighborhoods. Some had known each other for many years, while others were meeting for the first time. They lived in shacks or in RDP houses, which they could see giving signs of inevitable decay, day by day. Some had been party activists; others had already headed the episodic demonstrations against poor living conditions of the democratic era. Those of them who were already adults under apartheid also shared a certain experience of protest, forged during the various demonstrations and resistance movements that arose throughout that time. It is, in any event, through these women and men, aged between forty and seventy in the early 2010s, that the permanence of a whole "repertoire of contention" (Tilly 1986) has been ensured. From Grahamstown to Cape Town, Durban to Johannesburg, modes of action (stay away, shut down, etc.) and songs of resistance characteristic of the years of struggle against apartheid seemed to resurface unchanged, right in the heart of the democratic era. This, however, does not imply an overpoliticization of the older South Africans, a strategy that always helps to suggest the depoliticization and individualism of the postapartheid generations. While their repetition and intensity produced dispositions for, and familiarity with, collective action, the demonstrations organized in the townships during the 1980s did not systematically have the same purpose for all those who took part in them. For a large number of ordinary people, it was perhaps above all a matter of expressing dissatisfaction with issues that were expressly local and part and parcel of daily life—bread-and-butter issues, in short. Housing, transport quality, and cost of living generally limited the horizon of demands. Only a militant minority saw these first and foremost as a direct political protest against the ideology of the regime. This was most likely the case of Joseph, who would join the UPM in the mid-2010s after being one of the principal representatives of the United Democratic Front (UDF)[4] in Grahamstown thirty years earlier. Be that as it may, these moments of internal resistance helped to shape an activism that was largely insensitive to the traditional boundaries between the social and the political (see Chapter 10). Pamela Reynolds's study of young men committed to the struggle in the 1980s shows this very well (2013): their rebellion was aimed at defying a power that brutalized them and denied the most basic human rights, as much as at taking charge of the community.

In this way, a first moment in the emergence of the Unemployed People's Movement in Grahamstown could be seen. The consolidation of this momentum, in the days and weeks that followed, required the harmonization of several different dynamics. The organization had not been created *ex nihilo*. Not totally, at least. It appeared at the convergence of, or the rapprochement between, various small social worlds. The original group first went to different areas of the township to ask the most influential people for their help, and to hold public meetings to publicize its cause. Neighborhood relations and family ties also played an important and easily understandable role in that it is always easier to embark on this kind of adventure if you are guided by an acquaintance or someone you meet on a daily basis. The movement has regularly included cousins, brothers, and sisters, sometimes even parents and their children. Ayanda, for example, had no trouble convincing his cousin, a single man in his fifties, to follow him in the early stages of the movement. Local political networks have also proved useful. From the beginning, the UPM welcomed women and men who shared a past (and sometimes, indeed, a present) as activists in the African National Congress (ANC), the Democratic Alliance (DA, the main opposition party), and the Azanian People's Organization (AZAPO, a small party relegated to the margins of Parliament during the 2000s).

In general, the existence of prior social structures such as a circle of friends, or connections with one's neighbors, is in itself a resource. It provides essential elements for mobilization by ensuring, for example, the presence of groups that are more or less formally preconstituted, people who already know and trust each other, or individuals who are familiar with the ins and outs of shaping a collective (Oberschall 1973, 25). In this case, the original commitment of men and women who had long been involved in local life helped the UPM to integrate on the ground level and thus blend into the social landscape of the township. More specifically, this situation enabled the group to claim the status of "community-based organization"—a collective that had emerged from the "community" to defend and represent it.

Attempting to (re)embed South African protest in the social relations structuring lower-class neighborhoods involves taking stock of one of the main ways of shaping the "social" in these spaces. As can be seen in Brazil, a country to which South Africa is often compared,[5] the particularity of these neighborhoods is that they merge with a multifaceted entity: the community. Understanding what such a notion actually means is all the more necessary as, for UPM members, community lies at the heart of the "spatially situated sociality" that I mentioned in the introduction. It is thus within this community that are lived out many of the individual and collective experiences which make the domain of the "near." This is also where the activism of women and men at the heart of this book unfolds. Examining what the "community" is should therefore allow us to approach the very special connection that binds together UPM activists and this entity. It takes the form of what one might call *the sense of community*: the conviction of belonging to that *whole* whose unity and coherence rest mainly on the principles of reciprocity and interdependence. The individuals who possess this conviction thus have a *feel for the community game*—a knowledge of the roles and rules, even implicit, which prevail within this social order. While it is not a question of making this particular sensitivity a source of explanation in itself (notably an explanation of why people become involved), an examination of it can nevertheless help us to better understand the foundations of

Joza neighborhood, in the township

the commitment of postapartheid activists, and to grasp how changes in township life put this commitment to the test.

"Community" is an everyday word. It is also the mainstay of many public discourses (see Jensen 2004; Averweg and Leaning 2015) that have made of it "the rhetorical touchstone of democratic governance" (Ashforth 2005, 101). The success enjoyed by this notion does not, of course, make it any easier to give it even a relatively stable meaning, no more than the long history of divergent uses of which it forms part. Under apartheid, this term allowed the government to classify individuals according to racial categories ("Indian community," "Coloured community," etc.). It also replaced the words "'race,' 'ethnic group,' 'nation,' 'peoples',", thus legitimizing the fact that "since each is a distinct 'community' it must develop 'separately'" (Thornton and Ramphele 1988, 30). The reference to the "community" had also been privileged since the 1960s by liberation movements which used it to mobilize support in the name of the "common good" (35). That those who now resort to it sometimes prove rather evasive when it comes to defining this notion should not, however, lead us to underestimate its symbolic strength.

What may seem to be just a word in fact acts directly on the *social*, endowing it with boundaries, and conferring on it a meaning and a form.

The multiple contemporary uses of this term share a common basic definition. The community refers at the very least to the population of a space whose limits are never formally fixed but which most often corresponds to a street, a neighborhood, a district. The township is therefore a set of communities, though activists generally speak of it in the singular, thereby strengthening its symbolic dimension. In a very tangible way, the community is the parents, neighbors, friends, and "pals" whom we have known since childhood and whom we meet daily. It is, in a way, a "familiarity," in the term used by Bheki, a young UPM activist whom I asked to help me understand a notion that was, to put it mildly, unfamiliar to me as a European.

The result of these few elements is something that certainly comprises the main virtue of community in the eyes of those who invoke it: it constitutes a protection, a pledge of solidarity and, even more, the ideal framework of an "economy of affection," a "network of support, communication and interaction" among structurally defined groups connected by blood, kin, or other affinities (Hyden 1983, 8). The combination of these qualities opportunely shapes a model of the "caring community" that it is always tempting to offer to "outsiders" (Ross 2010, 25). However, the reality may sometimes be a little different, revealing the constraints that are exerted daily on those who populate this small social order. The community can even be perceived as a threat to the privacy that many lower-class households regard as a central pillar of their ideal of respectability (see Muyeba and Seekings 2012, 41–63). By the end of the 1990s, in some townships, as in Soweto, many of those who had succeeded in taking some advantage of the development of the "new" South Africa had erected walls around their homes. It was not only a question of protecting oneself from crime but also of keeping the neighbors at bay, of "excluding" them from the private sphere (Ashforth 2005, 102). Indeed, the increase in inequality observed at the same time in the Black population could feed envy and jealousy and favor the spread of gossip (Ramphele 2002, 102–122). Adam Ashforth (2005) has clearly shown how, beyond any question of rationality and education, fear of rumor and suspicion marked the daily lives of a large number of residents.

Beyond these nuances and contrasts, the community is perhaps above all an effective framework for regulating local social life. It has its guardians, who endeavor to reify it so that everyone will be more inclined to view it as a given. One example that has been studied by Rebecca Pointer and Peter van Heusden (2006) is the district of Driftsands. If several hundred kilometers separate Grahamstown from this area on the outskirts of Cape Town, the structuring principles in both cases are certainly the same. The two sociologists have examined the different processes that led to the "constitution of the community" in this relatively young district, which did not really develop until the early 1990s, when the residents from another area, Crossroads, took refuge there to escape the tensions between ANC and PAC activists. The authors of this study insist on the importance of the creation of the Driftsands Residents Association (DRA), a gathering of the type that exists in most lower-class areas (in the form of street and neighborhood committees, etc.). The genealogy of this type of structures goes back to the late nineteenth century (Bundy 2000, 26–51). Formed in 1993, this association originally rested on the activities of a dozen or so people. It gradually established itself in the social landscape by setting up various grassroots projects, such as opening crèches and creating vegetable gardens. These initiatives enabled the DRA to win a form of authority in the district, and thus to deal with an ever broadening spectrum of "problems." In an almost logical fashion, the association mainly managed to gain the right to speak on behalf of the whole "community" and, boosted by this claim, set itself up as an interlocutor with the political and administrative authorities when RDP houses were built in the district. Its officials negotiated with the authorities, participated in the setting of the level of financial contributions, and organized, from each household, the collection of the money necessary to buy land. The DRA was simply taking on a truly "disciplinary role" (van Heusden and Pointer 2006, 133) within the community, assuming the authority to exclude families who could not pay this sum from the program. Such developments highlight the foundations of the very principle of representation, and in particular the circularity under which "the representative creates the group which creates him" (Bourdieu 1991, 106). More specifically, "it is because the representative exists, because he *represents* (symbolic action), that the group that is represented and symbolized [in this case, the community] exists and that in turn it gives existence to its representative as the representative of the group" (204).

The preceding example shows quite explicitly how, like many social groups and groupings (the "working class," etc.), community is a social, cultural, and obviously historical construction. The objectification of "community" is indeed linked to the racist policies of apartheid governments. The emergence and consolidation of this entity in an urban environment were fueled in particular by the passing of two laws in 1950, completing several decades of segregation. Two years after the National Party came to power, the Population Registration Act defined racial groups based on biological and identity criteria. The same year, the Group Areas Act set out the urban apartheid system by assigning separate territories to these racial groups.[6] It thus put an end to mixed neighborhoods and authorized the eviction of nonwhites from areas designated as "white only" to segregated townships. Inevitably, the forced and supervised constitution of these racial enclaves created the conditions for a communitarian proximity, or even "cultural intimacy" (Hansen 2012), between those who were its subjects: "Africans," "Coloureds," and "Asians." This same proximity would, in turn, shape protest against the regime and turn the communities into veritable "site[s] of struggle" (Bundy 2000, 28). In her study of African women who lived in the Cape region during the second half of the twentieth century, Rebekah Lee clearly underlined how, in the 1950s and 1960s, "the sense of community provided by the township largely shaped the type of everyday resistance that was possible" (2009, 39): a "communal" protest, founded on the mutual encouragement induced by the number of participants and residential proximity. The protest campaigns that were launched at the same time, such as the campaign against influx control policy, also invigorated the communities. On these occasions, a generation did indeed become convinced of the effectiveness of its "organizational power" (39) and redeployed it into the establishment of a community associative network. This could all be summed up by asserting that the unity of the communities was mainly forged under the weight of the oppression and repression exerted by the segregationist regime. The most glaring example remains that provided by the civics, who most often emerged from "older representative bodies" at the end of the 1970s (Bundy 2000, 27) and organized the home front of the struggle at the level of township streets and neighborhoods. In his activist memoirs, Mzwanele Mayekiso (1996), one of the main instigators of this movement, states that "the driving force of black resistance that immobilized the coercive and reformist actions of the state emanated from below as communities responded to their abysmal local living conditions" (68). During the last decade of apartheid, this situation resulted in the development of a multitude of local collectives across the country. Mayekiso insists on the fact that the fruit of these initiatives—"township politics"—rested on the assembly and assent of the community, in particular through "general meetings" organized in the streets. The work of the local committees consisted in allowing the most concrete problems (high rentals, bad houses with no repairs, dirty toilets with no sewage system, high rate of crime, etc.) to find their place in "national liberation politics."

It is undeniable that this history fostered a very antagonistic understanding of the social world of apartheid: communities versus the State and its repressive apparatuses. Perhaps it is partly for these reasons that, even today, the community frequently apprehends itself in terms of adversity: it must be cohesive when confronting a threat that, most often, comes from *outside*. Mention of community also suggests the consciousness of belonging to a separate group within society. The kilometers that separate these neighborhoods from the rest of the city obviously reinforce this perception of things. They can certainly help to explain a conception of the world that, in the minds of a certain number of residents, rests on a separation between "them and us." This "us" includes, in a very general way, "the poor," those who have not benefited from the development of the country, insofar as it seems self-evident that all the poor live in the township or in the shack settlements.[7] As for "them," it is obviously all those who are outside the "community" and the places where the poor and the workers live—that is, the rest of society.

An episode described by political scientist Sally Matthews (2015) gives a palpable form to this way of seeing and dividing the social world. Several students from Rhodes University, members of Students for Social Justice (SSJ), had grown close to the Unemployed People's Movement in the first half of the 2010s, partly through the intermediary of several teachers from the Department of Political Science. The two collectives then undertook to carry out actions together—more specifically, development projects in the poorest areas of the city. Soon, however, the students encountered the suspicions of the locals and many activists. They experienced, even more, the disagreeable feeling that their only reason for being there was to respond to many requests for financial aid. However, the hostile and challenging attitude of the residents was not just aimed at young white people: it targeted with equal force their Black classmates, some of whom had grown up in such communities. They had studied at university, that is to say in a world commonly perceived as privileged: this seemed to *naturally* remove these young Blacks from "us" and set them apart as "them." Sally Matthews reports the unambiguous remarks of one Black student, a member of Students for Social Justice: "By being in Rhodes University, even if you're Black, you are also white in the township. You are called *umlungu* [white person] (quoted in Matthews 2015)."

I have, to a certain extent, had an almost similar experience on my first visit stay in Grahamstown, when I took advantage of an activists' meeting to introduce myself to those who did not know me yet. At first glance, the situation was quite unproblematic, but it took an unexpected turn after my intervention. A woman activist who was present that day spoke out loudly against one of the leaders present at my side and castigated him for welcoming "people" who would disappear once they had got what they were there to seek, to the detriment of the struggle of the poorest people. Beyond the suspicion of instrumentalization, I was especially reminded of my condition as a white middle-class man, even though I sometimes persuaded myself that my nationality placed me a little apart on the scale of the mistrust that my interlocutors are entitled to nurse toward whites. Didn't one of them assure me that I wasn't "too white," unlike some of the others, and that I didn't have a problem with my "whiteness"? Loïc Wacquant mentioned such a feeling in *Body and Soul*. Immersed in the practice of boxing in a club frequented by Black men, the sociologist seemed convinced that his French nationality granted him "a sort of statutory exteriority with respect to the structure of relations of exploitation, contempt, misunderstanding, and mutual mistrust that oppose Blacks and Whites in America" (Wacquant 2004, 10). In my case, although my nationality has sometimes aroused a certain curiosity, it has not diminished the weight of the past that I am supposed to bear as a white European. Here too, there was never a lack of opportunities to remind me of a certain order of things. One Saturday afternoon, while we were sitting in the living room of one of the supporters of the movement, discussing everything under the sun, Ayanda, one of its key spokespersons, spoke to a visitor who had just joined us, and said, "Yes, Jérôme is French . . . Jérôme from France [*laughs*]. He could tell us the story of the French Revolution. And I could tell him about the colonization of Africa by France [*laughs*]."

A few years ago, certainly motivated by the will to test and/or provoke me a little, one young activist also launched into a nonnegotiable praise of Robert Mugabe. The tone of the discussion led me to think that he was not totally unaware that the then-president of Zimbabwe was, at least in Europe, mainly known as the man behind the expulsions of white farmers and the source of regular diatribes against the "perversions" of Westerners.

This book is, whether I like it or not, written from *my point of view,* that of a Western researcher who every evening returns to the house he is renting in a white middle-class neighborhood and who can therefore at any time extricate himself from the often painful daily lives of those he observes. I want to believe, however, that the essential thing is perhaps less to try to resemble the women and men we study than to make them our familiars (Naepels 2011, 20).

The community is largely a sociohistorical construction. The effort to make it *exist* on a daily basis, however, is partly facilitated by the fact that some things may suggest that what it designates is almost *already there*—in the houses, in the streets and on the more or less extensive territory that constitutes the neighborhood or the district. The *self-evident* aspect that follows from this does not, of course, mean that everyone supports it without exception. Just as thousands of Blacks did not join the regular demonstrations against apartheid in the 1980s, or did so under the constraint of neighbors, there are of course individuals who keep their distance from what one, adapting the formula of the French sociologist Maurice Halbwachs, could call the "central hearth of the community."

In *La classe ouvrière et les niveaux de vie* (The Working Class and Standards of Living), published in 1913, Halbwachs described society as a campfire surrounded concentrically by social groups. The level of participation in community life was the highest near the hearth, the situation worsening as one moved further away from it. The most integrated classes in society, socially and culturally, were therefore those belonging to the first circle, where "social, religious, political, business affairs and so on" formed a dense and tight network. Conversely, the groups furthest away from this hearth (such as the working class, in Halbwachs's analysis) were marked by a "certain detachment from society and its customs" (1913, 76). Many people in South African working-class neighborhoods, of course, maintain a similar distance from the community in which they are supposed to live: they stay aloof from the various microsolidarities that extend through the neighborhood, and do not go to the community meetings where people discuss the issues that affect the neighborhood. Many of the UPM's young activists admit to having had little interest in their community before joining the movement. It is only through this commitment that they say they "discovered" it (see Chapter 8).

Immersion in the *center of the community*, near the hearth, as it were, is mainly through membership of one or other of these groupings that form the social mesh of many poor and working-class neighborhoods. As a Soweto activist told me in the late 2000s, "as a member of the community, you're always involved in a load of things in the neighborhood."[8] These may be the street committees that were particularly active under apartheid. Composed of residents of the same street or the same neighborhood (when they are called area committees), they are traditionally responsible for dealing with petty crime (including the recovery of stolen goods) and neighborhood disputes; they also provide assistance to households experiencing housing problems (particularly in the context of disputes over title deeds and occupancy rights) (Cherry, Jones, and Seekings 2000, 893). They are therefore likely to be as active in the public affairs of the district as in the private life of its residents (892). Entities as diverse as sports clubs, associations for the elderly, burial societies, vigilance committees, and the like cohabit with this type of structure. Most of the UPM's activists have moved around this central hearth on an individual basis, and often for several years. Many of them coach teams of young footballers and make sure that the latter become aware of what they owe to the community. These young players therefore have to make regular "rounds" in their district to ensure that the elderly have a tank in case of water shortage. Other activists are or have been active in residents' committees, although the omnipresence of ANC members in these structures does not make things any easier. We could go on and quote such examples as Joseph, a sixty-something activist who is helping an association that works for the elderly in his neighborhood, or Arthur, a thirty-something responsible for the Bible society in his area. One could also add to this list the case of Onke, who for a long time ran a *stokvel*, an authentic self-managed popular savings association (see Bähre 2007a) of a kind that brings together residents who, each month, pay a fixed contribution so that the sum thus collected can be paid to one of them on a rotating system. Emerging in the 1930s, at a time when many Blacks were leaving rural areas for the isolation and loneliness of urban spaces, the *stokvels*—or *umgalelo* clubs—continue to play a major part in Black neighborhoods, especially the less well-off. Such capital can help start up a small business or get over a "bit of bad luck." Because they weave social bonds, these collectives do indeed help to certify the existence of a community in the eyes of the residents. They are most often built on prior relations of acquaintance, formed at the level of a neighborhood or attendance at the same church. Their regular meetings are moments of sociability—a chance to maintain friendships, to exchange various pieces of information or to obtain support in the face of adversity (Buijs 1998). These associations are therefore real landmarks in environments that are affected by economic vulnerability as much as by uncertainty.

As I have already had the opportunity to write, it is possible to live far from community activity. This does not mean, however, that the residents who make this choice totally and systematically escape the various regulations that this entity generates. The threat of finding oneself alone when having to cope with a problem hovers over all those who risk this withdrawal. Thabo, a UPM activist particularly committed to the life of his neighborhood, had unambiguously explained this to me: "The one who does not come to the [community] meetings, we know who he is and he will not be supported in case of a problem."[9] The sense of community thus traces a relatively explicit dividing line at the very heart of local life. It includes as much as it excludes, by defining what is the done thing and what is not, and the like. In an essay combining memories and fragments of historical ethnography, Jacob Dlamini has discussed at some length what can be considered as the matrix of this demarcation. The author, born in 1973, describes a "moral economy of mutual exchange and obligation" (2009, 99), in which he includes the very standardized system that regulated money lending between households on the same street in the township of his childhood. The organization of support for bereaved families was also part of this moral economy. From the announcement of a death to the collection of donations for the family by the person put in charge of this function in the street (Dlamini's mother, as regularly happened) (103–105), it was indeed an entire informal system of rules, practices, and expectations that, under cover of solidarity, allowed this small social order to stick together, and excluded families perceived as "stingy, antisocial or contrarian" (98).

A study carried out in various lower-income parts of the country highlighted the propensity of members of associations such as *stokvels* to highlight values such as "camaraderie," "trust," and "socialization" to justify their support (Naong 2007). Such motives are obviously music to the ears of those who seek confirmation that lower-income neighborhoods are havens of mutual aid and participation, even though some sociological surveys have, on the contrary, shown that the poorest of them are often characterized by "weaker social bonds" (Muyeba and Seekings 2012, 48). Other studies have mainly emphasized how respect for these values sometimes only led to false pretenses or "reluctant solidarity" (Bähre 2007b). In his analysis of the treatment of a woman who lived the last years of her life on the edge of a community in a township in Cape Town, Erik Bähre has shown how, on the death of this resident, her neighbors experienced a "mixture of feelings: guilt for not being able to take care of the marginal; embarrassment for having the reputation of a street that does not care for its neighbors; identification with a poor woman who died of the fast spreading disease AIDS; as well as the difficulty to respect a person who was a disgrace to the neighborhood" (51).

References to "camaraderie" and "solidarity" do have one merit: they tell us what, in the view of most residents, can normally or fairly be seen as part of collective life and thereby the "community." "Solidarity," "selflessness," and "mutual aid" are also words regularly uttered by activists in the Unemployed People's Movement when they affirm their willingness to "fight for the community." It is not absurd to take the assertion of adherence to these values seriously, bearing in mind that this same statement is made in the always particular context of a conversation with an "outsider."

The importance of exposure to "community values" in the most fundamental moments of their childhood or adolescence is, in any case, regularly suggested by activists during interviews, regardless of their age. It gives rise to a sense of duty that can be applied in a concrete and regular manner: a sense of community. Zolani, a young man who had been active for two or three years in the UPM, talked about this sense of responsibility as we walked the streets of his neighborhood on a day in April 2016:

"You are involved in your community?" I asked.
"Of course," Zolani replied.
"And when you were a teenager?"
"Things were easier when I was a teenager. There was not a lot of crime. Everyone played sport or did something at that time . . ." He interrupted himself. "Those children . . ." He pointed to a group of four

or five children playing further away. "Now, there's always the risk that the young children are getting involved in crime activities, are getting involved in gangs. So . . . we have to take it to ourselves, just because we have young brothers now. It's like a free mentorship program."

These remarks echo those of many activists with whom I have talked over the years. The multivoice discourse that emerges from these exchanges is in fact a relatively specific discourse of legitimation. It is, more exactly, a *discourse of institution*. For the community is indeed an institution, that is to say a set of social relations that, as an aggregate, has acquired a life of its own and come to be associated with beliefs, practices, principles, and a culture. This discourse reveals more precisely, and very explicitly, the ideal model of the activist *at the service* of the "community," with its codes of conduct and its right ways of doing and being. Those who emphasize belonging to the "community" implicitly know that they must respect it at least a little if they want it all to hang together and provide them with a position of their own. This obviously goes without saying for the activists who grew up in, or near, the central "hearth." Thus inhabited by the sense of community, they seem indeed seized by the *illusio*: "invested, taken in and by the game" (Bourdieu and Wacquant 1992, 116). They view the community all the more as a reality, that is, as something that appears to hold by its own strength, as it lies at the heart of their *activist time* and their daily lives. It can justify the fact that, twice a day, Thabang makes a detour to ensure that work on the local school is making good progress. He knows that this is one of the things *the community expects of him*. And by doing so, this full-time UPM activist is obviously helping to consolidate this "bodyless being" (Boltanski 2011, 74). What is essential, then, is less any belief *stricto sensu* in the existence of an all-encompassing entity than this type of consensus about belonging to a set of more or less direct social interdependencies.

The phenomenon of the *influence* of institutions on those who inhabit them has been extensively and frequently studied by the social sciences (Douglas 1996). However, I argue that "community" exerts less of a grip on the minds of those who appeal to it than it meets certain dispositions within them. Take the case of Bheki. It is admittedly quite likely that this activist barely in his thirties was drawn into it by a man who, a few years previously, had coached him in football and helped him to find political words for the injustice he was experiencing. Nevertheless, the fact that he joined the UPM can also be read in the light of an upbringing marked by the recurrent memory of well-known "community values": solidarity, a certain idea of equality, altruism, the ability to resist all types of oppression, and so forth. During our conversations, the young man frequently mentioned the commitment his parents had shown to their neighborhood, its associations, and its meetings. They explained it to their children, most often establishing a parallel with Christianity. Bheki also has every reason to believe in these values insofar as he was able to see them regularly transcribed into the mobilizations of residents against this or that threat:

> I saw that solidarity when I was a child. I saw what solidarity is. I saw my neighbors, my friends, who were gathering. Meetings were organized in my neighborhood . . . when there was a problem. People were talking. They were struggling . . . against crime, floods. You see? That's the community, you see? We help each other. You know, people also used to give food to neighbors who needed it.

In the view of Bheki, the unemployed movement is able to defend the ideals with which he claims to have grown up. In other words, the actions of the UPM largely meet the expectations that are part and parcel of his socialization. The example of this young activist therefore sheds a slightly significant light on some of the springs of commitment. Sociology and social psychology have thus amply demonstrated how often membership in a collective is based on interactions, inclusion in social networks, or chance encounters. Numerous cases of people joining the UPM confirm this analysis. However, it seems to me that we should not neglect all that commitment owes to values "partly forged outside the organization" (Mischi 2016, 213), as the case of Bheki illustrates quite well. Of course, we should not go back to a form of idealization of commitment but rather try to understand that when individuals persuade themselves that a collective fits the values that they themselves have previously incorporated, their enrollment is more effective and perhaps more sustainable. This observation could apply to different types of structure—a party or a union, for example. However, it is even more evident within a protest movement. As James Jasper rightly notes, the public, collective and often intense nature of protest has the effect of deepening "the significance and emotional impact of beliefs and feelings"

(Jasper 1997, 5). Protest therefore comprises an unparalleled forum for expressing an indignation that combines people's sensibilities and their moral convictions.

Bheki's remarks suggest a kind of ethics of community and the relationship to others. In the past, in other organizations, some activists used a specific term to summarize all of this. They spoke to me about *Ubuntu*, the set of social and moral values often summarized by the famous formula of Archbishop Desmond Tutu: "A person is a person through other people." An activist from the Soweto Electricity Crisis Committee told me that she had "lived socialism" even before discovering it in books: "As Africans . . . we live it the whole time, with *Ubuntu*." Here again, everyone is free to see this as a mere idealization of what is supposed to have led people to put their words into deeds, and justified attachment to the cause. The choice of this register of justification nevertheless explains why, in many interviews, activists place on the same level, without hierarchizing them, their commitment to protest, the help they bring personally to an association of elderly people, and the educational support provided to children in their neighborhoods, for example. These few cases overlap in the concern for the "humanity" constantly invoked by my interlocutors to explain the meaning of their actions.

The essentially *self-evident* nature on which the idea of community rests is thus nourished by the fact that it can deck itself out in a relatively abstract form, woven from representations, values, and perceptions. The case of South Africa can be compared with those of other societies in the Global South such as Brazil, Chile, and Venezuela (see Fernandes 2010; Oxhorn 2011; Fischer, McCann, and Auyero 2014). The community appears at first sight as the almost ideal place of a *natural* solidarity, consubstantial with the worlds of the working class; a solidarity on which everyone can rely. This is all the truer in South Africa in that the very idea of community is deemed to carry with it the history of resistance and protest against the apartheid regime—a relatively recent history, still present in people's memories and words. I am thinking, of course, of the demonstrations, but also of the fact that the ban on "multiracial" parties and the Communist Party from the 1950s and 1960s had transferred part of the process of politicization to sports clubs, secondary school associations, religious groups, and all the collectives at the heart of community and local activity. Interviews conducted with women and men who spent their childhood or adolescence in the 1980s are thus almost always studded with references to these apparently harmless but, in fact, "highly politicized" groupings which helped to structure resistance or, more simply, awareness. This was true of the amateur football teams in the townships. Some of the founders of the UPM, aged between thirty-five and forty-five at the beginning of the 2010s, played for a long time in the very popular Cosmos Joza club. Everyone remembers the training sessions where you could talk without being heard by the regime's police. Recalled one activist:

> And people were talking, talking, talking [*laughs*]. . . . They talked about politics, they talked about what was happening in the country. And the older ones, who were in their twenties, those who were role models . . . they explained what was happening to the younger ones. They were very, very influential. They were community activists.

These memories and the stories they generate sometimes give the appearance of a golden age to this period of history, especially in the eyes of younger activists who are convinced that the problem now is that individualism is eating into their time:

> In the community . . . yes, we are selfish. We do something for ourselves, not for the community. I think it was different in the past. Now things are different. Our generation is so different. . . . I don't know why but things are so different. When I hear my parents telling me stories about their older days and compare to . . . now. Things are different.

Siphokazi, a twenty-two-year-old activist, is obviously evoking a time she knows only through the accounts of her elders and which can obviously give rise to a certain idealization. It is, for example, difficult to conclude that the residents of the postapartheid township are more "selfish" than in the past. On the other hand, it is not improbable that a context increasingly marked by uncertainty, but also by the simple fact of finally being able to leave the location when one wants, will have modified the relationship that individuals maintain with the community. From the interviews that Rebekah Lee conducted with young Black women born in the 1970s and 1980s, there emerges a more selective and distant attitude to the community-based associations created by their mothers (2009, 145). In the 1950s and 1960s, participation in these associations occupied a central place in the lives of individuals. It directly contributed to the construction of their identity as city dwellers and endowed them with a "sense of cohesion" (150). Nowadays, the relation is more distanced and looser. Taking part in collectives such as burial societies or savings groups is no longer an end in itself but one way among many to obtain certain resources in a consumer society. Quite logically, identification with the place of residence, where the community is supposed to take shape, is all the more weakened.

I have often witnessed the nostalgia expressed by Siphokazi, whether in exchanges with activists or with residents of poor neighborhoods. It has even become a fairly common theme in studies of postapartheid South Africa (see, among others, Reed 2016 and Paret 2018). While the condition of the poorest is generally placed under the sign of the temporariness of things (Appadurai 2003), this nostalgia reflects the simple and attractive idea that life in the township may at one time have been synonymous with permanence and continuities. In his aptly titled *Native Nostalgia* (2009), Jacob Dlamini paints a picture that may help us better grasp this contemporary feeling, especially in the Black townships. He notes that, while the townships were conceived as "dormitories of labour" (105) by the architects of segregation, they gradually became places of culture, stability, familiarity, and solidarity, following the activities and daily encounters of their residents. That they evolved into places of "embodied memories" (154) is therefore quite logical. Although their origin differed somewhat, the development was, in all likelihood, comparable in Indian and Coloured townships.[10] This obviously does not mean that the locations of the 1950s, 1960s, or 1970s brought together socially homogeneous groups. The wealthiest households, for example, were already competing in strategies of social distinction. Also, as Steffen Jensen notes (2008, 146), while the Group Areas Act (1950) assigned individuals to spaces based on their race, it did so on the basis of class for the Coloured population as well. However, the fact that these spaces were experienced as enclaves fostered the idea of a proximity, even a communitarian intimacy, among many of their residents.

The climate of uncertainty that prevailed during the last decade of the twentieth century swept away these reference points, especially in poor and working-class neighborhoods—whatever the color of their residents. The fault lay mainly in the impoverishment of the most vulnerable, under the effect of deindustrialization and the massive destruction of low-skilled and unskilled jobs. Local life became less structured, more anonymous, and less unitary; Thomas Blom Hansen even concluded that "the community has splintered very rapidly along lines of class, language, and religion" in the Indian township that he studied at the beginning of the 2000s (2005, 313). Hostility toward the intruder, that is to say, the person who, even recently, was above all "outside" the community,[11] has become a norm as the perception of a *brutalization* of social relations has spread. When Ayanda, a UPM leader, is disillusioned or tries to sensitize a foreign interlocutor to the situation of the township, he does not hesitate to speak about the "brokenness" of Grahamstown's communities. He obviously has in mind the poverty in which many of them are plunged, but he is especially thinking of the violence that makes the township a world whose balance is permanently threatened. The violence is something that most activists experience or have experienced in their daily lives. It can be domestic or sexual violence, or it may involve completely gratuitous acts on the part of a neighbor or stranger, one evening in the tavern or on a street corner, after a minor altercation. Violence has affected the movement on several occasions since the early 2010s, including the murder of one young activist's sister, and the time when one of its main leaders was found guilty of torture resulting in the death of another man. At times such as these, activists obviously notice a "differential between what should be and what is" (Boltanski 2011, 106). The community as an institution then produces a reality that no longer corresponds to its principles. We thus find ourselves at the very heart of those "hermeneutic contradictions" (106) which generally foster criticism. In the present case, however, the revelation of these contradictions merely gives rise to doubt and despondency that usually occupies little space in the commitment of these women and men.

These forms of alienation, which are part of a fairly precise historical context (the shift from one society to another), can, more generally, be an echo of what Loïc Wacquant calls "dissolution of place": "the loss of humanized, culturally familiar and socially filtered locale with which marginalized populations identify, and in which they feel at 'home' and in relative security" (2007, 241). The idea is also found in Leslie Bank's study of the Black location of East London (2011, 215–217), less than two hours' drive from Grahamstown. Bank does not hesitate to place this phenomenon in a long succession of trials endured and discourses of vilification whose origin he traces back to the beginning of the twentieth century. He shows how much this accumulation has inevitably fomented the self-deprecation of residents who have gradually lost all hope of seeing their daily lives improve. It would be hard not to find confirmation of such a phenomenon in the words and attitudes of the locals encountered over my years of research in Grahamstown. One need only remember the uncompromising words chosen by township schoolchildren to describe their daily environment (see Chapter 1). There are also, among the activists of the UPM, the moments of dejection of which I have already spoken and the analogies sometimes drawn, in moments of emotional outburst, between the township and a "concentration camp" (see Interlude 3).

However, this does not sum up the mind-set of the women and men who invest their energy in their community-based organization on a daily basis. Even with its shortcomings and constraints, the township remains the place where *their* domain of the near is shaped. The following observation gives us a glimpse of this reality. The mother of an activist I had known for several years died a few weeks before I made my final trip to Grahamstown in 2018. She lived in a small house in the heart of one of the oldest neighborhoods in the township. Her three children grew up in this building, probably built in the 1950s or 1960s. Over the years, an additional room was added to it, while the outside walls were repainted in yellow, as if to break

Nompodo street, in the township

with the monotony imposed on Black districts by the architects of apartheid. This embellishment certainly dates back to the 1970s, when the residential stabilization of urban Black households enabled some of them to transform their "sterile matchbox houses" into respectable "family homes" and to dream a little of the emergence of a "Black suburbia" (Bank 2011, Chapter 7). Although I have always known this activist as a resident of the Black neighborhoods that stretch from the limits of the old white city to the township, he has often told me that he only conceived his "home" within these walls, alongside neighbors he had known since "forever." He also knows, if we are to believe him, that he will return to live there one day. Almost every day, even since his mother's death, he manages to stop by in his old neighborhood, sometimes for a quarter of an hour. The many times I have accompanied him there, I have observed him, obviously relaxed, leaning against the fence surrounding the house, chatting and laughing with passing acquaintances. These repeated scenes bring out how much, for those who invest in it, community is above all a familiarity, in which an almost elementary social affiliation is affirmed. It seems to me that the contrast between these innocuous but everyday scenes and the episodes of resignation already mentioned explain quite well the tension that slips into the commitment of the activists of the UPM and, most certainly, that of many of their peers across the country. This tension is particularly strong when the xenophobic violence that the country has known since the beginning of the twenty-first century erupts. It is no longer the feeling of estrangement from an era that overwhelms activists, but that of seeing a crisis brewing in what is supposed to justify their mobilization.

Violence linked to hatred of foreigners—or to what some refer to as "Black-on-Black racism"[12]—has been the subject of sometimes contradictory analyses, variously emphasizing the frustration born from wretched living conditions, the maintenance of a system of exploitative migrant labor in a context of high unemployment, the identity contradictions entailed by economic globalization, a retreat into ethnicity due to the fact that the democratic citizenship does not keep its promises, and so on. Most commentators, however, stress the responsibility of political elites in these events. Xenophobia is even, in their view, "a structural feature of State discourse and practice, not an accidental occurrence" (Neocosmos 2006, 125). This, among other things, seems to be confirmed by the adoption of aggressive postapartheid legislation against immigration, the waves of expulsions of foreigners and the national-chauvinistic postures of many national politicians.[13] Relatively unanimously, the main actors of postapartheid protest, on the other hand, denounced violence as soon as it occurred. They usually called for the protection of their foreign "brothers and sisters," and put forward a vision of the community which could seem very inclusive in such a context but which, above all, respected a fairly literal definition of the sense of community. In May 2015, just days after the lynching of foreigners in a Black neighborhood in Johannesburg, I witnessed an unambiguous position taken by members of the Soweto Electricity Crisis Committee. During an internal meeting devoted to the movement's participation in a national demonstration against xenophobic violence, one of the leaders had made a point of recalling at considerable length what South Africa and its residents owed, according to him, to "other Africans." He had first of all evoked the memory of the apartheid fighters forced into exile and welcomed into neighboring countries during the 1960s and 1970s. But he had above all insisted on the benefits that everyone derived from the presence of foreigners within communities: from taxi drivers bringing them downtown to customers of spaza shops (convenience stores) run by Ethiopians known for their credit facilities. These are arguments that I sometimes also heard in Grahamstown, where certain activists sometimes physically interposed themselves between strangers and the crowd during the events of October 2015.

In the months following the looting, those with whom I spoke about the matter almost systematically emphasized the good integration of foreign traders into the neighborhoods and their participation in aid for the community—the help given to the poorest families, for example. UPM leaders condemned the unrest but also sought dialogue with its perpetrators. Several community meetings were organized to this end. As is often the case, those who spoke on such occasions engaged in a certain amount of pedagogy. They explained to an often mistrustful audience the very precise origin of the "self-hatred" and the "frustration" which impelled people to attack modest businesses that were nonetheless perceived as successes obtained at the expense of the "nationals": the abandonment of the poorest people and the evident desire of those in power to divide them. In other words, these activists sought to transform an issue that had been imposed on them in racial—or ethnicist—terms into a social and political issue: whether the ruling elite was white or Black, the poor had most in common with each other. By drawing somewhat freely on the work of Ernesto Laclau

(2005), we could therefore consider that activists, as self-proclaimed guardians of the unity of the community, promoted a *logic of equivalence* that offers to bring people together beyond cultural heterogeneity. Conversely, they castigated the *logic of difference* that it would be in the government's interest to promote.

I hope I have shown how necessary it is to take into account the "sense of community" in any study of a movement such as the UPM. Its understanding obviously does not say everything about the commitment of the activists, but it reveals important foundations. The sense of community sheds light, for example, on the meaning these individuals aim to give to their struggle. The following chapter will also highlight its influence on the form of actions and, more generally, on the positioning of the collective in its environment.

By perceiving and presenting themselves as being at the service of their community, the activists seek to preserve this sensitivity, which they see as now threatened by poverty as well as by individualism and the harshness of social relations in the township. This apparent abnegation (even if, in their eyes, it seems to be an obvious fact that is rarely questioned) requires reproducing every day the practices that are supposed to consolidate the community. Such an undertaking appears, it is true, all the more coherent as it holds the promise of continuity and stability in lives marked by unpredictability.

INTERLUDE 1: FOOTBALL, COMMUNITY, AND POLITICS

Among the different social worlds that make up the township, there is one that has, perhaps more than others, been an echo chamber for the discussions that preceded the birth of the Unemployed People's Movement. This is the world of amateur football (soccer). It deserves a little closer attention as, to some extent, it is a kind of half-open window that gives us a glimpse of some of the dynamics and rifts in the "community."

Just like religion, football is often a refuge for many township residents (see Withley, Hayden, and Gould 2013), and it can thus become a moral resource. It "brings meaning" and "contrasts radically with the dreary lethargy of township life," wrote one UPM activist in the pages of the local newspaper, before adding, "It's an act of defiance against the given, a struggle against the horror expressed in the eyes of our parents."[1] Football simply brings regulation and ritualization to lives that usually lack it (Jensen 2008, 177–183). The presence of a neutral referee, numerical equality between the two camps and, above all, the recourse to a set of "trans-cultural" and "trans-historical" rules (178) keeps the arbitrariness of daily life in the township at a distance, at least for a few hours.

In the center of the Joza district there is a large plot of land on which the boundaries of two football pitches have been drawn. The whole is surrounded by a high blockwork wall surmounted by barbed wire. You can enter the compound and park your car a few meters from the touchlines, not far from the groups of children tirelessly playing on an imaginary pitch. One Saturday afternoon I did so, at the request of the three activists I was accompanying into the township. We had spent about twenty minutes sitting in the car, in near silence, watching a team in blue jerseys giving a team in red jerseys a hard time. Every weekend is a succession of matches between teams of teenagers and young men. Whatever the time of the day, you can sit on the cement terraces and chat to those who are already there. People swap opinions about the technique of this or that player, find out about those who are absent, talk about the events that have occurred in the township that week, and so on. Even when feelings are running high on the pitch, the surrounding atmosphere remains generally calm and serene.

Some of the discussions that led to the formation of the UPM in 2009 took place here, or on one of the vacant lots more or less given over to football in the township. This sport plays a major role in the lives of several activists. Ayanda, one of their main spokespersons, trained a team of teenagers, some of whom joined the movement in the 2010s. The camaraderie that prevailed during training allowed him to speak quite openly to these boys, who were often not highly politicized. Ayanda encouraged them to analyze the injustice of their living conditions. Thabang is now doing the same, with whatever means he can muster. The teenagers in his care—some are just over ten years old—train four evenings a week in the middle of a big windswept plain. Little piles of coats are used to mark out the pitch. This thirty-year-old, with his solid, determined physique, sees these moments as opportunities to provide the young players with benchmarks and values. Regular "team building sessions," and the minutes that close the training sessions, are dedicated to their "consciousness-raising." While he was responsible for founding this club, and its survival rests on his shoulders alone, Thabang nonetheless considers that "it must belong to the community," since "moral leaders" may perhaps emerge from it.

In the eyes of Thabang, his coaching and his activism in the Unemployed People's Movement thus follow the same logic. It is true that, in the township, football fits easily into the places where a passion for sport overlaps with social-communitarian commitment. For some time, various members of the UPM had been planning to create an after-school academy based on this sport. It would have welcomed children and thus kept them away from petty crime or, more simply, protected them from boredom. Their access to the football field would have been on condition that they finished their homework. The project has gradually withered due to lack of financial means. The challenge lay mainly in obtaining a football ground from the municipality. But such hopes were in vain.

One afternoon in 2016, while we were sitting in the living room of the UPM premises, I asked Bheki what, in concrete terms, he was doing for his community. In a logical and predictable way, he first mentioned his activism within the collective: the meetings organized to convince his neighbors that there is nothing fated in their condition, the occasional help given to some of them when they have to cope with a sudden bit of bad luck, and the like. There was also the attention brought to bear on young people in his neighborhood to prevent them from falling into delinquency. He then mentioned the volunteer tutoring he did at his old high school—something he did, he told me, at the request of a teacher with whom he had been in contact. Then Bheki started talking about the time spent training the team in which he had played during his childhood. In his view, this investment of effort was self-evident, and the hours spent mentoring young people could perhaps help them find a path to a more structured life. One could obviously find this language, highlighting altruism and disinterested self-giving, as a little

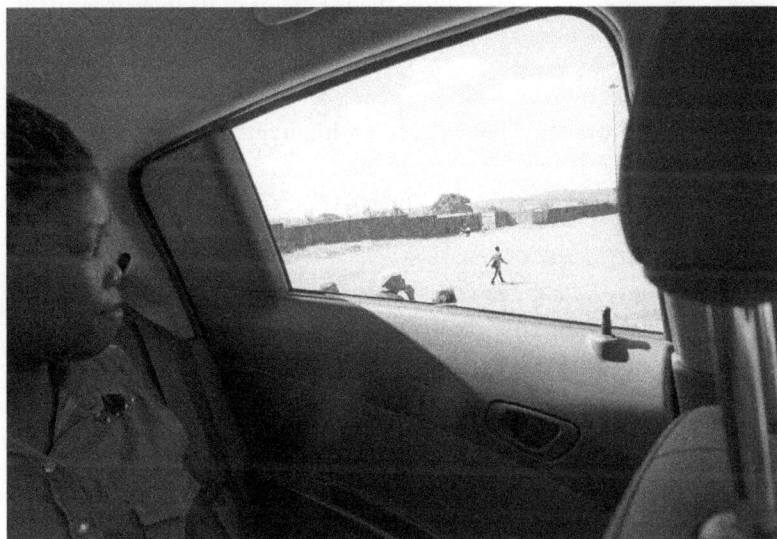

Match day in the township

suspect. But it would then be necessary to find other reasons to explain what drives Bheki and his comrades to spend so much of their time volunteering to help young footballers in Black neighborhoods.

While in other parts of the world it is certainly the dream of many amateur coaches that one of their players will be scouted by professionals, things are a little different in the township. Here, people's express hopes are both more rational and more political. They consist in not seeing these young people as being totally trapped in the "raw life" (Ross 2010) that often seems to await them. Comparison with the commitment to protest movements is thus never very far away, as Ayanda told me: "When you see someone giving everything for football, it gives you hope. When you see someone setting up a barricade or protesting, it gives you hope."

Football is therefore eminently "political" in the eyes of the activists concerned. From a historical point of view, first of all, it regularly offered a protected area for the struggle during the years of apartheid. The discussions made possible in the clubs often contributed to the political awakening of an entire generation in the townships. This political dimension did not disappear with the advent of democracy. If it can give an impetus to the youngest, football also closely follows the contours of the postapartheid universe of the governed. It reproduces the meanders of its injustices and its inequalities, and is imbued by the feeling of abandonment that the poorest say they experience. Said Ayanda:

> You've got the elite league . . . people with luxury cars. The elite league gets all the money and the grassroots soccer is neglected. The development structures are neglected. I mean . . . it's political. Football is also political.

> We must give young people a social conscience. They've got to understand why there are no soccer balls . . . why they have to share the soccer boots . . . why they don't play prestigious competitions. . . . Football and social ills, the brokenness of our society . . . you cannot separate the two.

3

"WE ARE THE PEOPLE WHO STAY WITH THEM IN THE TOWNSHIP"

It's a rather unusual photograph. There isn't really anybody in it: just legs and knees. A few hands. No faces. "They" are sitting in a semicircle on make-shift seats: breeze blocks or plastic crates placed on the dusty earthen floor. A classical, methodical composition would have revealed the features of the women and men who settle down every day in the yard of the man who brews *umtshovalale*, the alcohol that is held responsible for driving people mad. It has its equivalents in other parts of South Africa. In the informal settlements of KwaZulu-Natal, they refer to *isipikili siyeza* ("the pick is coming") or *ukhakhayi lwemfene* ("crown of a baboon"), a beverage that some people drink so as to forget that they have left their declining rural areas only to find themselves unemployed (Hunter 2010, 157–158). The same idleness hovers over this yard somewhere in the middle of Joza, the oldest district in the township of Grahamstown. It is lined by three modest houses and a few shacks and surrounded by a rickety wire fence. Leaning against a wall or sitting, the women and men gathered here drink the pale yellow alcohol out of plastic bottles that must once have contained fizzy drinks and now lie between the consumers, littering the ground or piled in a little heap in a corner of the yard. Whether you come in the morning or very late in the afternoon, you ultimately tend to find pretty much the same thing: haggard individuals, reeling under the effects of alcohol, barely exchanging a few words. Only the arrival of a stranger seems able to disturb this order. At least for a few minutes. On most of the photographs of the scene that I took, there are four or five of these individuals taking turns in front of the lens, some pretending to drink, others proffering the bottle in my direction as if in a commercial touting the merits of some fizzy drink. They started to act this way after I agreed to give a few rand to the owner of the premises, with the definite aim of bribing them into more or less tolerating my presence. The money immediately went to a round of drinks for everyone there.

The place is not a shebeen. There is no concession to sociability or relaxation here; it's a clandestine microbrewery for homemade liquor where customers can drink. For decades, in the slums of South Africa, men and especially women have been transforming their homes for this purpose. When the authorities found out about this activity at the beginning of the twentieth century, they first tried to criminalize it and then decided to smother it by entrusting the monopoly of the sale of beer to municipal beerhalls in the 1930s. This decision obviously roused the anger of the women selling their home brews: they threw themselves into organizing boycotts and demonstrations—in vain (see Walker 1982). This situation of unfair competition lasted a few decades. Because they were associated with white power by the township residents, the beerhalls logically became the first targets of the insurgency that swept the country in July 1976. This accelerated their decline.

In a clandestine microbrewery

The premises are run by a stern-faced man. His commercial survival rests mainly on two plastic containers. First, there is the large basin placed on the ground in his shack, at the far end of the yard. In it, a whitish and slightly sparkling liquid is macerating; the brewer presents it as a simple mixture of water, brown sugar, snuff, and yeast, three large bags of which are stored in a corner of the room. Rubbing alcohol, brake fluid, and detergent have occasionally been found on the premises of other producers in Grahamstown. The thick liquid thus obtained is then placed for several hours in a barrel, also made of plastic, in order to accelerate fermentation. At the end of these rudimentary operations, repeated every day, the *umtshovalale* can be served to these customers, more captive than faithful, who occupy the yard.

Without my asking, the master of the house suggests that I follow him into the backyard so that I can discover the basic process of alcohol production. Police officers took the same route a few weeks ago. However, they merely tipped over the basin and let the soil absorb the alcohol. They did not seize the equipment or issue a fine.

Strangely, it is Ndisa, a very young woman activist, who brought me here, no doubt thinking I'd find be impressed by the place. A few months back, however, the UPM launched public meetings aimed at educating the poorest people in Grahamstown about the harmful effects of this alcohol. Community buildings and school halls were the venue for these gatherings, which included representatives from the many township churches and heads of associations with expertise in health; more surprising, perhaps, was the presence of brewers eager to explain their activities. According to the protesters, the spread of *umtshovalale* needs to be understood as both a health and a social problem. While this beverage is suspected of having caused deaths in the township of Grahamstown, it is mainly an expression of the misery so widely shared by the residents of the lower-class districts of South African towns. Produced by unemployed men and women (single mothers, most often), *umtshovalale* is essentially sold to the poorest of the poor, or at least those who could not afford more than the two rand that are the usual cost of a full bottle.

The UPM initiative may surprise anyone interested in social protest in other parts of the world, particularly in the West. The same would certainly be true of the few hours of consciousness-raising about sexism and patriarchy that activists organized in three of the township's high schools in spring

2016. These actions reflect other activities through which the protest collective fully focuses on its most immediate social and spatial environment, even becoming a lookout or mediator for the latter. For evidence of this, you need merely read the newsletter which the UPM brought out for a few months. This document, about twenty pages per issue, was one of the fruits of the money paid by a German foundation close to the European Green political movement. Relatively rare, this type of financing is generally associated with projects related to environmental, democratic, or social issues. For a few months, above all, it guaranteed a regular income for the collective, in the form of various stipends. Before that, it was necessary for the leaders to prove their social knowledge of the township or the competence of their movement in mobilizing residents to take part in actions likely to improve their lives. In this case, the UPM had to "investigate" the xenophobic attacks that drew the interest even of the Western media and write a report. Reading the few issues of the newsletter also helps one grasp the field of expertise claimed by the movement. As well as reporting on relatively "traditional" struggles, such as the denunciation of housing conditions, the newsletter recorded reasons for anger that were more diverse, but equally rooted in the daily lives of the township's residents. The publication was thus a succession of "reports"—on the poor state of the roads in the township, on the proliferation of illegal garbage dumping, on the derelict state of certain cemeteries. All these problems had the same origin according to the editors: the "general disrespect of government for the people."

It seems to me that when rooted in everyday life, activism deployed by members turns out to be as much a set of practices and activities as a social relationship between them and the residents. Activism bears within itself the responsibility which the former claim to have toward the latter, in the name of this "sense of community." It also allows us to glimpse a proximity that, as I intend to show, is quite simply based on what activists actually *are*: "poor" *among* the other poor, *similar* to the other poor, or almost.

As it gained legitimacy, the protest movement ventured to extend the scope of its interventions to very specific issues, such as gender. Its main leaders sought very early on to engage in the fight against sexism. I have often seen how sensitivity to this theme was important in the self-presentation of certain men within the UPM. They often spoke to me severely about how women were treated in other organizations or, more simply, about ordinary interactions they had witnessed in their daily lives. In the 2000s and 2010s, some of the more politicized among them moved in activist circles that were open to different intellectual trends, including feminism. In any event, this sensibility is also linked to more personal experiences. On the one hand, in some cases their entourage had occasionally been affected by cases of sexual and domestic violence. One example is Likhaya, whose sister was tortured and then murdered by a neighbor. On the other hand, the arrival in the collective of people more directly concerned by these questions has helped to legitimize the attention paid to such issues. Thandazile, for example, is a young lesbian from a small town in the Eastern Cape. A state loan allowed her to study at Rhodes University, and she soon became very involved in the UPM. The fact that she is quite open about her sexual orientation explains, in any event, why she was entrusted with the task of setting up workshops, but also organizing community meetings on the situation of LGBTI people in the Black and poor neighborhoods of the town.

In many ways, this urge to look after the interests and ills of the community was somewhat reminiscent of the position adopted by the grassroots organizations that emerged in Chile in the aftermath of the military coup. These organizations were responsible for presenting to the authorities petitions drawn up by the residents of the *poblaciones*, the shantytowns of Santiago, whenever problems related to water or electricity bills arose. They also distinguished themselves in the fields of culture, recreation, and commerce (Oxhorn 1995). One can also think of the Argentinian *piqueteros*. In addition to blocking highways since the 1990s, in order to resist privatization and layoffs, these groups of unemployed workers have helped to create gardens, clinics, and bakeries within their communities (Osterweil 2014, 478). If the UPM has not (yet) ventured into these latter territories, one of its young activists told me that he frankly feels that his movement is also a "social service" which sometimes moves into the *almost intimate* sphere of the poorest Grahamstownians. This happens when UPM groups do their utmost to help bereaved families when the latter are unable to pay their funeral costs. In June 2013, Zandile, Amada, and Sibongile, three women activists, were approached by a family from Extension 9 who did not have enough money to bury one of their children. An internal meeting was organized at which it was decided that the UPM "would work with the family" to raise the necessary sum. In particular, the leaders of the unemployed movement sent an email message to their external supporters and contacts—a score of South African and European academics and researchers. In simple words, but sparing no details, they related the story of the child's family: the mother had been raped a few months before and had wasted away; the grandmother had resorted to shady measures to protect the child, who was also ill. The message ended with the call for a "financial contribution" to help pay for the funeral undertaker, transportation, and food. For several days, most activist activities were put on a back burner while money was sought, even though no member of the organization was directly affected by this misfortune. A few months later, when a similar problem raised its head in the course of the movement's everyday life, Ayanda told me that the UPM simply had to intervene when adversity struck a member of the community. The repetition of this type of intervention even led the activists to think about the creation of a burial society, this form of self-help group allowing people not to be caught off guard when misfortune strikes. The idea was finally abandoned after many discussions, the time necessary for the good management of such a system appearing too important.

Perhaps it is this same sense of responsibility, implicitly put forward by Ayanda, that regularly drives activists to try to resolve neighborhood conflicts. It was one such conflict that, on an April evening, took four members of the organization to the home of a couple living on a street lined with small dilapidated houses. Sitting in the living room, serious and concentrated, they listened as the woman and the man explained what had happened the day before and led them to lodge a complaint against their son's girlfriend. It was a quite ordinary story of a love quarrel that turned into a petty crime when the young woman, overcome by jealousy, deliberately broke one of the windowpanes in the couple's house and found herself taken into custody at the Grahamstown police station. The activists obviously took care to show they understood the plaintiffs' problem. But if they had come to see the couple, it was also in order to convince them to reconsider their decision, which was causing a certain unrest in the neighborhood. On the way back in my car, the activists were not very positive about the young woman; in their view, she was showing a "toxic" attitude toward her community. The next day, however, they went to the Grahamstown police station and managed to get her out, after negotiating with the officer on duty and hinting that I was a journalist.

These efforts at mediation are quite typical of the set of interventions that occur at the heart of the disorders and dysfunctions affecting the community. At other times, in other places, this activity can lead to organizing the collection of the rubbish strewn down the streets of a particular district or negotiating with the owners of shebeens in order to put an end to the night-time disturbances that residents complain about. Such interventions sometimes go further and become a real attempt to regulate certain aspects of local social life. In the early 2010s, UPM leaders were alerted to the brutal shutdown of an RDP housing construction project in Sun City, one of the most desolate areas of Grahamstown. Unpaid for several weeks, the workers had stopped working on this project, which aimed to build 440 houses: their employers had not received the funding promised by the Human Settlements Department of the provincial government. The activists then became involved in the dispute and sought to mobilize the residents, who had been waiting for years in the middle of this landscape of shacks and dilapidated buildings. Because the municipality was the developer of this project, funded by the province, a great march on the city hall was organized to "put pressure" on it. This intervention was as much a matter of helping the workers to obtain satisfaction as of ensuring the completion of the housing project and guaranteeing access to it for those waiting on the allocation lists.

These various interventions share the same more or less explicit ambition: they seek to demonstrate that the collective is a "community-based organization." The terminology, found in ordinary, administrative, and political language, designates those associations founded by the residents of a particular neighborhood to contribute to its *smooth functioning*. Whatever the purpose of the intervention, it must be made self-evident that the community is still the principal player. Returning to the investigations that the UPM was then conducting on the subject of resales of RDP houses by municipal councilors, one of the leaders of the movement explained to me in April 2016:

> We are going with this information to the community. The community will advise us. What should be the next step? We take our mandate on a daily basis right from there. . . . Those are the people who decide what problems they want to talk about and for which we will act. . . . We will not take decisions on their behalf. We will not say that there's no contradiction between our ideology and their thinking. . . . We just go there.

The mandate is thus presented as organization's moral compass, or even as its main driving force, in that the defense of the interests of a community can only be the result of a decision taken by that community. When in the winter of 2012 UPM activists sought once again to engage with the council so that it would take over the constantly postponed development of the eThembeni shack area, they did so only after a huge community meeting organized amid the huts and the mud houses. Their failure meant they had to return a few days later to obtain a "fresh mandate" for an action whose direction did not depend on them: it might be "a demonstration or something else," as Ayanda told me. From this order of things there emerges a twofold responsibility. The first responsibility is moral, and it is obviously reflected in this imperative of transparency expressed by the idea of "accountability" that crops up repeatedly in activist speech but also in certain ways of doing things—witness the mandatory "report" to the community that most South African protest organizations produce: an organization must always get back to the community after having acted or negotiated on its behalf. Whether in Grahamstown, Thembelihle, near Johannesburg, or on the outskirts of Cape Town, the principle is always the same and ultimately encapsulates the supposedly almost organic link between the collective and the community. In eThembeni, Sibahle knows this all too well: often several times a month, she has to assemble her neighbors to keep them informed about what was said at an internal meeting or an encounter with a local councilor.

A second form of responsibility could be described as *social*. This time the initiative comes from the organization, but always in the interest of the community. It gives life to projects of social and community entrepreneurship, such as the vegetable gardens that the UPM is trying to develop in several neighborhoods. This is an ambition that can be seen well beyond the limits of Grahamstown. For example, there were traces of it in Cape Town, where activists of the Anti-Eviction Campaign were transforming an unused building into a "school" open to all children whose parents could not afford the tuition fees of the official system. The principle seemed to be the same in Kayelitsha, where members of Abahlali baseMjondolo had been setting up a nursery for the children of the community.[1] These actions are clearly driven by the desire to occupy a space abandoned—or more simply, ignored—by the public authorities, insofar as the problem concerns services (health, education, etc.) that the authorities provide in other places. In this way the organization, acting as lookout, mediator, and sometimes even guardian for the community, goes beyond its primary purpose of shaping, monitoring, and expressing social discontent. In doing so, it moves outside the space of protest,[2] which one can well imagine is too specialized and thus ultimately too narrow for it, and finds a more adequate place in the larger space of the community.

One last example will demonstrate this rather clearly. One evening in July 2012, just after receiving news of the nonrenewal of their employment contracts by a subcontractor from Rhodes University, four women went to the UPM offices hoping to get help. Various options were envisaged by the activists present that evening: they could send a delegation to negotiate with the employer, threaten to hold a demonstration outside the university gates, or write a press release that would probably be published in the local daily, whose editorial board had elected Ayanda—one of the main leaders of the movement—"Grahamstownian of the Year 2011." At the end of a somewhat feverish discussion conducted in a mixture of English and Xhosa, it was a somewhat less chaotic route that, at least at first, was recommended to the four employees: they should consider that the missive from their employer contravened labor legislation, since no notice had been given, and resume their work the following Monday as if nothing had happened. Here, it is perhaps less the meeting itself that we should note than the reasons behind it. Why, indeed, did these women employees turn to the Unemployed People's Movement, an organization in which they seem not to have known a single activist personally? Would it not have been more logical to turn to the trade unions, which were well represented among campus employees? Certainly not, if we are to believe Ayanda: for him, it was a foregone conclusion that the four women workers would turn up at the UPM premises: "They know we are the only ones to be active in the community!"

Even if it is rather summary, Ayanda's formula has the merit of highlighting the deficiencies of postapartheid syndicalism. This question deserves a few moments of attention. Casual workers are not at the heart of the preoccupations of the most powerful trade union organizations, any more than are workers in the informal economy. South African trade unions generally seem "reluctant to devote resources to organizing contingent workers who are unable to pay regular dues" (Barchiesi 2011, 78). This can also be seen as the result of certain sociological developments. A structure like the Congress of South African Trade Unions (COSATU), a loyal ally of the ANC, has thus seen the profile of its members gradually move away from that of the average South African worker: while, in 1994, 60 percent of them were semiskilled or unskilled, the situation has been diametrically reversed since the beginning of the twenty-first century. The majority of this population now consists of junior executives, office workers, and skilled workers (Buhlungu 2008). By the mid-2000s, 92 percent of federation members also had secure, full-time jobs (Buhlungu 2006, 9), which mostly meant they could live in households with incomes above the average South African income (Seekings and Nattrass 2005, 373). The gap between union representation and the social reality of millions of South Africans is also reflected in the nature of the respective demands of the unions and the organizations of the social movement. Admittedly, since the beginning of the twenty-first century, COSATU has campaigned against toll roads in Gauteng and for the establishment of a National Health Insurance scheme. These two examples are not just issues of "workers in the workplace but of individuals dealing with commodification in the realm of everyday life" (Scully 2016, 309). Nevertheless, by focusing primarily on working conditions and wages, trade unionists from COSATU and the other major federations place their action and their desire to exert influence at the heart of the production process, whereas the demands that the protest organizations put forward all focus on the level of consumption (of services, housing, etc.).

In the 2000s and 2010s, various formations on the nongovernmental Left failed to establish a common front between "the community" and the world of the workers. So it is a vacant space that the UPM occupies at this evening's meeting. On several occasions in the second half of the 2010s, its leaders helped poor farmworkers who were helpless in the face of landowners. They were often able to draw on the experience gained during the many workshops organized nationally by supporters of the social movement. They also relied on the knowledge accumulated over several years in contact with an NGO specializing in rural issues. Internal discussions, however, took another turn when the movement was contacted by some of the employees of a small supermarket on Beaufort Street. One of them had just been fired after having forgotten to charge customers for a plastic bag. If at first the leaders of the UPM sought to engage in a dialogue with the manager to make him reconsider his decision, the failure of this initiative convinced them to contact an association of lawyers with whom they were in regular contact. The justice system eventually reinstated the worker. In the weeks following this success, the UPM's offices were visited by other employees from the supermarket, dissatisfied with their working conditions and eager to see the movement of the jobless take an interest in their cause. In the course of the discussions, these employees suggested one main idea to the activists: Why not transform the movement into a local trade union? The idea seems since to have made headway in the minds of the leaders, who perhaps saw it as a way of reconnecting with the tradition of "community unions," those structures that, in the early 1980s in particular, managed to connect struggles in the community to struggles in the factory.

Spending time with the women and men of the UPM also makes one aware of the activities involved in militancy on a day-to-day basis. This theme is now quite fully incorporated into the analysis of social movements, especially in sociology and political science. Everyday activism is thus often described as covering these individual (but "not consciously coordinated") actions and words inspired by a social movement and "consciously" oriented to produce the change sought by this same social movement (Mansbridge 2013). Unlike everyday acts of resistance, such as rumor, sabotage, concealment and theft, daily activism is said to be a question of "open resistance": it is "visible and even confrontational" (338).

This definition makes it possible to break away from the exceptionalism which sometimes prevails in the study of militant actions. However, in my opinion, it neglects a certain number of apparently insignificant, nonconflictual tasks, moments, and interactions that do not interfere with the core features of protest action in the strict sense of the term but nonetheless are capable of clarifying the conditions of mobilization. They work to maintain things over the life of the organization, either because they maintain visibility, and thus the potential to attract new members, or because they are involved in the integration of militants in the collective by giving them a role that convinces them of their social utility. This can obviously involve such essential but relatively underrated things as opening up the premises each morning, bringing help to a household that cannot cope with the complexities of a water bill, or greeting those bold enough to cross the threshold, usually to beg for a little food or (though this is obviously less common), to donate food.[3] This is expressed even more vigorously in the small services, apparently unconnected to the cause, that an activist may render and that draw most often on the resources provided by the organization. Anyone from outside the organization can easily witness this, if he takes the trouble to spend a few hours in its offices. He might observe a resident who has come not to ask the movement to intervene, but to type up and print out his curriculum vitae on the collective's computer equipment. Or there may be some high school girls, neighbors of one of the activists, who have come to use the internet connection to do their class assignment. In the same vein, the car of a foreign researcher—myself—may become a resource for the movement.[4] Regularly, as I take activists to the site of a gathering, one, two, or three people who I know to be external to the organization but who are (more or less vague) acquaintances of one of the activists, take their places in the vehicle, without any asking my leave and usually without even speaking to me. I then have to make a detour to drop them off at their homes or near a store.

The help provided by the collective can be particularly crucial for certain residents. This is the case for those who sought support from Joseph, who was on duty during the second half of the 2010s. This man, just short of sixty, with his emaciated and smiling face, had been jailed three times under apartheid because of his membership in organizations banned by the regime. In particular, he paid the price for his involvement in one of Grahamstown's major Black organizations affiliated with the United Democratic Front (UDF). The "police harassment" to which he was subjected in the late 1970s also forced him to abandon the law studies that he had started at the University of Fort Hare. From the early 1990s, Joseph was employed, however, by an association of lawyers active against apartheid, and this enabled him to undergo legal training. These qualifications, subsequently recognized within an NGO, now allow him to provide valuable assistance to those who come to see him, including parents who have got lost in the bureaucratic machinery and are therefore unable to obtain their child support grant. Joseph helps them to fill out the administrative documents properly. Sometimes he even accompanies them to the offices of the South African Social Security Agency (SASSA), which is involved in several mismanagement scandals. Here he attempts to assert the rights of those who have requested his aid against employees who, as he told me in 2018, have "no empathy" even though "things are not properly explained."

These services are certainly less trivial than they seem. They help to maintain a link between neighborhoods and the collective. Through them, the collective retains a certain usefulness, disconnected from its periods of activism, and asserts its presence even more clearly as a community-based organization. In other words, it is nothing less than a social relationship that is established through this activism on a daily basis.

The status of community-based organization also serves as a base for the identity that largely cements this gathering of women and men. The notion of collective identity is central to the analysis of political activism and social movements insofar as it helps to explain their allure: it is succinctly but usefully defined by David Snow and Doug McAdam as "a sense of 'one-ness' or 'we-ness'" (Snow and McAdam 2000, 42) anchored in a set of experiences and attributes (real or fantasized) shared by the members of the community concerned and involving the idea of a "collective agency." "One-ness" and "we-ness" therefore suggest a sense of unity, which logically goes hand in hand with an awareness of the existence of "others," of "them." So here again we encounter the notion of a social boundary which gives meaning to the definition of the community for a large number of residents. Collective identities often appear in the dynamics of mobilization (Melucci 1995, 41–63), and are shaped by the most committed activists, who emphasize the sharing of a social condition, of various characteristics and experiences. In the context of the UPM, the identity prioritized in the activists' discourse, whether or not they are particularly committed, is that of "poor people": the UPM is a "poor people's movement." Such an assertion lays claim to a certain *ordinariness*, underlining the fact that those who stand under the banner of the UPM are people *like any others*, often from the majority who brought the ANC to power before being excluded from the forward march of development. This identity also has certain undeniable virtues—it is designed to emphasize that these women and men do not as such have any vocation to rebel: they are forced to resist by the socioeconomic aggression fomented by a political power that is also quick to criminalize their revolt. The fabric of this collective identity, however, is a little more complex, as suggested by activists' speeches at the community meetings organized in the township. Two conceptions of "we" intermingle in them: the general "we," which takes the same shape as the community as a whole, and the more restricted "we" of the protest collective; in other words, the "we" of the "poor" and the "we" of "the poor fighting for the poor." For those who commit, therefore, it is a matter of endorsing an identity that is valued and confers value. This identity thus emphasizes a form of self-denial, even sacrifice, as evidenced by the threats and physical attacks to which activists are exposed. Since the beginning of the 2000s, UPM activists, like those in other South African protest organizations, have in fact been exposed fairly regularly to police brutalities, physical intimidation of political activist and legal proceedings. The violent arrest of one of the leaders of the movement could almost seem trivial in comparison to the killings of members from Abahlali baseMjondolo, the squatters' movement, in which police and ANC activists in Durban were allegedly involved.

Because it is relatively minimal, this collective identity means in particular that the greatest number, whether they are unemployed people or workers in the informal economy, residents in an RDP house or shack dwellers, can see themselves reflected in it. Such a feature is obviously essential. Here as elsewhere, individuals join collectives for many reasons. They are obviously less inclined to do so if the identity of the group is not in line with the idea they have of themselves (Friedman and McAdam 1992, 164).

Finally, this identity has one last virtue, a fairly obvious one, all things considered: it certifies the absence of social distance between those who lead and supervise discontent, and those who supposedly live it. This closeness is in itself neither unfounded nor misleading. It develops within the similar experiences. The activists of the Unemployed People's Movement share the conditions of life of those whose cause they are defending. It is pretty easy to see this from a few brief portraits, which also highlight the diversity of poverty in the township.

Let us first consider Arthur's case. Now in his thirties, he lives with his mother and his brothers and sisters, as do hundreds of thousands of young adults across the country. After being occupied as a casual worker, he found a place in the Community Work Programme (CWP) launched by the government at the end of the first decade of the 2000s. This program aims above all to support jobless young people by giving them various tasks that will contribute "to the development of public assets and services in poor communities."[5] These activities (fixing community assets like schools, roads, and parks, setting up food gardens, etc.) keep Arthur busy for only two days per week and do not earn him more than R600 a month (less than $45 in 2017). But, as he explained to me: "I have to provide at home. . . . I do put something on the table, and my principle is 'something is better than nothing.' So they give me something at least." Arthur's case perfectly illustrates one of the paradoxes of the postapartheid state. Between 1994, the year of the first democratic elections, and the mid-2010s, social spending more than qua-drupled in real terms. This result was largely due to the gradual extension of social assistance programs (child support grants, disability grants, and old age pensions). In 2014, one in three South Africans received a grant or pen-sion financed by general taxation (Seekings and Nattrass 2015, 136). These guidelines obviously contradict the accusations of "a drift to neoliberalism" laid against ANC governments. They tend toward a decommodification and redistribution almost reminiscent of the principles at the heart of the social democratic regime. According to official statistics and several spe-cialists in the field (147), they above all "massively" reduced extreme poverty (US $1.25/day) in the early 2010s. These trends, which favor cash transfers, illustrate an international movement that began at the end of the 1990s. Their roots are certainly in Latin America, particularly Mexico and Brazil (Ferguson 2015, 12). In spite of their relative effectiveness, however, they re-veal how much the system is out of step with reality. The state takes the decision to protect huge groups traditionally considered as dependent (children, mothers, disabled, old people) and manifestly ignore others, even though these latter are weakened by developments in the economy, namely, the (male) working-age unemployed. As James Ferguson suggests, this appar-ent deficiency must partly be read as the result of "a persistent . . . fantasy" (116) according to which, if they are not "lazy," able-bodied men should all have a paid job allowing them to live with dignity. In a context of massive and lasting unemployment, such a model leads to the marginalization of co-horts of young (and not so young) men trapped in a social reproduction crisis. More broadly, this shows the distrust of postapartheid government circles with regard to the alleged risks of fraud and dependency on state aid (Barchiesi 2011, 97–137). The establishment of several public employment programs, such as the CWP which employs Arthur, was therefore a move toward a "philosophy" centered on "the opportunity, the dignity and the rewards of work," to use the very words of a government spokesperson in the early 2000s (quoted in Barchiesi 2011, 130).

By her own admission, it was thanks to these very same cash transfers that Salinda's family was able to survive. Having become a mother when she was nineteen, this young activist lives with her daughter, younger sister, and mother in an RDP house in Vukani, one of the poorest places in Graham-stown. No one works in this household, which therefore depends on the pay-ments of the two child support grants of R750 monthly. The young woman also says that she cannot count on the help of her child's father. The results she obtained in the matriculation exams, at the end of high school, were not good enough for her to go to university. She turned to a private college to quickly pick up some "marketable skills," with one of her uncles agreeing to pay the fees. He, however, dropped her after a few months, forcing her to terminate her studies prematurely. Her presence in various NGO networks has finally allowed Salinda to again obtain financial support to improve her matriculation results and thus have the possibility of studying law at university. Such a situation would obviously involve having to look yet again for hypothetical financing.

Dumisa's life is another example of these living conditions. This sexagenarian, who worked as a domestic worker and then a hawker, lives on one of the hills that surround Grahamstown down a very rugged dirt road. The place was almost deserted when she moved there in 1983, accompanied by her two children and her mother. Her husband was then working in Cape Town. She now lives alone. Her husband died in the mid-1980s, and her children, who live far away, are experiencing the shaky trajectories of young Black people in the townships. So she sometimes wears the orange jacket emblazoned with the Community Work Programme logo that her eldest son, who is unemployed, was given in exchange for a few hours of work. Her two-room shack looks like most of the ones I've been in since 2009 in the informal areas of Johannesburg, Cape Town, and Durban. It is skillfully cobbled together out of corrugated iron and plywood sheets. Several very worn pieces of linoleum have been placed on the floor and of course completely fail to hide the irregularities of the ground. One of the walls is covered with newspaper pages printed with gaudy commercials. The premises are legally connected to electricity, but access to water is made through an external collective tap. However, this shack and those around it are not just mere assemblages of recycled materials. As James Holston has observed in the favelas of Brazil, their construction often seems to respond to a specific aesthetic sense (Holston 1991). There is nothing surprising about this: these are mainly homes that their residents are trying to make as comfortable as possible while obviously hoping that they are just temporary. This hope justifies the fact that Dumisa's name has, since the late 1990s, been on a list that was supposed to enable her to move into an RDP house. Like thousands of people in Grahamstown, then, she lives in this state of waiting which, because it generates an uncertainty that fosters a feeling of submission,

In Dumisa's shack

remains "one of the privileged ways of experiencing the effect of power" (Bourdieu 2000, 228).

Although it gives you a roof over your head and protects you from regular gusts of wind, an RDP house does not completely solve the housing problems. One simply needs to listen to Thozi, a mentally handicapped activist in his thirties. He is a young man who lives with his parents in one of those neighborhoods of RDP houses where, though it is not clear why, the water can be cut off for several days at a time. He mainly describes the cracked and fissured walls of this house built in the early 2000s and the water that seeps in during the periods of heavy rain that regularly falls on the Eastern Cape between May and November.

The last portrait is that of Onke, one of the founders of the movement. During the 1980s, while still attending high school, this woman, now in her fifties, became very active in the underground networks of the anti-apartheid struggle. She regularly assisted exiled freedom fighters who had returned to South Africa on a mission. Most often, she had to find them clothes and a place to hide, and then make sure that their movements were safe. Having become a locally influential political activist in the early 1990s, Onke has been very involved in the UPM since its inception. She also became a schoolteacher a few years ago, after working in various small jobs. After several years of unemployment, her husband found a job in an NGO. The location of his employer in KwaZulu-Natal province, however, forces him to spend the week in Durban, where he plays a part in programs for orphans. Although their income is relatively modest, the couple now seems to enjoy a comfortable situation, especially when compared to their peers and neighbors. The changes their home has seen in recent years seem to testify to this: the two original rooms of this matchbox have gradually been augmented by another five. Despite this apparent comfort, Onke and her family consider themselves to be living in poverty. Such statements are understandable only if one looks more closely at the composition of this household. In addition to the couple and their three children (the eldest daughter studies at Port Elizabeth University but has only a small scholarship), the house is home to several cousins, as well as young children whom their parents (relatives or neighbors) left there one morning for "one or two days" before more or less disappearing. There is nothing really surprising about this: Black South African households "frequently include a variety of kin and even non-kin, in a variety of ways" (Seekings 2008, 28). It is not uncommon to entrust one's child to a better-off close relative so as to facilitate access to school, care, and food. Sometimes these movements are also found within neighborhoods or communities, as seems to be the case here. The wages of Onke and her husband therefore enable a dozen people to live in a situation that is certainly not radical poverty but is far from the relative comfort experienced by the Black middle classes.

These five lives are all at least different from each other, while each one gives us an idea of what "being poor" can mean in postapartheid South Africa. The diversity they display lies as much in the forms as in the degrees of poverty: you certainly do not live in the same way in a shack and in an "RDP house," and it is certainly not quite the same thing to depend on a regular social grant or on sporadic help from your friends and family. I had once accompanied Ndisa, Onke's daughter, to a fish-and-chips restaurant in the city center. Her mother had asked her to go and buy food to take away for the evening meal. The place was certainly modest, but it testified that the fate of her family was still different from that of Dumisa who, a few days before and through Ayanda, had asked me to buy her a bag of three kilograms of frozen meat. Dumisa had immediately boiled it because she did not have a refrigerator in her shack.

In view of these differences, one can quite legitimately wonder what makes it possible to subsume this small world into the same cause and collective identity even though, in a movement as localized as the UPM, everyone can compare their conditions of life to those of their peers. I maintain that, beyond statistical data, the very term "poor" is fairly unanimously associated by those who perceive themselves as such with the feeling of having been left out—notably by "those who eat first (the elite)," to use the terms of a poor people's movement in Cape Town.[6] These people have in common the conviction of being excluded from something, of not being among those for whom 1994, the year of the first democratic elections, corresponded to a total change of life. Activists also share this perception of things far beyond the borders of the protest collective: with their neighbors, their relatives, their friends. Within the movement, however, this phenomenon has the virtue of weaving "equivalential relations" (Laclau 2005, 77–100) between noticeably social situations and distinct expectations. It is this chain of equivalences that generates and maintains a mobilizing "We."

The cases of Dumisa, Thozi, Salinda, Onke, and Arthur provide a glimpse, however schematic, of the personal situations in which UPM activists move.

I am not referring to these statements for any miserabilist reason, of course. Studying the poor neighborhood of El Alto, Bolivia, where the living conditions of the residents seem to be quite similar to those observed in East Grahamstown, Frank Poupeau remarked:

> The lack of running water in the home does not seem shocking to most of the residents surveyed, because they have never had access to this level of comfort, because they have not developed any need for it, and because other things take priority on a daily basis. And it is precisely this fact that must be questioned instead of simply perceiving it as a moral and political "scandal" against which it is always easy to wax indignant—not to mention the academic and political profits that can be derived from it. (Poupeau 2008, 17)

The threat of ethnocentrism obviously hangs over descriptions of poverty, even when sincere. More generally, there is a great risk of approaching these situations via one's own conceptions of a "normal life," conceptions that are inevitably foreign to those of the people one is studying. However, the situation is a little different in the case of South Africa, since from the mid-1990s onward, millions of poor citizens grew accustomed to the promise that there would be improvements in their living conditions. This "better life for all" was to take the form of a roof, sanitary facilities, and connections to water and electricity, which, even today, millions of people still lack.

Listing these situations, all too common in South Africa, is mainly a way of highlighting the social nearness between activists and the "ordinary people" they seek to mobilize. This community of existence and destiny is, without question, a resource in itself in a context where anything outside the township can sometimes be perceived with suspicion. This is exactly what one UPM leader said as he explained that his movement had managed to dampen the outbreak of xenophobia in October 2015 by holding many large public meetings and maintaining a "dialogue" with the residents: "The community was with us. Because they identified us as people who stay with them in the township, who fight together with them. . . . They did not perceive us as politicians. . . . Dumisa lives in a shack; I live in a shack. We're struggling just like anyone!"

While there is nothing artificial about this nearness, it does lose some of its clarity when we focus on one last characteristic that distinguishes certain activists from the majority of those who listen to them at public meetings. The youngest of them, or at the very least those who came to adulthood after the fall of apartheid, are often marked by a level of education that is not the norm in the poor and working-class neighborhoods of South Africa. The vast majority of people who are now forty or fifty years old and went to school in the 1980s suffered from the climate of violence of the time and were very often irreparably held back in their schooling (Manona 1994, 357–362). The 2001 census showed that less than a quarter of the adults in Rhini, the township of the city, had passed their matriculation ("matric"). Moreover, a large number of residents (38 percent) at the beginning of the twenty-first century had no education after high school.

The most active militant circles nevertheless welcome a certain number of individuals who passed their matriculation, a minority even undertaking studies at university, in a technical college or trade school. In general, however, these student careers are precarious and limited. In 2016, for example, Bheki was hoping to complete his training as a schoolteacher in Port Elizabeth, 130 kilometers from Grahamstown. A few months later, the economic situation of his family forced him to give up his course and take up a job opportunity in road building.[7] This fragility also runs through the biographies of those who make up the small nucleus of six or seven people aged between twenty and thirty who, in the mid-2010s, gathered daily on the UPM premises. A few were still taking courses at Rhodes University, where teachers close to the organization sometimes helped steer them towards scholarships. These young activists in fact mainly benefited from the National Student Foundation and Scheme, a scheme for student loans, renewable every year, the amount of which varies with each institution. Mark and Siniko obtained such a loan in Rhodes, unlike Lungile, who was forced to study away from home at the University of the Western Cape (Cape Town). He returned to Grahamstown at the end of the first year, as his loan did not cover all of his expenses. And the situation does not seem to have been much better for Mark, unable to pay the rent on a room on the Rhodes University campus and forced to settle in one of the rooms in the small house that then served as a UPM office.

The essence of these social characteristics gives an a priori coherence to the "regime of the near" in which the organization lives. The political cause and one's intimate experience meet and mingle at the heart of commitment. The activists' social condition also raises the very prosaic question of their livelihood: What do these women and men live off, when some of them devote all their days to the movement? The question is all the more insistent in that the welfare system is particularly limited: What income can they draw on when they have no children, are not retired, and do not suffer from any recognized disability? These are sensitive questions, often avoided during interviews—even when I dared to ask them. Activism, however, comes at a cost, especially for those from the most modest backgrounds. These women and men are sometimes reduced to making their day-to-day choices with very little room to maneuver, most often confined to simple questions of subsistence: "Do I use these R20 to take the taxi to the office, or do I use these R20 for bread?" The question obviously makes complete sense when we realize that more than half of South Africans were living on less than R26 per day in the mid-2010s.[8] These are the choices faced, for example, by those who in recent years have started a family and are now facing economic realities that quite logically mean they have to put their commitment on a back burner. This was obviously the case with Bheki: his job on building sites now keeps him away from the full-time activism that was so important for him in the mid-2010s. More generally, you may hear in the course of a conversation that one person is employed as a casual worker for less than twenty-four hours a month,[9] or that another can sometimes count on picking up a few rand from an informal economy where his handyman skills can be useful.

Sometimes, too, activism provides access to jobs funded by NGOs. The intensity of commitment can indeed generate a visibility likely to attract the attention of structures that need extra connections out in the field. In Durban, for example, in the late 2000s, some Abahlali baseMjondolo members were paid by an NGO to conduct sensitization workshops on the ravages of AIDS. Behind these relations, however, lies a mixture of dependence and mistrust which is not unique to South Africa. We may remember, for example, the Indian writer and activist Arundhati Roy's critiques of the "NGO-isation of resistance" (Roy 2004, 36) in the world. Roy was denouncing the propensity of these entities to bureaucratize discontent and to keep those whom they were supposed to help relegated to the status of victims. In other words, these support bodies are most often accused of coming with a hidden agenda, aimed at subjecting the fight of the poor to the more policed interests of their donors. The latter thus hover between "neocolonialism" and "elite project" (Gibson 2011, 36). In South Africa, this suspicion has often been extended to "city-based comrades," those whites—academics, journalists, independent researchers, students—who claim to support postapartheid protest. It is a suspicion that was perfectly summarized in a formula we owe to the leaders of Abahlali baseMjondolo, tired of seeing the squatters' struggle reinterpreted in the terms of political strategies: "Speak to us, not for us" (see Chance 2018).

On the ground, however, activists can hardly give up the funding these groups provide (either directly or as intermediaries). Even though it is not an NGO in the strict sense of the term, one renowned European political foundation paid the UPM's rent for a while, and paid a salary to the movement's administrator. A German association specialized in "ecology, sustainability, democracy, human rights and the fight against all forms of discrimination" also finances several of its projects in the township. Some activists have also been employed as "community workers" by a local NGO working in development and education in poor rural areas. The benefits of such a situation are not just individual, according to one activist: if you have a monthly salary, you'll engage in the struggle with all the more intensity now that you are rid of material worries. An activist who draws a salary, moreover, can assume responsibility for some of the expenses of his organization. The real challenge is not to fall into the logic that the "management" of NGOs almost intrinsically fosters: setting the interests of the individual against those of the movement.[10] Said one UPM activist to me in 2014:

> In fact, NGOs act like politicians. . . . They take themselves very often for messiahs and treat people as victims. They think they always have the answers, that they're the only ones with brains and that we're just pawns or numbers, victims or spectators who have to be told what to do. . . . Or they tell you: 'you mustn't do that or you mustn't say that, because some book says that it's wrong.' . . . But in fact, you see, they're not involved in the fight most of the time. We [the social movement] are.

This distrust also takes on a character that we have already seen in the preceding pages: it slips along the boundary that encloses the community and separates it from the rest of society in the minds of many of the township's residents:

> I personally don't like NGOs because I think that NGOs are just like the government and political parties. The role of NGOs is providing funding for social movements but the funding comes with an agenda so I would

not say that they are contributing because they control my politics yet they are not in my situation. I do not understand why they have to ask for funding on my behalf without my presence if they are going to use the funds to assist me. We are excluded from those conversations yet we are told that they are working for us but they are not accountable to us, instead we are accountable to them. There are a lot of rich people in these NGOs and you can see that they are rich because of the cars they drive. I just ask myself how does a servant of the people, poor people in particular, live in such luxury while their comrades are poor, where are they getting the money to buy these luxury cars? How much does an executive in an NGO earn?[11]

When the European foundation stopped paying the rent on the office, the representatives of the unemployed urgently had to find other patrons and solicit the support of white sympathizers. In any case, this material dependence arises at other times and in other areas of militant activity. Take this Sunday afternoon on the premises of the UPM, for example. There are four people in the office today, studying the latest invoices submitted by members of the group. These may include the purchase of small equipment for the premises (e.g., cups and mugs), transport tickets (to get to Port Elizabeth, in particular) and, most often, food purchased for forthcoming internal meetings. One of the invoices, relating to the purchase of doughnuts, is problematic: "Usually, you just buy bread for meetings." One activist is obviously embarrassed, and I can't make out whether she is directly concerned by the purchase; she tries to find some justification by consulting other invoices that do not seem to have any direct link with the one that has raised eyebrows. There's a slight hesitation. One of her comrades turns to tell me that they need to be constantly on the alert, since some activists try to get payment for personal invoices. The issue of doughnuts is finally abandoned. The following invoices do not seem to raise any suspicions until one invoice catches the attention of one of the young women sitting around the table. This time, it is neither the amount nor the nature of the goods purchased that are in question, but the time of the purchase. The piece of paper passes from hand to hand so everyone can be a witness. One of the activists turns to me again and explains: "If you have a meeting between 10:30 a.m. and 1:00 p.m., and 15 hours is written on the invoice, there's a problem." He adds that it's especially important to be precise in checking expenses, the only way of being "accountable" to those who finance the organization.

This anecdote shows that the question of money arises regularly, even if some people such as Dumisa like to recall that "the UPM was a social movement even before it had an office." On a daily basis, food has to be bought for an internal meeting that may be attended by thirty people, the transport costs of those who live at the other end of the township have to be met, and various activities need to be funded, such as sending representatives to a workshop about the Russian Revolution organized in Johannesburg. At these different times, the money comes mostly from outside, since the sums that can be collected through membership fees are quite derisory (R5, i.e., 40 cents in US currency). Quite apart from the fact that it repeatedly renders the movement dependent, money is a thorny issue. The short history of postapartheid protest bears the scars of this, just like those suspicions of misappropriation that have spared no organization. Some remember the rumors about the "over-luxurious shirts" of a leader finally forced to leave the squatters' movement he had helped found in Cape Town a few years before. The UPM has not been spared this kind of problem. The circulation of money within it sometimes raised tensions and rekindled disagreements. Salinda, a young woman activist who will be discussed again in Chapter 8, experienced this when one of the leaders suspended the stipend that a European foundation was paying her in return for her participation in a program in which the UPM was a partner. There followed threats, blows exchanged with another activist right on the movement's premises, an accusatory letter addressed to one of the main donors of the movement, and finally a dramatic split with the UPM. The violence of this episode instilled doubt even among some of the most committed activists like Thabo. Finally convinced that the money was not always being used wisely, this young man also distanced himself from an organization to which he had devoted most of his time for several years.

These events mainly led the organization financially supporting the movement to suspend its assistance, forcing the UPM leaders to seek new funding. As well as reminding us how much money, especially when it is scarce, can be used to reaffirm implicit hierarchies and relationships of internal domination, this example helps to relieve us of one illusion: the illusion that a group whose members affirm their attachment to solidarity and

Internal meeting

collective strength will inevitably be cohesive. Like any protest group, the Grahamstown unemployed combine expectations and interests that may well be different, even divergent, and that regularly threaten the unity highlighted by the leaders. This was also the case on the eve of local elections, when some activists hoped to stand for a party while drawing on the popularity of the UPM (Chapter 10).

The existence of UPM activists is therefore similar to that of a large number of people in the township. This lack of social distance also allows them to present the movement as the *natural* spokesperson for the poor of the city ("we're struggling just like everyone"), while seeking to neutralize the suspicion of appropriation that often accompanies this status ("We'll never just sit here [in the office] and take decisions on behalf of the people").

If a certain number are forced to "improvise" in order to live, or depend on help from family and friends, a majority relies on social grants that are modest in amount but at least, one may feel, have the merit of existing. These cash transfers are the sign that the postapartheid state is not absent from the lives of these women and men, who nevertheless perceive themselves as having been forgotten by institutions. In the mid-2010s, the National Treasury claimed that "60% of non-interest spending in the national budget [was] allocated to social spending and programmes to alleviate poverty" (Friedman and van Niekerk 2016, 1–2). Such a figure conveys a significant piece of information: even though the populations concerned are socially and spatially marginalized, they are nonetheless in contact with policies, measures, and practices emanating from one of the main pillars of the postapartheid state. To use a now classic formula, these populations are "seeing the state" (Corbridge et al. 2005) on an almost daily basis, through social grants, non-fee-paying schools, housing programs, vaccination campaigns, and the like.

This quite objective reality does not contradict the fact, of course, that poverty remains one of the best shared things in South Africa. Nor does it diminish the feeling of many poor people that they are despised by their rulers. The poor people's vision of the State can also be very blurred. Dumisa, for example, is on the registers of the indigent policy, the program managed by the municipalities that provides beneficiaries with a certain level of electricity and water free of charge. She claims, however, that she does not receive this benefit, due to the "incompetence" and "corruption" of the municipality. Other people sometimes mention the brutality with which they are treated by employees of the South African Social Security Agency when they go to their offices to inquire about the possibility of collecting a particular social grant. As is often the case for the most vulnerable, even within liberal democracies, South Africa's poor actually face a State and policies that may hesitate "between protection and coercion, welfare and exclusion, invocation of formal rights and violation of human rights" (Fassin, Wilhelm-Solomon, and Segatti 2017, 166).

4

"MY BLOOD IS STILL HERE, IN UPM"

It is early afternoon, and there is a little less activity here on the premises. Amanda, Zandile, and Ayanda are in the main office, leaning over the computer and writing a press release. The place is, to say the least, sparse. The bareness of the walls is interrupted only by the A4-size photos of Vladimir Ilyich Lenin, Frantz Fanon, Steven Biko, and Neil Aggett.[1] The floor, meanwhile, is permanently littered with stacks of files and folders. Thabo, Max, Bheki, Lungile, Mark, Arthur, and I are in the living room, sitting on the couch and the two worn armchairs that the activists have salvaged. The average age of the group I have joined hovers between twenty-two and just over thirty. Their jeans, T-shirts, and tennis shoes, sometimes with Western brand names, initially give them a similar look to many young people from around the world. On this autumn afternoon, I have before me a rather well-defined sample of the younger generation that I have already met in other protest organizations, in Johannesburg or Cape Town, since the end of the 2000s: students who are struggling to make ends meet, thirty-somethings who have never had a job in the formal economy, as well as young parents and others who are finding it hard to live as a couple as they cannot afford to leave the family home. Despite their differences, they all ultimately form a sort of community in which they share the same condition and, sometimes, the same destiny.

The conversation soon starts to revolve around "girls" and polygamy, including the polygamous relations of the then-president of the Republic of South Africa, Jacob Zuma. I am asked for my opinion. Is this to help the group make up its mind? Its members are obviously split. Arthur has launched into what is evidently a somewhat forced encomium of the mari-

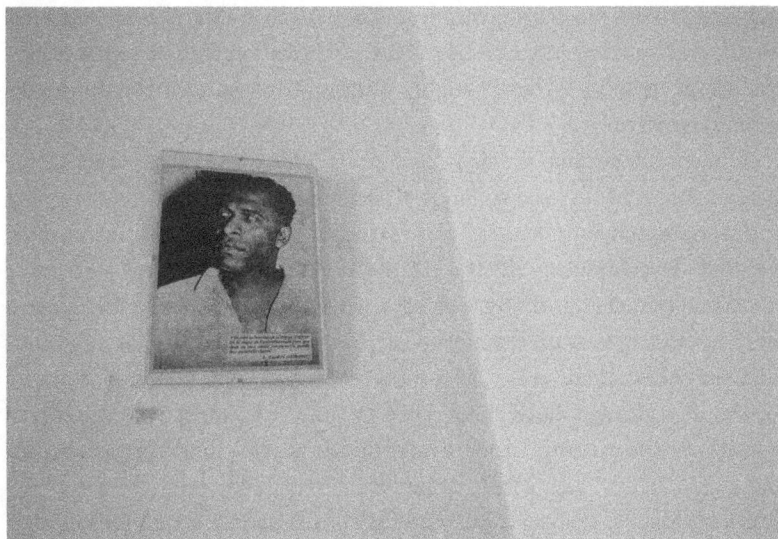

Frantz Fanon, UPM office

tal choices of the "Zulu boy"—the nickname given to the man who is also the ANC president. He enjoys provoking his "comrades" by acting as the devil's advocate in an organization that follows an antisexist line. The conversation then focuses on the "romantic" reputation apparently enjoyed by the French. When we are joined by Siniko, a psychology student at Rhodes, we move to the room in which the organization's leaders recently allowed Mark to settle. His scholarship money was not enough for him to rent a dorm room. Some sit on the floor, others on an old mattress. For half an hour, the young people chat about music, helping themselves from the packet of potato chips that Lungile has popped out to buy for lunch. Siniko makes us listen to a song she has downloaded on her phone. Earlier this same morning, when I had asked her about the sources of her politicization, she had spoken at length about the influence of the Fugees and, even more, of their singer, Lauryn Hill. Her interest in a music that she seemed to view as "committed" distinguished her, she felt, from the "bourgeois" students and their taste for performers like Beyoncé.

Some of the young people in the room grew up in the same communities and mention friends they have in common. A few days ago, I also realized that Mark and Siniko had been dating for a few months. They are the only ones in this small group not from Grahamstown: she is from Port Elizabeth, and he from Johannesburg. The conversation shifts to what everyone wants to do on Saturday night. Mandisa's Tavern seems to meet with general approval.

It is not uncommon for this small group, plus two or three other members of the UPM, to head to Fingo Village on Friday or Saturday to spend the evening in this tavern. The place is in fact a vast courtyard surrounded by single-level buildings. By the end of the afternoon, the very broad pavement that borders it is filling with cars, which are immediately surrounded by men offering to wash them or to keep an eye on them. Not far away, outside the entrance, several groups of women and men, young and not so young, are talking loudly, encouraged by the music whose volume will increase over the evening. Inside, everyone can watch a sports broadcast on a big screen, dance, have a beer, or buy meat to grill on one of the three barbecues available. During these moments of relaxation, few of the activists mention the cause: conversation turns mainly on the football championship or more personal and everyday topics. In the course of the evening, they also encounter other comrades of all ages who have come to spend an hour or two at this great nocturnal mingle.

Such moments occur in close proximity to the heart of activism. They barely disturb militant activities—in fact, they actually help to weave and strengthen the bonds that link commitment to other dimensions of the lives of these young people. They also include various elements that help one understand the persistence of people's investment in the collective. Environments that are conducive to commitment and its continuity over time are often characterized by an entanglement of various links, whether friendly, familial, or emotional. These situations can potentially lead to dense bonds which foster loyalty to the institution or, at the very least, a form of solidarity "mediated by loyalty to the people we meet" (Duriez and Sawicki 2003, 18). The importance of this emotional attachment is clearly summed up by Arthur in a conversation with me in October 2017. Unlike many people, this young man did not join the UPM after a meeting organized in his community or on the advice of a friend. Drawn in by the hubbub, he simply dared to cross the threshold of a premises that he regularly walked past:

> "I was just passing in front of the UPM offices. I got curious and got inside. I saw the UPM abbreviation and they told me: 'It's an unem-

ployed people's movement.' And Zandile, she welcomed me warmly . . . very well. . . . Ayanda was there with Zandile, and they explained everything to me. In the very good manner . . . nicely. And to be honest with you, I like the UPM. I like it."

"Is it like a family?" I asked.

"Not per se, not per se, but slightly . . . I joined those people and got along with them and got used to them, so they've become all my friends . . . My blood is still here, in UPM."

In interviews, people often refer to the friendly relations within the movement. These friendships have sometimes been forged after they join, but they may also have been present beforehand and led to their entering the organization. This is true of Simthandile, for example. This young activist, about twenty years old, joined the movement mainly as a result of regularly hearing about it from Ndisa, her neighbor and best friend, whose mother is one of its founders. Tshepo, the younger brother of the same Ndisa, has managed to recruit five of his friends into the movement. According to Tshepo, who says he has been an activist since he was fifteen, this was done in two stages. He first undertook to "conscientize" them at the most innocuous moments:

With my friends, we sit in a room, playing games . . . like checkers, dominos, cards. And we discuss politics, history, revolutionary, all of those things . . . discussing about the icons like Malcolm X, Martin Luther King, Steve Biko, and all other heroes. So my duty to them is to show them: "Ok, this person did that and this person sold out the nation and its people." Sometimes, I come back to my room at 11 p.m. . . . We discuss these things, discuss, discuss, discuss . . . all the time. We do it every day . . . because people are landless . . . too much poverty. . . . We talk about what causes those things.

Tshepo then convinced his friends to accompany him to a political school organized by the UPM. For two days, they were able to listen to some of their more politicized elders, and two academics close to the movement, holding forth on the Russian Revolution of 1917 whose centenary was then being celebrated. Obviously seduced by the experience, and particularly by the parallels established with contemporary times, Tshepo's five friends decided to join the ranks of the movement, thereby reinforcing a relatively frequent pattern. In fact, the various events organized by the collective are often attended by women and men who have been persuaded to accompany a friend. If attending a public meeting sometimes leads to an increased awareness of the cause which will, for example, justify taking part in an event a few days later, it may also lead to a more sustainable membership of the organization. However, the mere fact of knowing someone who is already committed does not explain everything. These "prior ties would appear to encourage activism only when they (a) reinforce the potential recruit's strong identification with a particular identity and (b) help to establish a strong linkage between that identity and the movement in question" (McAdam 2003, 287). Accompanying a friend, neighbor, brother, or sister to such meetings certainly simplifies access to the collective, but above all it potentially confirms that other "ordinary people," who are experiencing the same distress and the same threats as you, have decided to confront them. In other words, I believe that these identification processes are all the more important as they make it possible to make commitment something self-evident. This is clearly true of Thozi, who one evening in February 2012 accompanied his sister, already an activist, to one of the public meetings that the UPM organized in his district. He says that he then had a "revelation," as he listened to "poor people like [him]," committed to a movement of which he became, a few months later, the organizer in his own neighborhood. In addition to ensuring the mobilization of their community, the organizers also have the task of recruiting new activists and, above all, acting as a bridge between residents who face problems and the leaders of the Unemployed People's Movement. The case of this young man, who suffers from a slight intellectual disability, also emphasizes that, in addition to being a framework of identification, the organization can be an area of inclusion, especially for those who have to face the hostility of their social environment. According to one of its leaders, entrusting this young man with the coordination of the operations carried out in his neighborhood was first of all meant to help him gain confidence, as "the simple-minded, AIDS patients and the disabled are regularly discriminated against or made fun of in the townships." The UPM was not the only thing that counted in this young man's life. He was also active in his church and an activist in the Congress of the People (COPE), a breakaway party from the ANC.[2] However, it was within the protest movement that he seemed to feel "at home," in a place where he was most valued, where he felt most justified in being assiduous in his commitments, making many "visits" and engaging in many discussions in his neighborhood and regularly traveling to the premises of the organization to relay requests, attend meetings, or simply be with his "comrades."

While their depth and intensity should not be overestimated, friendship and intimacy do have their place within the organization. People meet or make friends and acquaintances there. Arthur attends regularly, and his answer is ultimately quite enlightening: the collective is not a family, but that obviously does not stop one from feeling a strong attachment to it. This can be accompanied by a sense of protection. I had already sensed as much while carrying out research in Soweto a few years before. One resident told me that she no longer felt threatened by power cuts and evictions since she had joined the ranks of the local protest group, the Soweto Electricity Crisis Committee (SECC). She obviously counted on the solidarity of her "comrades" in case of difficulty and, above all, on the fact that her membership in the SECC could dissuade potential evictors and disconnectors, the latter preferring to avoid any resistance. This type of belief is certainly not a sufficient reason for becoming committed, even among the less politicized. It is even likely that this woman, who only occasionally participated in public gatherings and SECC events, was not aware of it when she joined the organization. However, it may be one reason among others for remaining, as much as the prospect of picking up a few rand when the collective obtains funding or benefiting from what may be considered its social capital. Despite the poverty of her family, Simthandile, a young UPM activist, told me she believed in her chances of studying at university one day, "thanks" to the movement. She had obviously observed the links between the collective and several lecturers at Rhodes University, as well as the benefits (help for scholarships, information on diplomas) that some of her comrades had drawn from it. Maintaining commitment, therefore, is not only based on friendship and the sense of serving a "just cause."

Attachment to the cause one is defending or to the collective is not in itself sufficient to explain the initial stages and the persistence of individual commitment over time. Nor are the setbacks and failures of a movement enough to fully explain why people move away from it. The collective Voices of Africa appeared in the aftermath of the xenophobic violence of 2015 and brought together many of the wives of foreign traders targeted by lootings. However, this UPM-sponsored movement broke down in a few months.

Beyond the classic funding problems, Voices of Africa suffered mainly because the women who had given it life pulled out. The cause of these departures was relatively simple and did not reflect any divergence as to its substance. As businesses reopened, these women simply reassumed their places alongside their husbands and therefore had no time to devote to the movement.

The reasons for disengagement and withdrawal are therefore not always (and not only) to be sought in the hopes raised by activism and the disappointments it leaves in its wake. They are also to be located in other spheres of activist life. Even among "full-time activists" (to use the formula often used by those concerned), life is indeed an intertwining of different spaces that have their real and symbolic boundaries, their own logic and dynamism: the "sphere of work, of study (if the person is in education), the sphere of family and emotional bonds, the sphere of his or her political commitments, leisure activities, and so on" (Passy 2005, 115). Activist commitment can thus vary with decisions and situations that are a priori foreign to it because they are inscribed in existential territories distinct from that of activism. The activist circles of the UPM have often changed since 2009, in line with the success of the mobilizations or, conversely, reflecting a certain lassitude and divergences of opinion. But beyond that, perhaps more prosaically, the morphological evolution of the collective, and especially of its ruling group, has often followed changes in people's personal lives, following a pattern observed well beyond the borders of South Africa. Without completely disappearing, some of the very young activists who flocked to the forefront of the demonstrations in 2009 have ceased to be less prominent, making way for other faces, sometimes just as young. Some started a family while others found jobs.

Such a phenomenon is represented rather well by Melekile's experiences. Wearing long dreadlocks most often held together by a red or black turban, this thirty-year-old was unemployed when the protest organization was set up in 2009. Until then, he had devoted most of his days to the activities of a street committee and the development of various art projects for the young people in his community. At our first meeting, in 2012, he was one of the mainstays of the movement, and in particular he acted as its spokesperson. At that time he was separating from his wife and lived alone in a small, cold, damp house in the heart of the township. The following year, however, Melekile was recruited for a few months as a "community worker" by a local NGO close to the protest organization. Activist and professional spheres were thus relatively in sync since this status, based mainly on being present in the region's communities, allowed him to maintain a relatively high level of commitment. Changes and developments in the emotional and professional spheres, however, disrupted this order. First and foremost, Melekile and his wife reconciled and settled back under the same roof with their five children. The return to life as a couple quite logically forced him to reconsider the time spent on activism, as he told me in July 2018.

> "Was it difficult to be both married and a full-time activist?"
>
> "Yeah, my brother, it's difficult. That's what made me end up looking for a job. Because I'm not a job person. I'm a person who . . . who was independent. But at some point I had to make that decision. I've got five kids, you know? Five! I have a wife. At home . . . we were very very poor. . . . I'm a man, you know."
>
> "That means that you have to put something on the table?"
>
> "The fact to be unemployed rips off anyone's dignity. Because even at home, they don't look at you the same way when you're unemployed. Even your partner will not look at you the same way when you don't have the money and when you have. It's not supposed to be like that but . . . this is what happens. Even the children begin to disrespect you because you can't do so much for them. . . . So you're forced at some point to actually look for a job."

So Melekile started looking for a lucrative and regular job. He finally found one by joining the Department of Arts and Culture ("An advert came out, I sent my CV"). Now working "for the government," he is responsible for providing logistical support to artists living in communities throughout much of the Eastern Cape. He also runs workshops to introduce young people to video techniques, his favorite artistic domain. Inexorably, Melekile moved away from the protest collective even though he had helped to found it. His wife also saw her situation develop over the same period. She was recruited as a schoolteacher. They now comprise a couple that can easily be seen as forming part of the South African Black middle class. This social rise over just a handful of years led them to look for a home in central Grahamstown. The very high prices and, according to Melekile, the "obstacles" regularly placed in the way of those seeking to leave the township, however, led the couple to reconsider this ambition. Melekile and his wife finally moved into a bond house, one of those relatively comfortable houses whose acquisition was funded by bank loans, in the township of the neighboring city of Port Alfred.

Melekile's new social and professional condition has obviously put him at odds, especially vis-à-vis his new employers. Although he had previously worked for the Department of Arts and Culture, running occasional projects within the township, he acknowledges his difficulties in adjusting to a logic that he describes as "bureaucratic." He accuses it "neutralizing" artists' work by separating it from the social context in which it is created: "When you come with a social activism background, it's a bit difficult because you're dealing with people who do not want to deal with the holistic picture."

But it is also vis-à-vis his comrades that things may have been ambiguous, even if most of them claim to "understand" a situation that does not contradict his support for the cause:

> The UPM . . . obviously, my heart is still there. But now, you have challenges. One of the challenges is that . . . the UPM is a social movement which is leftist obviously, which is my home. Political home. The challenge is . . . because obviously it's controversial for them . . . for me to be involved. . . . But my involvement is still there, in the UPM. I'm not physically there because most of the programs happen during the day and during the week and obviously I must be at work. . . . But what I do is that I make sure that in the work that I'm doing, I raise the consciousnesses. . . . That's what I do: when I go out and do workshops, I make sure that I conscientize. People must be able to interpret what is happening. It's my contribution. But obviously I'm not as active as I was in the UPM.

Mandla, another very committed activist, also experienced this withdrawal, but for very different reasons. Affable, and wearing an eternal cap, this sexagenarian with his emaciated face was a model of full-time activism during the first five years of the movement's existence: almost every day he was there in its premises and he attended all its internal meetings. This commitment, however, faded in the middle of the 2010s without leading to a complete break.

Mandla, who was close to the Black Consciousness Movement during the apartheid years, also likes to recall that he was present at Steve Biko's funeral in Port Elizabeth in 1977.[3] In contrast, the "heroes" of the African National Congress no longer find favor in his eyes, even though he may have believed in them at the beginning of the democratic era. One rainy morning in July, it was he who showed me, in a corner of the township, a wall tens of meters long and covered with graffiti hostile to the ruling party. He even insisted, that day, that I take a picture of him in front of a large and explicit "Mandela Sell Out."

In the 1980s and 1990s, like thousands of men from the Eastern Cape, Mandla was forced to leave his family to work in the gold mines in the Johannesburg area. However, he abandoned this job at the request of his wife, who wanted them to settle in Port Elizabeth, the capital of the province. Mandla then joined the informal economy, doing welding jobs on demand: fences, gates, car components, and so forth. Finally separated from his wife, the former miner succumbed to alcohol before deciding to find the way back to his hometown, Grahamstown. He returned "broken," according to one of his friends.

At our first meeting, Mandla was still a little too young to collect an old age pension. He survived thanks to the disability grant that was meant to compensate for an arm wounded during a welding operation a few years before. Also, he lived in a spartan dwelling: a dark room whose earthen walls had been whitewashed. The furniture consisted mainly of two chairs, a table, and a bed. Against all odds, Mandla nevertheless gained ownership of an RDP home in 2014, the year in which he also began to collect a retirement pension.[4] Mandla, on the waiting lists since the mid-1990s, had however come to the conclusion that his commitment to the protest movement made this expectation totally futile. According to him, the local ANC power could be tempted to prevent a house being allocated to anyone considered to be an opponent. Despite the obstacles, UPM investigations verified that the activist's name was indeed on the list of residents meant to receive a grant so as to obtain property—a list established by the provincial administration but placed under embargo by the municipality (see Chapter 7). The activists then simply had to put the local councilor "under pressure" by coming along regularly to point out to him that Mandla's rights had been denied. The latter's activism then gradually decreased. We could see this as one of those withdrawals into private life that, depending on satisfactions and disappointments, alternate with phases of sociopolitical commitment (Hirschman 1982). Lassitude has managed to overwhelm this sexagenarian, whose life has often placed him on the side of the vanquished.

Mandla, in his previous home

Mandla's withdrawal certainly has other, more prosaic roots. The satisfaction of finally moving into a proper house has been accompanied by a new geographical location: after having lived for a long time in Fingo Village, in the neighborhood of other UPM activists just as committed as he was, Mandla moved into a house that, as the luck of the draw would have it, is located in a new out-of-center district in the conurbation, a great distance from the organization's premises. The round trip via collective taxis would now cost R20, a significant expense, especially if it needs to be paid several times a week as full-time activism requires. This situation also reminds us that commitment has a cost and that material constraints inevitably demarcate the horizon of possibilities of the poorest activists. In the first months after this move, the neighborhood also experienced frequent break-ins, since the absence of neighbors seemingly encouraged thieves to be bold. Forced to stay at home to protect his property, Mandla spent his days on his couch, listening to the radio.

Despite the price of transport and his fragile health (he suffers from asthma and knee pain), he briefly returned to the premises after a few months, showing that for those who feel that their lives are a matter of indifference to their rulers, protest is "a time when they feel justified, accepted and appreciated" (Auyero 2003, 11).

Despite their respective withdrawals, Melekile and Mandla have not completely disappeared from the activist landscape. Their names still crop up sometimes in conversations between UPM members. Some say that Melekile clearly still supports the cause—at least on a "moral" level, as one of his comrades puts it. He can also be available to help should the need arise. Mandla, meanwhile, is the movement spokesperson at neighborhood meetings in his young community. He also says he keeps abreast of "what's going on" within the UPM. So their place in this small world does not seem to be in any doubt.

Such a situation is certainly not unrelated to the fact that the boundaries of the movement are relatively shifting. There is indeed the matter of membership, fixed at R5, but it is difficult to know who pays it. Maybe that is why I have never found out exactly how many people were actively involved in the movement. The information was not kept secret. It just seemed meaningless to those I asked. Perhaps it is also for this reason that I have never seen any avowed withdrawals from the movement in six years of observation, with the (rare) exception of those caused by deep and sometimes personal disagreements. Some people may be less frequent attendees at meetings or in the local premises, but they do not disappear completely. They are sometimes encountered in the township, especially at community meetings. We talk about them in the movement's offices. They are above all neighbors, friends, and relatives, people whose living conditions mean they cannot stand aloof from the movement's struggle.

It seems to me that the most committed activists can have a form of tolerance toward those whose commitment weakens at times. Once again, the sensitive link between activism and living conditions helps to shed light on this. On the one hand, any activist may be constrained in his or her commitment by the need to meet the pressing needs of his or her family. As one said, "I'd like to be a full-time activist but everyone has to grow up, socially, and I have to provide at home." On the other hand, opportunities can sometimes arise, such as the business of T-shirts that Lungile, a young activist who was also the chairperson of the movement, is trying to launch.

Finally, this same connection between personal situation and collective destiny makes it easier to understand the opposite situation: the maintenance of commitments over time, even at the cost of a few periods of absence. One of the main peculiarities of the poor people's movements (compared to other forms of mobilization) lies, in my opinion, in the fact that their struggle is actualized on an almost daily basis in the social and moral experiences of each of their members. Very concretely, the cause advocated by the organization is nothing but what people curse about all day long, whether at home or with "comrades": the water cut off for several days, the refusal of elected representatives to come and see the state of decay of the houses, the streets flooded by sewage, the bucket system, and so on. These experiences shape the condition of the activists, whose belief in the merits and necessity of their combat becomes more focused as a result. They thus contribute to a form of continuous reassurance. This situation is further reinforced by the fact that "all this," that is, private life and activism, unfolds in the same space and, more important, in a "spatially situated sociality" (Pithouse 2013, 105). The fact that certain neighbors may be activists or sympathizers generates a "process of mutual encouragement and cajoling," which is, if not "indispensable" (Gould 1995, 55), at least essential to mobilization. A certain social pressure cannot be excluded either. Perhaps we can detect the fusion of these two phenomena in the arrival on the movement's premises of activists (sometimes in groups) whose shacks or houses are just tens of meters away in the township. But beyond that, this spatial configuration also helps to normalize commitment, preventing it from being too separate a sphere, too isolated within activists' lives. The reason is quite simple: activism is practiced primarily in the neighborhood and is not systematically disconnected from the activities and the most banal moments of an ordinary day. Under such conditions, while withdrawal is obviously possible, an open, a clean break is rarely the most obvious and natural solution.

The fact that the movement's boundaries are not always drawn very clearly has often led me to wonder about the status of Archie. His personal situation has in fact made him part of those Black middle classes still living in the township but in conditions that have little in common with those of the poorest residents. Just over forty, Archie lives with his wife and two daughters in a bond house. He has become one of the managers of the parks and gardens department of the municipality, after studying social sciences at the University of Rhodes. A photo representing him at the graduation ceremony sits on the big TV in his living room. His social success assumes an almost ideal shape both in the form of this house but also in the imposing 4 × 4 that he parks in front of the entrance. It is also to some degree embodied in the two young purebred dogs that welcome visitors. Their presence is indeed surprising (even incongruous) in a neighborhood where, as throughout the township, stray dogs are legion.

Despite these clearly telling signs, I have never known whether Archie was "officially" a member of the UPM. Ayanda himself hesitated a bit before finally answering that he was a "sympathizer." The two men have been friends for several years. Ayanda regularly visits Archie's house without even needing to tell him in advance. Most of the time, they sit on the sofas in the living room and discuss anything and everything, mostly politics and football. At other times, especially during his lunch break, Archie goes to the UPM offices, sits in a corner, and talks to the activists present.

Archie is a "child of the township." By that I mean that he is often careful to point out how much what he *is* and what he *does* is related to the "community." He continues to live there even though his social status would certainly allow him to move closer to the city center, near the private schools. In the 1980s, he was part of the Amabutho, the "small soldiers" of the township. Internal resistance to the apartheid regime was partly supported by these adolescents, most of whom were dropouts or petty criminals. They spent their time in the street, ensuring that people respected the consumer boycotts and stay-aways (injunctions not to go to work, so as to weaken the regime's economy). The effectiveness of their actions helped make the townships "ungovernable" in the middle of the decade: "One day, there was a big meeting. And someone told us: 'There's a message from Robben Island.' That message was: 'Freedom today, education tomorrow.' So we stopped going to school to fight the power."

When he had barely entered his teens, Archie spent five years away from school, roaming the streets. However, he managed to find his way back in the late 1980s, unlike many of his comrades who subsequently paid a high price for those years without education. In the next decade, Archie received a scholarship to study at university. He obtained a bachelor's in primary education before moving to the social sciences.

Archie's sensitivity to the township's troubles and, more generally, to the UPM cause finds explicit expression. At the helm of an amateur football team, Archie works with children and teenagers in poor communities in the city. In particular, he has initiated a scheme for collecting shoes for children who live on the farms around Grahamstown and sometimes have to travel up to eight kilometers a day to attend school. He has also helped set up partnerships between his sports association and schools and libraries in the township to develop a "reading culture" in poor and working-class neighborhoods. The idea behind these initiatives came to him during his studies. At university he realized, sometimes at his own expense, that you must "speak academic English" if you are to have any hope of escaping poverty—and this is a language unknown to the children of the township.

One last thing, of a more personal nature, convinces one of the sincerity of Archie's attachment to the township. The often wretched situation of most Black neighborhood schools leads many middle-class African families to enroll their children in private establishments in the old "white" part of Grahamstown. Archie has always refused to do so for his two daughters. He is even a little critical of those who have made this choice. Listening to him, it is quite easy to understand that staying in the township and accepting its shortcomings is a moral obligation that everyone should fulfill.

However, it is not Archie's awareness of the township's woes that makes Ayanda hesitate a little when I ask him to describe the bond between his friend and the UPM—nor the fact that this same Archie is often present on the outskirts of the movement. Ayanda hesitates above all because the apparent discrepancy between the social condition of this employee and the struggle of the unemployed of Grahamstown is actually a false problem. This is why some members of the UPM feel that their fight should not exclude the Black middle classes, and more precisely the population of small employees and public-sector workers who, without leaving the township, have managed to own houses with three, four, or five rooms. These activists, among the most politicized of the movement, have very definite ideas on the matter. As one told me:

> These people, the middle classes . . . the black middle classes . . . they are not like the white middle classes. It's different. That's what they don't understand. If you lose your job tomorrow . . . the house is not yours. It belongs to the bank. The car is not yours. It belongs to the bank. You have nothing of your own. Everything belongs to the bank. You're living a false life. It's a life of debts, you see? You don't pay the bank two months, you're out of the house. . . . The Black middle classes, they don't have more than

the poor, but they don't know it. It's different when you're a white middle class because the white middle classes have the capital. When you're Black, you rely on your salary.

According to this activist, it would therefore be essential (and, ultimately, inevitable) that everyone, beyond the class to which they belong, become aware of the existence of objective alliances within the Black population. Such an analysis overlaps some of the ideas that have been spreading at the intersection between South Africa's activist and intellectual worlds since the beginning of the twenty-first century. A number of researchers, often very close to the protest movement, have suggested that the unemployed, semi-employed, self-employed, and employed belong to the same community of fate and, more generally, that "the long term interests for the poor and workers [were] similar, unlike those of workers and capitalists" (Alexander 2013, 30). If these rapprochements between predominantly Black social groups are sometimes justified by political considerations, they have been partly confirmed statistically by several economic studies carried out in the second half of the 2010s. Contrary to the vision of a deracialized post-apartheid economy, these studies have emphasized that the South African Black middle class was not as homogeneous as a public debate focused on some fantasized "empowered class" might have suggested. Within this population, it is claimed, there are groups that are weakened because they consist of women and men living just above the poverty line. This "vulnerable middle class" includes households and individuals who have been poor in the past and who might well be poor again if some unforeseen event might happen.[5]

This picture of postapartheid society needs to be fleshed out, however. Achille Mbembe suggests that if "race is still a crucial marker of privilege," "the forms of social polarization, inequality and exclusion are becoming increasingly complex."[6] More precisely, he adds, "racial antagonism no longer simply opposes the two generic blocks of blacks and whites . . . It now cuts through both categories and in between." Inequalities have thus increased markedly within the Black population itself since the start of the twenty-first century, while they have remained stable or decreased in other racial groups (Statistics South Africa 2019, 145). The emergence of the "new black middle class" (Southall 2016) plays a part here, despite the economic vulnerability of some of its members. But one of the most striking features

Middle-class neighborhood in the township

of the postapartheid social landscape is certainly the formation of a wealthy Black elite cherished by ANC leaders. Aided by the African nationalism adopted by the majority party from the 2000s onward (Glaser 2011), this "small African capitalist class" (Mabasa 2019, 178) was, in time, meant to announce the political and economic emancipation of the entire Black population. Its creation took place through various laws, but also via encouragement and political pressure exerted on the most powerful companies so that they would promote Black candidates to positions of responsibility or open their capital up to Black entrepreneurs. All these measures took place in one of the most emblematic policies of ANC power: Black Economic Empowerment (BEE).[7] In fact, only a minority of individuals benefited from it, since the majority of the Black population did not have the necessary qualifications for their integration into the sectors concerned by the BEE (Wesemüller 2005, 102). Above all, the visibility in the public space of this Black bourgeoisie, which in no way threatened the property rights of capital, enabled governments to affirm that they had successfully deracialized the economy without depriving the ANC of the possibility of resorting to "racial appeals" (MacDonald 2004, 631) when this could be electorally or politically profitable.

The lifestyle of this Black elite obviously has nothing to do with that of people like Archie and his wife. While they have a nice car, two dogs, and a house, the two lead a sober life, like their neighbors in this unostentatious part of the township. Does this sobriety of life lead this fraction of the population to show solidarity naturally and spontaneously with the poor Blacks and workers who are defended by the members of the UPM, however? This is not obvious, and there are some subjective elements to be taken into account. Even if they have often done so at the cost of incurring heavy debts, which justifies this clearly described "precarious ownership" mentioned by the activist, the new Black middle classes have nonetheless entered the consumer society. Whatever they have been able to acquire, whether it is a house, a car, or the possibility of enrolling their children in better schools, it allows them to project themselves into the future and to free themselves from that temporariness which characterizes the poorest people (Appadurai 2003). Above all, access to new lifestyles can encourage these households to try to distinguish themselves (and therefore to detach themselves) from those in the lower strata of society. This is reflected in the choice made by some to leave the township to settle in the former "white" suburbs of large cities. But this, admittedly, is a choice that Archie himself has not made.

"Blood." "Heart." The words chosen by some activists to describe their connection to the movement are, to say the least, evocative. They express rather well the extent to which commitment is not just a matter of joining a cause. It also marks immersion in a collective—in a configuration of exchanges, recognition, loyalties, and various bonds.[8] Such an observation could be verified in many organizational forms, but it is certainly accentuated by the specific nature of the poor people's movements. For reasons that largely depend on the feeling (most often justified) of sharing the same trials and tribulations on a daily basis, an organization such as the UPM may indeed appear as a group of peers or fellows in the eyes of its members, in spite of the greater or lesser social differences between them. Attachment is undoubtedly nourished by this type of perception.

INTERLUDE 2: WHAT REALLY MATTERS

"I have a base, you know?" It's a late November afternoon, and Ayanda and I are strolling down the long street that runs along the buildings of the social science departments of Rhodes University. A few minutes ago we were in one of the main pubs in the city. He ordered a pizza to go. I paid without him having to ask me, as if it went without saying. I was almost surprised that he should choose this place which, to my eyes as a foreigner, embodies perhaps a little too well the white face of the city, with its clientele of students, families, and single men who have come to drink a beer while watching a rugby match.

Once out in the street, we resumed a conversation that may well have begun six years ago, at our first meeting. I wanted him to talk to me again about the conditions of his commitment:

> I have a base. My sister, for example, she lives in Cape Town. She's the one who buy me clothes and she sends them to me. There's also Paul,[1] who can help me. And you see, tonight, I'm going to eat the pizza you bought for me. It's my base, you see? I'm surrounded by people who care about me.

The "base" evoked by Ayanda—these people around him who "take care" of him—has allowed him to be a full-time activist since the beginning of the 2010s. The movement seems, moreover, to have colonized almost every aspect of his own life, occupying him from morning until night and leaving only Sunday free for his passion for football.

Ayanda is undoubtedly the most famous figure of the movement, in Grahamstown and beyond. He has also become one of the unofficial spokespersons of postapartheid protest, one of those to whom the media turn when they are dealing with the "revolt of the poor." He is sometimes interviewed on the radio, in the daily papers, or in television reports. So he is one of the few people whose identity I felt I did not need to anonymize. His notoriety is, however, less than that of Trevor Ngwane, the main leader of the Soweto Electricity Crisis Committee in Johannesburg, or Z'bu Zikode, president of Abahlali baseMjondolo in Durban. These two men spent part of the 2010s acting as the "travelling ambassadors" (Burawoy 2017, 24) of protest. His fear of flying may have prevented Ayanda from following this path, which would otherwise have led him to present the South African case to activist audiences around the world.

Over the 2000s and 2010s, postapartheid South Africa became an iconic textbook case for many actors in what could be called the international alter-globalization galaxy. South African protest activists first started to crop up in the essays of Naomi Klein, Michael Hart, Antonio Negri, and many others, where their fight appeared as a striking illustration of the resistance to the "trickery" of the globalized order. And it is true that these struggles ideally brought together individuals who had spent part of their lives fighting for their freedom and dignity before being betrayed by their former leaders and finally handed over to "neoliberalism." Thus, the protest movement in South Africa has, little by little, found its place in this mesh of interlacing networks that NGOs, intellectual and political friendships, and the solidarity between activists weave and foster on an international scale. It is in this way that Ayanda, in spite of his fear of flying, participated in the Marxism Festival in London in the early 2010s, at the invitation of an academic who also ran a small Trotskyist party. His travel and living expenses were borne by a British university, which also agreed to invite him to take part in a seminar organized by its department of African Studies.

Paradoxically, it is actually Ayanda's ability to play with boundaries that comes to mind when I have to describe him—physical and social boundaries, in this case. In fact, the choice of this pub should not have surprised me. As a child, Ayanda came to town quite often, unlike most of his classmates. He accompanied his mother, a domestic worker in the home of a white academic who was close to anti-apartheid organizations. He also likes to tell how, when he was barely a dozen years old, he left the township one day armed with his "broken English" in order to buy a soccer ball in the city, when apartheid was still in force. Ayanda has obviously kept the self-assurance that some may interpret as a form of rudeness. He does not hesitate, for example, to make himself a cup of tea without being invited when he goes to the premises of the lawyers' association that the UPM regularly calls on. Then he goes straight into the lawyers' offices, even he is not always expected there. He concedes that he can be a bit of a "bully" or "bossy" when he wants to get something: "When you're in the social movement, you've got to hassle." All this, of course, may seem very by the by. It seems to me, however, that this mixture of ease and self-assurance also expresses the conviction that his social status should not stop him doing anything he wants. Being poor *and* Black does not mean that you have to hold back. To a certain extent, the fact that he walks into these offices or those of the sociology department without being announced is also a way of challenging the social order or, more exactly, to defy it a little.

These few characteristics might suggest that Ayanda is not at all representative of the Grahamstown collective of the unemployed. Although he is distinguished from his comrades in certain respects, his social condition is in no way different. His life is, furthermore, shaped by the political, social, and economic realities that run through postapartheid society. His case simply underlines the fact that "no life is outside of its times" (Fassin, Le Marcis, and Lethara 2008, 234).

When our paths met for the first time in the early 2010s, Ayanda had just turned thirty-five and lived in a misshapen house built on rough terrain and eaten away by weeds. As for being a house, it was mainly just the two rooms constitutive of a big shack, sturdy enough but little more than an assembly of sheet metal and various bits of recycled material. He later made his home on the other side of the street, in a building that was cramped but made of "hard" materials—a kind of cement covered with pink plaster. However, the solution could only be temporary, as the building also housed one of his two sisters, as well as his nephews and nieces. A few months later, Ayanda decided to rent another shack not far away. This is a sheet metal construction of approximately seventy square meters divided into three dwellings. It is built on a plot vaguely surrounded by a rickety fence, at the foot of which lies a pile of torn plastic bags, wastepaper, and soft drink bottles. The landlord is a kind of *rentier* in the informal economy; he collects rents from the five shacks that his mother built in the neighborhood several years ago. The part occupied by Ayanda consists of a room whose only window is obstructed by pieces of cardboard meant to replace the missing glass tiles. There is not enough space to accommodate much more than a bed and a chair. In the evening, Ayanda sometimes goes to eat at his sister's house. More often, he joins his girlfriend, who lives in her brother's house a block away. For lack of "means," Ayanda cannot live with her and their young child. His two older sons, whom he had with another wife, live at their aunt's house with their cousins.

He also spends a few hours at Mandisa's tavern. This belongs to a woman of about sixty who receives various influential local people in the apartment she has built in one of the wings of the tavern. Ayanda has been a visitor there since Archie, a friend who works for the municipality, introduced him to Mandisa. In the course of these evenings, he sometimes rubs shoulders with ANC local councilors whose incompetence and corruption he has denounced during the day at community meetings. In his view, this is part of his commitment: "You shouldn't be aloof if you want to be influential."

Ayanda was born in Grahamstown in the late 1970s, but spent a few years in Cape Town. He first studied management at a university of technology, while living in one of the many informal settlements that surround the Western Cape capital. It was also in this city that he found his first job. He was in charge of training and assessing the employees of one of the call centers of a catalog company. According to him, however, he was often taken away from this assessment in order to defend employees threatened by the company's management. This attitude eventually led to his being summoned by the head of human resources on a Friday afternoon. The tense and stormy discussion he had with her, however, did not prepare him for what awaited him on his return the following Monday morning: dismissal, motivated by the accusations of physical aggression brought against him by this woman. He found another job in a furniture store but resigned a few months later after again defending an employee.

These setbacks, which he links to the racism still lurking at the heart of postapartheid society, came with other disappointments. Ayanda has always loved politics. As much as football. It would certainly be more accurate to say that he has always had a special love of *political commitment*. He often told me about the photo on which, at the age of seven, he appeared on the front lines of an anti-apartheid protest. The image made the front page of the Grahamstown newspaper in the 1980s, thirty years before the newspaper's editorial board named him "Newsmaker of the Year 2011." While he consistently speaks in favor of concrete political action, which incidentally means that he can denigrate the action of political professionals and their "empty promises," Ayanda also loves ideas. I was very often able to observe him printing out highly theoretical political texts that I imagined he would read at night in his shack. At internal meetings, he will also sometimes quote Lenin or Trotsky. It is Steve Biko, however, the founder of the Black Consciousness Movement, assassinated in 1977 by the apartheid regime, whom he most greatly admires.

The thought of Biko, a celebrated martyr of political struggle, could certainly be compared to that of Frantz Fanon and James H. Cone, one of the main theorists of Black Liberation Theology.[2] Steve Biko elaborated a critique of white liberals opposed to apartheid. He judged them guilty of adopting, in reality, a "master's perspective" seeking above all to "integrate" Blacks into South African society (Biko 1987; Gibson 2011). Biko's thinking, and more generally that of the BCM, did not remain suspended in the sky of ideas, nor was it a secret confined to the intellectual elites of Black activists of the 1970s. It soon spread among Black youth, at university or in high schools, appearing as the most appropriate (i.e., most "radical") response to the white state that drew its strength from the most violent repression. Biko's history is linked furthermore to Grahamstown. He was arrested at a police roadblock near the town in August 1977 before being imprisoned and tortured in Port Elizabeth. A few years earlier, in 1968, the National Union of South African Students (NUSAS) had also organized its congress on the Rhodes University campus. The leaders of this multiracial and "progressive" union had invited along their counterparts from the South African Students' Association (SASO), founded a few months ago and chaired by Steve Biko, then a medical student. Because Blacks were forbidden by law from spending the night on campus, the SASO delegation was forced to fall back on the township. Biko and his friends settled in Saint Philip's Church. Ayanda's shack was a few hundred meters from the red brick building of the church to which he had often steered our steps as we walked through the neighborhood. For a time, there was talk of the unemployed moving into the ruined building facing the church. The organization even received support from the bishop, who had to yield, however, to the opposition from some of his flock who were close to the ANC.

Ayanda discovered the life story and thinking of Steve Biko in his early teens, when most of his friends still swore by the ANC leaders. This happened via one of his neighbors who was at that time very involved in the clandestine activities of the Azanian People's Organization (AZAPO), one of the main political groups associated with the Black Consciousness Movement. This same neighbor would be one of the founding members of the UPM a few years later. Ayanda quickly progressed through the AZAPO, where he soon assumed major responsibilities for its youth league. The marginalization of the party within parliamentary space inevitably stoked internal dissent. The political tendency to which Ayanda belonged criticized the way the management was slipping toward the center of the political spectrum. The opposition members were in a minority and had to leave the AZAPO, sometimes under physical threats from their former comrades. They initially sought to create a new political group that could claim to be the heir to the BCM. In a political field then dominated entirely by the opposition between the African National Congress and the Democratic Alliance, any other political enterprise or attempt at dissent seemed destined to fail. "It was quite a trauma in my life," Ayanda told me. "None of us could imagine our life outside AZAPO. It was a trauma . . . it was one of the dramatic years of my life when it became clear we had to find a political home outside AZAPO. I felt soccer would do it good . . . 'cause I was frustrated.

Shack in which Ayanda rents a room, Fingo Village neighborhood

Nothing was going right." Feeling weary, Ayanda entered Grahamstown in the mid-2000s and devoted himself to amateur football. He took on provincial responsibilities and, most important, coached a team of young players from the township. Repeated discussions with other residents convinced him to help found a movement to express dissatisfaction with poor living conditions.

His shift from the sphere of political parties to the sphere of the social movement is far from being an isolated case in postapartheid South Africa. The gradual closure of the political field from the end of the "Mandela years" (1994–1999) onward resulted in a hunt for dissidents within the ANC and its allies (the COSATU trade union federation and South African Communist Party), both at national and local levels. The world of social protest then allowed a certain number of former political and trade union activists to change career (Tournadre 2018, 66–71).

In 2009, when the UPM was founded, Ayanda had just found a job as a casual worker. He unpacked goods after their delivery to one of the city supermarkets. He suddenly left it one day so that he could fully devote himself to the new organization: "For once, I found life outside AZAPO. I had a political home. For once, I could do something that I love." These few words give a pretty clear idea of how Ayanda says he lives his activism: as a vocation. Activism thereby becomes a *lifestyle* or, more importantly, a way of inhabiting the world. This does not, however, tell us why the movement, and devoting body and soul to it, are so important to Ayanda.

In a book published in 1951, *Minima Moralia*, the philosopher Theodor Adorno asked a question which could be expressed as follows: "Can one lead a good life in a bad life?" Sixty years later, Judith Butler sought to adapt this question to the contemporary world: "Can one lead a good life for oneself, as oneself, in the context of a broader world that is structured by inequality, exploitation and forms of effacement?" (Butler 2012, 9). The lives of Ayanda and his comrades, as well as the lives of women and men around the world who are struggling to improve their living conditions and those of their peers, provide an initial answer to this question.

The conception of the good life obviously varies with individuals, and certainly with the periods of history and across the lives of individuals. In Ayanda's case, the "good life" seems to merge with his activism or, more exactly, with the meaning he gives to his commitment. Because it is associated with selflessness and an acceptance of sacrifice, commitment is indeed a sociopolitical as much as a moral experience in which "what really matters" (Kleinman 2006) is defined.

By putting himself at the service of the "community" and, more concretely, of those who are enduring the same things as he is, Ayanda first and foremost finds the resources to create a good image of himself. He thus protects his self-esteem from the humiliation that is the daily lot of the poor in South Africa—a humiliation related to their living conditions, but also to what they perceive as the indifference, even the cynicism, of the political elites. These initial virtues can be reinforced by what a large number of people outside the movement say about him.

Regularly, people whom I do not necessarily know, and whom I meet at random in my wanderings across the city, point out his "devotion" and his "humanity" to me. When these scenes take place in his presence, he seems both embarrassed and proud. These testimonials and these marks of admiring support certainly bear fruit. It is likely that they reinforce a form of reassurance—that, in particular, he is serving as he should a cause that he deems to be "right." In any case, the expression of this recognition also helps him to transcend his own condition. It helps to remind him that he is not "only" an unemployed man living in a shack, when so many others would be gnawed by envy, resentment, frustration, or the "self-hatred" that he sometimes says he can perceive among certain residents. Thus his concept of the good life also develops in this feeling of being able to act on his own life through activism. He knows how rare it is for this ability to be within the reach of those around him in the township.

5

"IT IS MORAL TO REBEL"

The Unemployed People's Movement has moved its offices four times since my first stay in Grahamstown. This is a clear sign of the precariousness and uncertainty in which the organization operates, since each of these moves was the result of difficulties in paying the rent. In any case, in spite of what differentiated them from each other (both in size and location), the four places I knew shared this appearance of transition and ephemerality. Nothing seemed to make them places where one could feel at home. Some "revolutionary" photographs or posters brightened the walls, but not much more. Even the small garden attached to the house in McDonald Street, rented by the movement for a few months, had been abandoned. Only the youngest activists would sometimes sit there and talk, in the midst of the tall grass and rubbish of all kinds.

It is in the premises that they moved into a few weeks ago, behind the Day Hospital, that an internal meeting has been convened for this October morning. Thirty or forty activists are present—women and men of all ages, from all four corners of the township. I recognize many people whose intensity of commitment does not seem to have weakened over the years. They have sat down in a circle in a large empty room, in the center of which an oil heater mounted on wheels is endeavoring to mitigate the coldness of the place. A large number of those present have come on foot. The others, especially those living in the most remote areas, have had to bear the cost of a minibus trip. In both cases, there is nothing innocent about their presence here this morning, which underlines the fact that "the more important a group becomes in the life of its members, the more sacrifices the members are usually willing to make in its name, both from love and from duty" (Mansbridge 2001a, 254).

The discussions focus initially on the difficulties encountered by the organization. They are the direct result of internal conflicts that have led one of the UPM's financial backers to suspend its assistance. Former activists have written to the NGO that had been supporting the UPM's efforts for a few years, accusing some of their comrades of mismanaging the funds allocated.

Some suggestions are made of routes that the movement might follow so that it "rises again." Dumisa, a grandmother who held the position of chairperson a few years ago, recalls that the UPM was in any case "a social movement even before it had an office." "Before, the meetings were outside. We forgot that we are a social movement," she adds, in the brusque tone that she adopts regularly in meetings, one that disarms her opponents. One activist also mentions the need to "punish" those who have apparently betrayed them and suggests setting up a disciplinary council. Many of his comrades immediately object.

The conversation gradually takes another direction as these internal problems are reinscribed within the broader context of the "oppression" of the poor in South Africa. Gradually, the activists come to talk about what in their eyes justifies the existence of the organization. The speeches are unequivocal. They emphasize the shared feeling that, as a poor person, you are regularly attacked in your integrity as a human being. "If you have no dignity and no roof over your head, you're forced to revolt!" asserts one of the activists. "We must resist these people [of the municipality] who make us suffer and attack our dignity," storms Dumisa. Athandile, who lives in Extension 7, a district of the township created in the 1990s, also warns about the continuing lack of rubbish collection and what it says about how poor people are treated by their rulers: "Because of them, we live like animals now." "We have to occupy the streets. This is where our freedom is, even if we are desperate," seems be Ayanda's conclusion.

It is always a little unrealistic to describe an atmosphere, since subjective impressions count for so much. However, as I observe these people holding forth, I cannot help but think that something has got these women and men in its grip—something that needs to be explained. Of course, I recognize the long-nursed frustration that runs through interviews and even the most innocuous conversations. But it is not merely frustration that seems

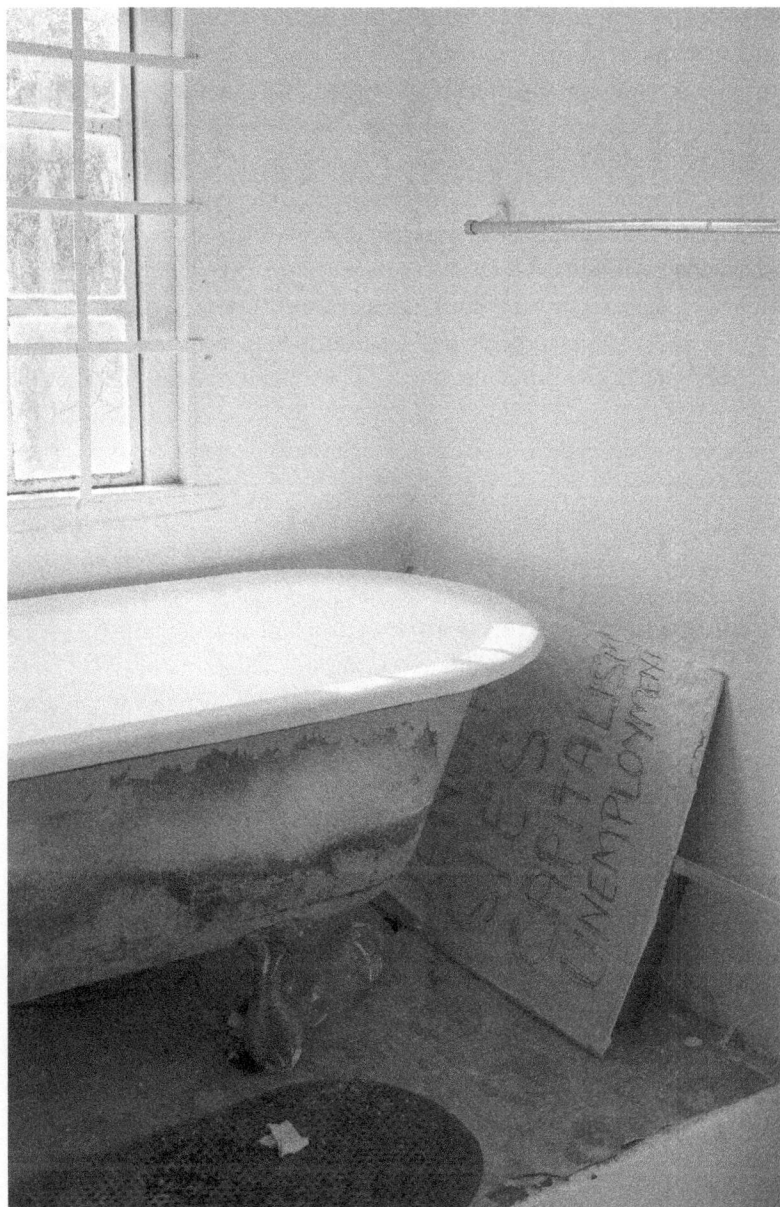

In the premises of the UPM, McDonald Street

to imbue the timbre of their voices and to lie behind their choice of words. Added to this there are a suppressed anger, indignation, and diffuse forms of resentment. It is at the heart of these mixed feelings that the "subjective roots of protest" grow (Mansbridge and Morris 2001). Admittedly, these concentrated emotions and feelings are not enough in themselves to launch a protest movement. The world is bursting with anger, humiliation, and frustration, but there is little sign of systematic rebellion on the part of those who suffer from them. A catalyst, whether it is an organization or networks of mutual acquaintance, remains indispensable. However, it has no raison d'être unless these incorporated elements help to maintain the motivation of these people, and can nourish the "oppositional consciousness" of the group (ibid.).

In an attempt to define the concept of oppositional consciousness, Jane Mansbridge has suggested thinking about "what people have meant with the words 'class consciousness' and apply the same logic to other groups, such as women or African Americans" (2001b, 1). Oppositional consciousness is therefore an "empowering mental state" that prepares members of an oppressed group to act against a "system of human domination" (4–5). It is this, too, that makes it possible to transform a "subordinate identity" into a "positive identification." I regularly ascertain this when my interlocutors claim to be "poor" and thus oppose the stigma that most often accompanies this condition with a sense of collective honor. This "consciousness" makes it possible to conclude that the other members of the group share the same interests, and thus contributes to changing the aspect of things: "suffering" can become "injustice." It is, therefore, this awareness that justifies the way these activists have traveled to the meeting this morning, in this cold room.

As the exchanges of opinion at this meeting confirm, the subjective roots of protest are firmly rooted in the social and physical worlds that individuals deal with every day. The feeling of injustice is experienced above all in one's ordinary relationship to the world; it then reveals raisons d'être that are, to put it mildly, perfectly objective. It is built, among other things, on water cuts, damp walls, and leaking roofs. It can also arise from wounds more deeply internalized by individuals. A few months after this meeting, I asked Onke if she remembered how "all this," that is, her entry into activism and then her commitment to the UPM, had begun. We were in front of her house in the heart of the Joza district, and I think I expected her to tell me about neighbors struggling to survive or the exasperation aroused by the ANC's "betrayals." Spontaneously, however, she evoked memories of her childhood, and especially of those times when she accompanied her mother, a domestic worker, to the homes of her white employers. It was on these various occasions, she told me, that she felt she had first experienced injustice and, perhaps even more, humiliation.

> They were not bad. They were very welcoming. They were nice bosses and they liked us because we were their domestic worker's children, but . . . there were things I didn't like. At eating time, we ate outside while they were sitting around the table. Inside. And . . . they gave her beans to take home while they ate very expensive things. I asked my mother questions. I asked her: "Why are we eating outside when the family is eating in the house?" Things like that. I used to question. But my mother laughed. She saw no problem, or maybe . . . she didn't want to encourage what I was asking her. I knew it wasn't normal and it was hurtful. I've always wondered about that kind of things.

Answering the same question, one of Onke's comrades, Thabang, had also returned to what he perceived as the causes of his own discontent. Like others before him, he first described the feeling of being left out of contemporary South Africa. Then, as if to convince me of the widespread injustice of postapartheid society, he decided to tell me about another case than his: that of his uncle, a former "freedom fighter." Thabang, both moved and concerned, had described to me in broad terms the existence of this man, imprisoned on Robben Island during apartheid, alongside various ANC leaders such as Nelson Mandela and Govan Mbeki. Now sixty-six years old, physically and morally diminished, Thabang's uncle continued to fight destiny, even in a South Africa rid of apartheid: "If you could see him, you could see a man that has been betrayed. . . . Most of the people who are now reaping the fruits were not there during apartheid. So they do not know what these people were fighting for."

Conscious or not, the choices made by Onke and Thabang as they answer my questions are not trivial. They emphasize personal wounds that are closely connected with the UPM's struggle and, more generally, the collective destiny of the poor. In recalling these memories, Onke is more generally speaking of the sense of indignation at class-based contempt and barely euphemized racism. Thabang's story, meanwhile, describes a self-respect flouted by the blindness and ingratitude of the "new" South Africa. Their replies, but also the various statements at the meeting mentioned at the beginning of this chapter, highlight one and the same thing: protest (also) has a moral dimension. This moral charge is one that comes up regularly and in other forms when I am talking to residents and activists. Some people may summon up the past to justify postapartheid discontent. The "unfulfilled promise" of power, they say, broke the pact established between rulers and ruled at the birth of South African democracy in 1994. The story is simple enough to understand: supported by the population of the townships, the new power was indeed supposed to deliver "a better life for all." The ANC even made it its campaign slogan in the first democratic elections, and then the core agenda of the early governments. The "raw life" of a large majority of South Africans symbolized this break and justified the fact that it was now "moral to rebel," in the terms used in a press release issued by the Unemployed People's Movement.[1] True, revolt does not arise directly from such a perception of things. On the other hand, it may lead to the expressing of moral motives which help to justify revolt in the eyes of the women and men who resort to it. Above all, it gives a certain ethical sense to their action.

The fact that discontent and its expression as protest can have moral springs is not surprising (see, among others, Jasper 1997). This almost banal reality is undermined, however, by the discourse that has dominated South African public debate since the beginning of the twenty-first century. The increasing number of demonstrations has indeed justified the emergence of a generic term supposed to encompass them all and reveal their essence. This is the term "service-delivery protests." This category, very widely used in the worlds of politics and journalism, inevitably tends to present discontent solely from the material angle. If one follows this logic, one could immediately counter the protestors' arguments and undermine the coherence of their anger by pointing to the construction of more than three million homes since 1994 or the progressive electrification of poor residential areas in the country (Palmer, Moodley, and Parnell 2017). Political scientist Richard Pithouse, close to Abahlali baseMjondolo and the Unemployed People's Movement, sees the bases of a "service delivery myth" at the heart of this reading of the social world. In his view, this myth is built on the idea that the people are "passive consumers . . . who just need to be plugged into the grid of serviced life by a benevolent state."[2] He continues,

The myth assumes that . . . as backlogs are steadily overcome people who aren't yet plugged in will join the rest of us and enjoy a better life. It makes us assume that patience is a virtue and that dissent at anything other than the pace and efficiency of service delivery is perverse and probably the result of malicious conspiracy.[3]

As so often, this type of categorization may tell us more about who uses it—mainly the political and media elites in South Africa—than about what it is supposed to describe: the anger of the governed. It is as if this discontent were being expressed directly and without complexity.

This is obviously not to diminish the material dimension of the demands being voiced. The anecdote shared by James Ferguson in the pages of *Give A Man a Fish* puts it quite well. Ferguson recounts that, at the end of a housing rights workshop organized by an NGO in a neighborhood of shack dwellers in Cape Town, one of the participants took the floor and explained that he did not want to have the "right to a house" that had been discussed throughout the meeting. And the man added, in front of stunned workshop leaders, that he simply wanted "a house" (Ferguson 2015, 48). Socioeconomic factors therefore remain an essential cause of protest or, at the very least, of the discontent that may lead to revolt. But just as the uprisings against the price of wheat in eighteenth-century England were not only "revolts of the belly" (Thompson 1971), postapartheid demonstrations cannot be reduced to the mere expression of material demands. UPM activists affirm this, moreover, in the most explicit way possible. Responding to a journalist questioning him about the reasons for the anger in the township, Xola, one of their first spokespersons, summed things up in two short sentences: "It's not just about 'service delivery,' it's about dignity. When you don't have a toilet, what does that do to your dignity?"[4]

Xola's words remind us of something essential that we are sometimes tempted to forget: protest is very often "a multilayered and complex phenomenon" (Salman and Assies 2017, 59). It involves material demands that monopolize signs and banners, and more symbolic and moral aspects referring to demands for respect or the defense of what is perceived as *due* or *just*. There is nothing contradictory about this: symbolic struggles are never devoid of more concrete stakes, just as redistributional conflicts are never independent of immaterial issues (see Lazzeri 2009). The reason is simple and relatively universal: "all the axes of oppression in real life are mixed"

(Fraser 1997). In this case, the poverty in which millions of South Africans live has elective affinities with the disrespect (Honneth 2007) they feel they have suffered and which justifies the raising of the broader question of their social status,[5] and even of their place in the "New" South Africa.

This last question is all the more legitimate as postapartheid citizenship is absorbed in another feeling widely shared by the poor: that of being denied in their subjectivity, even in their "being." "They don't listen to us. They don't see us"—these are words I regularly hear from activists and residents when we are talking about those who govern them. This perception of things can be fueled by the overt tendency of the public authorities to sometimes fail to consider these women and men as beings capable of making a reasoned judgment about their condition. The passivity to which they are thus reduced is, it seems, fully endorsed by the officials. Antina von Schnitzler, who has studied the installation of prepaid water meters in Soweto, supports this idea, pointing out:

> As one elderly man in Phiri[6] has explained to me a couple of years earlier, residents never got the chance to "sit down and discuss" the project. Instead, utility officials "simply come and dig here [to install pipes] . . . without asking us about what we want." The postapartheid democracy, while granting them the right to vote, increasingly appeared to many residents to be defined by such technocratic interventions in their daily lives. (von Schnitzler 2014, 346)

In Grahamstown too, there are plenty of examples. In October 2012, the municipality sent an expert to the informal neighborhood of eThembeni, where the UPM has several activists and supporters. The aim was to launch an environmental impact study that would provide guidelines for a potential development of the zone. Because no resident was informed of the existence of such a project, the outside observer was soon regarded with suspicion and fear by the community (Pillay 2012). Its members then decided to send a delegation of five people to the city hall to set up a working relationship with the mayor. The small embassy, however, was confined for several long hours to a waiting room before being informed that the city councilor was too busy to see them. This is one example among others: similar cases are frequent and in any case they can, in the minds of those who are its victims, create an impression of being excluded from the community of citizens. It is therefore not surprising that, like other organizations, the UPM relies on this grievance to call for a "democracy that includes the poor and allows poor people to plan their own communities and their own future."[7]

This impression of exclusion can sometimes be transformed into a deeper feeling of *invisibility*—an invisibility bordering on the negation of one's own humanity. This perception of things is forged daily, through attitudes and situations experienced as humiliations. Once again, the residents of eThembeni could provide a convincing illustration, just like those who, in the unhealthiest parts of the city, continue to experience a bucket system that the municipality had still not totally eradicated in the mid-2010s. Residents of these districts may feel that they are living in real "zones of social abandonment" (Biehl 2005). "Nobody is looking after us in eThembeni at all," explained one mother while she pointed out to the journalism students filming her the holes her neighbors had dug in the ground to compensate for the lack of toilets.[8]

However, should this scene, revealing as it does the daily lives of hundreds of thousands of women and men, mean we should follow Arjun Appadurai when he evokes a "bare citizenship" to characterize the "large masses of the urban poor" all around the world? In his view, these individuals are "invisible in the eyes of the law, stripped of many normal rights and privileges, and placed in much the same status as refugees, prisoners of war, aliens" (2013, 118–120). At first glance, the case of South Africa does not seem to contradict such an assertion. We need merely note the apparent ease with which this logic of "expulsion" has taken root: it is now omnipresent in contemporary societies.[9] Periodically, in democratic South Africa, public authorities or private owners resort to the services of security companies to ruthlessly dislodge the residents of squatter camps or households that have moved into unoccupied buildings. The systematic destruction of the property of those expelled, and the (sometimes lethal) violence that falls upon those who resist, might suggest that the lives of the poorest are of little importance to the rulers.[10]

The citizenship enjoyed by the poor is nevertheless more *paradoxical* than *bare*. The fact that the social security system is particularly redistributive in terms of cash transfers (see Seekings and Nattrass 2015, 15) tends to convince one that the social dimension of postapartheid citizenship is not *merely* formal or theoretical, even if it still remains deficient (see Chapter 1).

In the township

Judges have also enshrined several basic socioeconomic rights, even though activists and lawyers working alongside them have experienced many disappointments in this area (Langford et al. 2014). Finally, the political bond uniting the rulers and the poorest of the ruled is, at the very least, ambiguous. If the latter can feel in turn diminished, humiliated or instrumentalized *by, on the orders of,* or *in spite* of the former, they nonetheless remain potential voters who must sometimes be reassured and convinced that they do indeed belong to the polity. The repeated promises of successive ward councilors in eThembeni confirm this quite well. The postapartheid citizenship of the poorest therefore mainly resembles an unfinished project.

The idea that the poorest still have to fight to be respected in postapartheid South Africa sums up quite nicely what has been said earlier. The very term "dignity," as we have already seen, also comes up very frequently at those times when activists get together to discuss their living conditions and those of their friends and relatives. It is especially ubiquitous when members of the group address outsiders—either to take the latter to witness, or to blame them for not acting. The second scenario is illustrated by the appearance of thirty activists in City Hall one morning in May 2018. They came laden with plastic buckets filled with the cloudy, turbid water that had for several weeks been running from the taps in some areas of eastern Grahamstown. A few days before, traces of *E. coli* bacteria had also been found, even though the residents had not been warned by the authorities to boil the water. Cases of fever, diarrhea, and rash had been reported in several children. Standing in a semicircle in the middle of the main room in city hall, the activists wished to "assert the dignity and humanity of the residents," to use the words of one of their number, and to force the officials to explain themselves.

Often criticized for its vagueness or its normativity, the notion of dignity does nonetheless have one merit that the present case highlights: it means that activists can present as inseparable the undermining of a physical and material integrity (being exposed to disease, not being protected from cold and rain by a roof, etc.) and the negation of a moral status, that of being the member of a common humanity. For these reasons, the UPM's fight to change the most concrete aspects of the daily lives of the poor is also a struggle for the recognition (Honneth 1995) of this population. Recognition struggles, as Barbara Hobson reminds us, "often involve making claims for resources, goods, and services through state policies: care allowances via women's movements, social security benefits for gay couples, or building access ramps for the disabled. But claims in recognition struggles are also connected to membership and inclusion in the polity" (2003, 3). The question of housing alone, which lies at the heart of the demands of the UPM and, more generally, of most poor people's movements around the world, demonstrates this perfectly. Leaving a shack and moving into a house should of course make it possible to gain shelter from the cold and damp, or to protect one's property. But whether in Grahamstown, Mumbai, or Rio de Janeiro, formal housing acknowledges the urban citizenship of individuals, including allowing official access to networked residential services.[11] Housing also delineates the boundaries of the intimate (and therefore of a certain idea of humanity), providing in particular "a sense of respite from . . . the noise of everyday life's intimate details" to which one is exposed by "the close living of informal settlements" (Ross 2010, 65). Perceived as the bedrock of "normality," that is to say, of inclusion in a society, housing is an initial answer to people's aspirations to lead a decent life.

The expression of this need for recognition on the part of the most destitute runs through postapartheid protest. There is particular evidence of this in the "right to the city" regularly demanded by poor and Black populations since the beginning of the twenty-first century—those same populations that had been deprived of it by apartheid for decades. Being in the city means being able to access what most townships cannot offer: decent schools, jobs, and shops. It is also a question of citizenship or, more precisely, a question of recognizing the status of citizens. As the anthropologist David Harvey (2008), sometimes quoted by South African activists,[12] suggests, to demand the right to the city is to claim a fundamental and radical shaping power over the processes of urbanization, that is, the ways in which cities are constantly being transformed. This is another expression of the demand to no longer be treated as a second-rate citizen whom the rulers can keep at bay or move around just as their policies dictate, like the hundreds of poor households forced to move for the purposes of the 2010 World Cup (see Tournadre 2018, 128–129), or those residents of eThembeni "forgotten" in a waiting room of City Hall.

I would like to return, however briefly, to the part played by one's personal history in the formulation of discontent, but from a slightly different angle than with Onke and Thabang at the beginning of this chapter.

The sincerity of this collective struggle to escape from the social, spatial, and political margins to which these individuals consider themselves relegated does not stop activist discourse and the language of those who take part sporadically in demonstrations being imbued with more personal reasons or, at the very least, more related to an individual trajectory. The way Joseph looks back at his life as he enters his sixties partly illustrates these ambiguities.

Though he joined the UPM only in 2015, after losing his job, this warm and considerate man has a rich activist past behind him. In the early 1980s, along with his two older brothers, he helped to set up an association struggling to improve the living conditions of the Black population of Grahamstown. Well established in the township, this group was quickly enrolled in the wake of the United Democratic Front, the national structure that embodied the internal front of the fight against apartheid for a significant part of that decade. A few years later, Joseph threw his energy into founding another association whose goal, this time, was to provide financial support for young Blacks wishing to study at high school and university. His commitment cost him dearly. The police harassment he was subjected to forced him to stop the law studies he had himself begun at the university reserved for Blacks in Fort Hare. Above all, he served three prison sentences and considering going into exile to join the paramilitary branch of the ANC.

Today Joseph, his daughter, and his wife live in a house whose comfort may seem surprising in this neighborhood whose streets are nothing more than bumpy dirt tracks. The inside of the house is rather attractive. The living room is occupied by two sofas and various pieces of imposing furniture. I have frequently observed such things in seemingly more modest households. Some analysts would like to see them as the signs of "conspicuous consumption" (Veblen 2000). In their view, furniture, objects, and decorations serve to affirm a fantasized social status, that of the middle classes, and the way of life associated with it. However, the consumption of these goods can also be considered as a means of feeling included in society and as simply conveying the desire for a "normal" life. It does not matter in the present case, since Joseph and his family actually did belong to the middle classes when the husband still had a job. In a few years, the house has grown from three to six rooms, as its owner told me with some pride. Nowadays, however, the household lives on the sole salary of his wife, who is employed in one of the municipal libraries. I do not know quite how much they earn, but I feel that this household is now quite typical of the "floating class" that international organizations such as the African Development Bank deem to be living above the poverty threshold though not really in a position to claim they are "doing quite nicely." For example, the couple do not have a car.

Early one morning, while we were still alone in the movement's premises, the conversation turned to "disappointed hopes." Joseph first told me that he had left the ANC in 1996, considering that "it was not the party that [he] thought [he] knew." In his view, it was already in the hands of those who sought only to "hold positions." The rest of society had quickly succumbed to this kind of behavior. Today, he added, power, especially at the local level, was held by "puppets" whose incompetence protected those who had given them access to these positions. The identity of the latter was quite clear in Joseph's mind: the "mistake" of the first democratic years had been to let former "exiles" seize the "key positions" within the ANC and the country. This had been done to the detriment of those "who had their feet on the ground . . . who know what people want inside the country."

The current mayor is incompetent. She knows nothing about politics. She used to be a nurse. She was never involved. The people of Grahamstown, they know that. That's why I am doing this kind of work . . . consultation . . . helping people. Last year, the mayor even offered me an office so that I could advise people, as I do here. They have also tried to attract other comrades. It's a team of novices. They don't know the city. I have a good example: my neighbor, she is an ANC ward councilor. The day before the election, she came to my house because she was going to be interviewed. And she begged me to tell her the story of her party . . . because she knew nothing. But you see . . . every day I meet people who tell me that I should be the one to be mayor. But that's impossible. A few years ago, I had a friend who should have been the mayor. He was a councilor, and he has a master's degree in law. But he was too educated and too critical. They don't like that. They want puppets.

Realizing that he thought he was one of the people ousted from the "New" South Africa, I decided to make my questions a little more precise:

"Would you say that people like you have not been rewarded enough by South Africa?"
He nodded in agreement.
"I mean . . . you said that some of your former comrades are now in the national and provincial governments, while others like you are still struggling with unemployment and poverty. Do you sometimes think about this gap?" I added.
"Yes, yes, I do think about this. You know, these days, if you're critical about the issues . . . because the ANC is the ruling party . . . if you don't subscribe to this school of thought, you battle. I even battled to get my special pension. I applied, you know? But my application was turned down."

The "special pension" mentioned by Joseph is reserved for "individuals who made sacrifices or served the public interest in establishing a democratic constitutional order in South Africa."[13] It mainly concerns those whose political commitments landed them in jail in the years of struggle against segregation. It is thus a question of compensating "the time they lost" on behalf of the liberation of the country, Joseph told me—compensating them "because these people couldn't save for their children." Imprisoned for his activism by the apartheid regime in 1977, 1985, and 1988, Joseph could logically expect this form of recognition. Onke's husband, who was also arrested in the 1980s for his involvement in AZAPO's underground networks, faced the same problems before finally winning his case.

This was not the first time I had heard such a story. A few years before, Jacob, an activist with the Soweto Electricity Crisis Committee (Johannesburg), also in his sixties, had told me he was in a similar situation. He had then divulged a few details of a life that was quite similar to Joseph's. At a very young age, he joined the Communist Party in the 1960s, and Steve Biko's Black Consciousness Movement in the next decade. Meanwhile, he studied at the University College of Soweto. Threatened by police because of his clandestine activism, he went to the USSR, as did many opponents of apartheid in the 1970s, and then returned to South Africa on the eve of the Soweto uprising (June 1976). It was then that he joined the PAC, a dissident organization of the ANC, and participated in the activities of its armed wing in Tanzania. Despite his challenge to the apartheid regime, weapons in hand, this man did not receive the pension paid by the democratic state to former soldiers of the struggle. He attributed this situation to the presence of individuals who were hostile to him within the commission in charge of allocating pensions. Only the veterans of the armed wing of the ANC, he explained to me, received this compensation. One could see these difficulties as an additional sign of the tendency to consider that "only the ANC has a history in this country," as the novelist André Brink lamented.[14] It is not insignificant that, during the interview, Jacob recalled Tokyo Sexwale, whom he got to know at school in the late 1950s. Like him, Sexwale joined the Black Consciousness Movement in the 1960s and campaigned in the South African Students' Movement before engaging in turn in the armed struggle, in the ranks of Umkhonto we Sizwe (MK), the military wing of the ANC, and going into exile in the Soviet Union. But unlike the SECC activist, unemployed since the mid-1990s, Sexwale attained high positions within the ANC and the Republic after 1994, before making his fortune in the diamond, energy, and mining sectors. Here too, there are similarities with Joseph's life story. Indeed, the regrets expressed in the UPM activist's responses seem intensified by the fact that many of his former comrades have met with favorable destinies. On several occasions, Joseph told me about an ANC government minister of the 2010s, and insisted that he had "known him very well" during the mobilizations he organized in Grahamstown in the 1980s. He also told me that other leading figures, at the national and provincial levels, had been able to finish their studies in the 1980s thanks to the support of the second association he had helped to found.

This way of comparing a personal situation with those of individuals who have managed to get by is quite common in the interviews I have been conducting since the late 2000s. In the middle of a conversation you can perceive the frustration felt by someone who has had to wait for years on a housing allocation list while others soon manage to get a house, or the anger aroused by a clientelist system that, in Grahamstown as elsewhere, reserves most jobs in the municipal sphere for members of the ANC or those who know how to exploit the rules. In the mid-2010s, Thabo, a young activist, had three interviews for a position in the Grahamstown municipal administration. The last one seemed conclusive. The job, he explained, was eventually awarded to a candidate who was less qualified but who did not hesitate to bribe the recruiter.

It sometimes becomes clear, even without needing to read between the lines, that having been an activist for years in the ranks of the main South African party without having drawn any benefit from it can be a good reason for taking part in the protest movement: "I fought and campaigned for the ANC, but the ANC gave me nothing." Such comments are generally delivered as if the speakers wanted to call me to witness a flagrant injustice. A first reflex would see this as the sign of a commitment motivated only by resentment and thus out of sync with the collective good that the movement defends. The way some activists view nepotism and clientelism then seems to be part of a fairly similar logic. When it comes to this point, leaders often adopt a moral stance that allows them to point out the flaws of electoral democracy; but some of their comrades, admittedly less invested, take a very different position. If they criticize this system, which organizes part of life at national and local levels, this is mainly because they feel that it excludes them. In their eyes, it is fundamentally unfair because it keeps them away from networks of access to certain goods and information, and even from certain rights, such as that of seeing their years of waiting on the lists for RDP houses finally rewarded.

Once again, one must be wary of postures that are too ethnocentric or unnecessarily virtuous. All this reveal, first and foremost, one of the implications of the "regime of the near" to which UPM activism is closely attached. The notions of "common cause" and "collective" are not enough to capture this commitment as a whole. It must also be remembered that individuals enter the organization with a "lived experience" (shaped by personal grievances, such as the absence of a home) and that they may naturally seek to defend the interests generated in this context. More generally, the same desire, which in no way contradicts the collective cause, is apparent in these different cases: the desire to be granted the right to conduct a "normal life," built on the sense of security that a job and a decent home can provide.

Leading a "dignified" or "normal" life therefore remains the primary goal of UPM activists and those they represent. Logically enough, a normal life is a life finally freed from any reasons to complain—a life where it would not be necessary to fight for land, jobs, decent schools and homes, safe streets, equality between men and women. It is also, and perhaps above all, a life without humiliation.

Humiliation is obviously the negative double of dignity. It refers to those situations and behaviors that hurt the self-respect of individuals. Since the beginning of this book, it has been possible to see how many opportunities there are for the residents of the township, especially the poorest, to feel this kind of thing.

The quest for dignity and the need to protect oneself from the daily threat of humiliation outline an ideal that, in some respects, may recall what the philosopher Avishai Margalit (1996) has called a "decent society": "A decent society is one that fights conditions which constitute a justification for its dependents to consider themselves humiliated. A society is decent if its institutions do not act in ways that give the people under their authority sound reasons to consider themselves humiliated" (Margalit 1996, 10–11).

However, humiliation is not necessarily the outcome of an explicit will, Margalit adds when he focuses more specifically on the link with poverty. It can result from "life conditions" that institutions or individuals have sometimes unintentionally created.[15] Resorting to Margalit's concept obviously does not mean drawing an elegant theoretical veil over the lives of the poor residents and UPM activists. The "decent society" simply helps us to better understand the meaning of the struggle on which these women and men are embarked. In particular, it solves a particular riddle: Why, in a country whose Gini coefficient makes one feel giddy, do these activists so rarely refer to socioeconomic inequalities? Their discourse, after all, focuses on "poverty" and "suffering," which are obviously not the same thing. There are differences between the "decent society" and a "fair society" concerned with fighting against inequalities. The latter can appear as an ideal justifying the creation of new balances and, more simply, the emergence of a social order better than the previous one. Conversely, the quest for the former is based on a certain pragmatism that must above all aim to avoid the worst by focusing on the current situation of the humiliated. One could associate with this cleavage the difference that James Holston makes between insurgence and protest, within the framework of urban "rebellions" that have occurred since the beginning of the twenty-first century (Holston 2019, 134–135). Insurgence is, in his view, an "objection to current conditions by articulating alternative proposals" that individuals formulate from their own experience and with the ambition of seeing a new society—or a "new city," in Holston's case—take shape. Protest, on the other hand, is also an "objection to current conditions," but it is framed by requests directly addressed to public authorities that the protesters feel they cannot do without. These nuances may partly explain the discrepancies that sometimes occur between activists of the postapartheid social movement and certain "radical" intellectuals committed to their struggle. Even if some members of the UPM claim to follow "socialism," their goal is not ultimately to try to overthrow the social order but to draw the attention of the authorities to almost immediate needs. "We fight for electricity. We make barricades. But when we have it, we don't connect illegally," as one of the activists summed up the situation when I questioned him about the organization's relationship to illegal activities.

This form of pragmatism is nevertheless based on a discourse of rights that does not always systematically adjust to the expectations of some people in the township. If rancor toward rulers and their "broken promises" is obviously very evident, it is above all the expression of an urgency that imbues the discourse of "ordinary" residents: the government and the municipality have to intervene *because* the poor "suffer," because "[their] kids are sick. [Their] grannies are sick. Everybody is sick," as one woman resident of eThembeni put it. Once again, South Africa is no exception: the emphasis the weakest lay on necessity or need echoes the observations made by Javier Auyero (2012a) in his study of the long queues that form at the entrances of welfare offices in Argentina. Welfare clients "in need" understood their benefits not as "rights" but "aid" or "help" (122) explained the sociologist. Such a conclusion emphasizes the way that the urgency of their conditions can place the poorest in a form of subordination and, even more, lead them to accept poverty as destiny. Inevitably, the demand for dignity and rights as ultimate goals is overwhelmed by a reality with which activists have to deal.

From the preceding pages, perhaps we should especially remember this tendency that activists often have to draw on their personal experience to morally justify their commitment and the struggle of their organization. We see this quite explicitly with Onke: according to her, the indignation that pervades her activism dates back to the humiliations she felt during her childhood. Just as eloquent is the way Joseph compares the cronyism his organization denounces and the fact that his years of sacrifice under apartheid have not been given due recognition. I argue that these forms of intersection of the individual and the collective support the thesis that the cause defended by the movement is rooted in the familiar worlds of its activists. Perhaps this is even more evident with Thabang, who goes so far as to refer not only to his own case but to that of a relative (his uncle) to assert the fairness of the fight of the unemployed. In the same vein, I could finally have spoken of another of my interlocutors, who linked the legitimacy of the actions of the UPM to the failing state of health of his cousin: the latter had, for many months and without protection, maintained the famous bucket system on behalf of the municipality. These resonances between collective and individual experiences are decisive. They smooth out the differences and nourish the oppositional consciousness that the movement needs to come together. More generally, they confirm that when you militate in a South African poor people's movement, what you denounce alongside your "comrades" during a demonstration cannot be distinguished from what touches you in your private daily life.

6

"WE DO NOT DISCUSS POLITICS"

It is early in the evening, and darkness and a fine April rain are falling on Grahamstown as a handful of activists climb the low hillock where the public meeting they have called is about to take place. Yesterday, two of them, Amanda and Zandie, took advantage of my vehicle to drive around the streets and announce, with the help of a megaphone, that "the UPM [has] invited the residents of Phaphamani, Zolani, Pola Park, and Extension 10 to discuss the housing problem." We drove for almost an hour through the arteries of these neighborhoods of RDP houses and shacks, halting at more or less regular intervals so that the two activists could, without leaving their seats, hand out these leaflets with the same invitation written in Xhosa. More often than not, it was children, drawn over from their games by the amplified voice, who came up to one of the car doors. They barely hesitated before grabbing three or four of the leaflets and running off to the small groups of adults chatting nearby at street corners or on the doorsteps of their houses.

The path that starts from the road and follows the shape of the hillock was clearly traced by the regular and repeated passages of residents from the surrounding shacks. It winds up between rocks, succulents, and heaps of refuse, then runs along the broad block of cement which caps this small hill. Some people believe that this bunker is actually a water tank. In any case, a metal fence bristling with spikes and more than two meters high protects it from curiosity. Gradually, in twos and threes, the residents of the shacks—including women, some of whom carry a baby on their backs or are wrapped in thick blankets, together with men, and several children—converge on the meeting point. They do not always greet the UPM activists or even address a single word to their neighbors, but they are here to consolidate the circle that has started to form. Some lean or sit against the fence. Most remain standing. Eventually, over fifty have taken their places, while a dozen children play nearby. Their faces are quite serious, reserved, and sometimes tinged with a certain distrust, though I do not know for whom exactly this distrust is meant. Today, a dozen of them have spoken out after Dumisa, Thabo, and Ayanda did. Some did so with vehemence. Even when this discontent is not directly aimed at them, the activists have to deal with it: they need to explain things, display their understanding, and denounce the negligence of the political and administrative powers that is apparently behind the evils that people experience in everyday life.

Walking through the ranks of such an audience means that one can see a fairly faithful cross-section of the faces of those who take part, more or less occasionally and more or less intensely, in the different expressions of postapartheid discontent. These faces are those of women and men of all ages, the faces of "ordinary people," to use the term that activists love.

"Ordinary"? The qualifier is meant as proof that these people obviously have no vocation to rebel or to protest: they are forced to do so by the economic and social aggression that has plagued them for years. If they do not

Community meeting at dusk

comprise the heart of the organization and are not part of its activist circles, these individuals nonetheless form the population that is there to be mobilized, a population that the UPM needs if it is to give substance to its main actions.

A more insistent or focused gaze would certainly suggest there are three different groups among the audience gathered tonight. First of all, there are people in their twenties or thirties who most often have no choice but to live with their parents. As some of these young people have never worked, they are also excluded from the social security system, except if they themselves have children for whom they are paid the child support grant. These are the people who are suffering the most from the intergenerational "crisis of social reproduction" (Comaroff and Comaroff 2001). This phenomenon stems partly from the collapse of the model of "modern industrial man" (Hickel 2014). As early as the 1950s, in order to counter the uprisings, the apartheid regime tried to build a sort of class compromise in the townships around a specific figure: that of the "married male breadwinner living in a formal township house and working a stable job in manufacturing, mining, or the civil service" (Hickel 2014, 106). This model however rapidly "crumbled as new strategies of capital accumulation undermined the conditions for such aspirations and cast Africans into a state of abjection" (106–107). Trapped in unemployment and the housing crisis, some young men in particular live in the fantasy of this model. They indeed have the feeling they have no control over their destinies, and note that they cannot get married and establish their own respectable homes. The frustration of a large part of this population has often seemed to resonate with Jacob Zuma's patriarchal posture and, even more so, with the many and varied stagings of his manhood. Zuma, who was president of the Republic of South Africa between 2009 and 2018, was indeed able to embody the reaffirmation of a traditional and respectable male power capable of ensuring the material well-being of his children and his wives (Hunter 2011). Unlike Thabo Mbeki, his predecessor and rival, who was viewed as too technocratic, Zuma thus connected the private and the political, promising to restore "men's dignity" in the domestic as well as the economic realms (1119).

A second group is made up of individuals in the prime of life, some of whom occasionally live in what is commonly known as the "informal economy." Tonight, it is possible that there are residents dispersed in this small crowd who, during the daytime, put on high-visibility vests and, in return for a handful of change, find themselves an improvised job keeping an eye on the cars parked in the traffic arteries of the city center. There may also be waste pickers here, or people who have set up a clandestine bar in one of the rooms in their house. The informal economy, however, is not as evident in South African society as it can be in most regions of the Global South, where it sometimes represents over a half of nonagricultural employment (Skinner and Watson 2018). In South Africa, in the mid-2010s, only one in every six people who work, work in the informal sector (Fourie 2018). The majority (64 percent) are employees who work in formal firms or private households.[1] In Grahamstown, however, the informal economy remains one of the main horizons for the poorest people. In a paper published in 2016, Makana municipality even found that more than a third of the city's jobs were in this part of the economy and noted in passing that this proportion had more than doubled between 1995 and 2015 (Makana Municipality 2016, 81).

Zolezwa may be here tonight. She operates in one of the most visible forms of this economy. Every day, from 9:00 a.m. to 6:00 p.m., she sells fruit in the city center, a few meters from the minibus station. She is not quite sixty, and she knew the time when there was a big market in this part of Grahamstown. She bought fruits and vegetables in the early hours of the morning and then divided them up into four or five units in small transparent plastic bags. She tells me she can remember earning as much as R200 a day. The market has disappeared, replaced by shops run by Indians. These traders now enjoy a real monopoly when it comes to supplying the street vendors with whom they have also decided to compete directly. They do not merely sell five-kilo bags of oranges, which are too bulky for Zolezwa's potential customers, who have to cram themselves into crowded taxis. They also sell fruit retail at much cheaper prices than those of street vendors. A bag of four apples costs R10 on Zolezwa's stall, and only R5 in shops that are less than fifty meters away.

Zolezwa says that she now earns no more than R20 per day, just enough to supplement what her husband earns as a bagger at one of the main street supermarkets. The man who mends shoes about ten meters from Zolezwa's stall probably does not earn any more. To a certain extent, however, they both know they will find their place in this market tomorrow and the following days. This is not always what defines the informal economy, often characterized by day-to-day survivalist activities (Du Toit and Neves 2007). These realities, in fact, shift attention from the figure who usually attracts the attention of policy makers and international organizations, even though he or she is still marginal: the self-employed worker giving work to other informal workers in a business that is the result more of choice than of any constraint.

The informalization "from below" (Theron 2010) of a part of South African society is primarily the work of those who have had no choice but to create their own job, or at least something similar. As I have already had the opportunity to explain in my first chapter, most of the poor and the marginalized no longer seem of much interest to capitalism. These populations have become "surplus" to the needs and expectations of capital. This situation is in sharp contrast with the apartheid era, whose creators regarded the Black population of the "homelands" as a reserve army. Through the migrant labor system, the regime could benefit above all from a steady supply of low-wage labor by sparing itself the demands, whether political or wage-linked, that might have arisen with a permanently settled workforce (Ferguson 2015, 10).

The "surplus" thesis is not confined to South Africa. The beginning of the twenty-first century has witnessed a proliferation of analyses of these "outcasts of Modernity" (Bauman 2004) around the world. These lives set aside seem to originate in the very nature of a contemporary capitalism that Saskia Sassen describes as increasingly borne by dynamics of "extraction" and "destruction" that favor the emergence of "new logics of *expulsion*" (2014, 1). Now without economic value, growing numbers of people are, in her view, simply "expelled from the core social and economic orders of our time" (1). According to Tania Li, who has focused on the case of Asia, this situation does not result from a "strategy of global capital," but reflects a more prosaic reality: the "very limited relevance" of these individuals to capital "at any scale" (2010, 67). Partha Chatterjee draws the same inference in regard to India: increasingly capital-intensive and technology-dependent forms of production make it unlikely that the "victims of primitive accumulation of capital" (peasants, artisans, and petty manufacturers) will be absorbed into the "new capitalist sectors of growth" (2008, 55; see also Smith 2011). In this view, the fear of a class conflict engendered by such a situation has at the same time led to the establishment of welfare programs. This hypothesis about India seems to fit South Africa.

A number of UPM activists who were between the ages of thirty and forty during the 2010s have benefited from the general movement to raise the level of education of the Black population. They often managed to graduate from high school. Some were subsequently able to study at college for one or two years in the hope of quickly obtaining "marketable skills." Finally, though this is much rarer, a handful of them obtained state loans to study at university or technikons. These different qualifications have not saved these women and men from a lack of perspective, however, and this can obviously feed intense resentment and a sense of hopes disappointed. The experience of the formal world of work that some may have had can lie several years in the past. They seem to be absorbed into this population that capitalism no longer wants. Ironically, the shadow of capitalism is not entirely absent from the poor areas. In the township, it certainly does not have the flamboyance of the one in which the new upper-middle classes of the "New South Africa" move, but it can take, for example, the form of the Western-brand sports shoes that some young people wear, whether or not they are counterfeit. Sometimes some of the debris of this capitalism or its trappings (such as advertising posters praising its products) are used for the interior decoration of shacks built from recycled materials.

Finally, what is perhaps most striking when one observes the people gathered tonight is the large number of people in their sixties and seventies and, more precisely, of "grannies." Usually wearing a headscarf and decked out in long dresses, these "old ladies," as activists often call them, have regularly been highlighted by journalists and photographers in their reports on postapartheid protest. Tonight, yet again, they seem to be overrepresented in the audience. When they speak, they are among the most vehement in denouncing their living conditions. These women look like Dumisa, one of the UPM chairpersons, who is standing one or two meters away from me. There are different possible reasons why there are so many of them. Since the first years of the twenty-first century, women have mainly seen changes to their position in poor households. Faced with a male population weakened by unemployment and therefore challenged in its traditional role of breadwinner, women who, when they are responsible for a child, receive the child support grant have gained a more central role.[2] This situation is even more pronounced for the oldest among them: the fact that their descendants are unemployed regularly makes their pension the main source of income in many of these households where three generations sometimes live side by side. They "increasingly bear the financial, social and physical burden of caring for their children, grand-children and extended families"

(Mosoetsa 2011, 74). They are the ones who, among other things, pay the water and electricity bills. The magnitude of the devastation of AIDS has also led a number to raise their grandchildren and, as a result, also to receive state support.[3] Added to this is the fact that until 2008, women could collect their old age pension from the age of sixty, as against sixty-five for men. The state and the social welfare system have thus become the "new backbone" of these women's personal and collective security (Bank 2011, 166). All these elements have not undermined the patriarchy officially denounced by the UPM, but they have contributed to a significant change in the relationship between the sexes, sometimes at the cost of an increase in domestic violence (Mosoetsa 2011, 57–80).

That these elderly women have often lent their features to postapartheid protest as portrayed in the South African and foreign media is all the more logical in that, let us repeat, this group is overrepresented at protest rallies. In any event, they have also attracted media interest because of what can be said about their presence at demonstrations. Is this not a population that suffered segregation and challenged it (at least through the hundreds of local demonstrations that punctuated the 1980s), a population that is now, after having brought the ANC to power, struggling to fully find its place in postapartheid society? These women often share their disillusionment with those of their children who sacrificed their youth by exposing themselves to the regime's violence in the 1980s. For the latter, who became adults in a democratic South Africa that had consigned their resistance to oblivion, there remains, in general, only anger: "anger about the lack of skill training or employment opportunities as recompense for opportunities lost" (Reynolds 2013, 103).

The gathering that is gradually taking shape at Phaphamani is a community meeting, an almost commonplace and routine moment in the life of these neighborhoods. These public meetings are held most often in a community hall. When the neighborhood does not have such a hall, it is frequently on a corner of their township or the center of the informal settlement in which they live that women and men converge at the behest of a street committee, community leaders or a concerned residents committee.[4] These meetings are an opportunity to talk about the insecurity that, at night, is invading the area around the taverns and shebeens (pubs), about the refuse piling up in one part or another of the neighborhood, the repeated power cuts, or, as tonight, the allocation of RDP homes that have been promised for years. All those who have made their way here listen to the organizers of the meeting describe the evil that threatens the neighborhood, an evil that justifies the protest. Then some of those present speak, occasionally with a certain vehemence but most often respecting an implicit protocol and a certain order: their outbursts quickly cease, to allow for an answer or another intervention.

Like other postapartheid protest organizations, the UPM is regularly behind these gatherings. Politics in its most official guise has long occupied an ambiguous place in them. This characteristic is not confined to gatherings organized by the torchbearers of social protest. It is a frequent trend in the various more or less formal networks that extend through communities and in which many activists are caught up. In a study conducted at the beginning of the 2010s in two informal settlement areas of Grahamstown, focusing on one hundred people at the head of a poor household, Yeukai Mukorombindo has shown how much discussions in *stokvels*, burial societies, and other types of very local self-help associations were expressly disconnected from themes perceived as "political" and from "current affairs":

> No we don't discuss politics. . . . We do discuss issues such as unemployment. We talk about such things. No we do not discuss political issues or things that are happening in political parties like ANC or COSATU. . . . We are discussing that our cars are being damaged by the roads that need to be fixed. Those are the things we talk about.[5]

The general framework of the discussion is strictly defined by what affects the community—things that no one seems to expect "politics" and its agents to be able to tackle: the state of the infrastructure, but also such problems as alcoholism, crime, teenage pregnancy, and the like. Things are not so different at community meetings. It is also at these gatherings that the inclusive properties of reference to the community become apparent. The community is deemed able to overcome most antagonisms, especially those of political parties. In these crowds which come to listen to the UPM activists, there are obviously people who vote for the ANC, the DA, Inkatha, and so on. In the same way, some of the residents present could certainly be described as "reactionary," "conservative," or "sexist" if judged by the ideological criteria of the UPM. This, however, is less important than the fact they share a social condition that binds communities together. It was by virtue of such a principle that, in 2015, activists organized large community meetings in the places most marked by xenophobic violence. It was not a matter of blaming, but of listening and trying to reason with those who, a few days earlier, had looted businesses run by foreigners who had been living for years in the communities of Grahamstown.

Imperviousness to "politics" has also often been interpreted in terms of some supposed loyalty of the townships toward the ANC. This loyalty made it an indisputably delicate matter to launch any frontal attack on the party in power. So critics concentrated on the "incompetence" and "corruption" of local officials, of which everyone was inevitably a witness. This thesis—the idea that the poorest people will stay loyal to their former liberators—is all the more attractive in that the party in power is in fact never totally absent from these meetings. Tonight, not far from Dumisa, who is castigating the "corruption" of the ANC municipality, stands a young woman whose blanket, thrown over her shoulders, does not completely hide a T-shirt with the yellow and green colors of the ruling party. As paradoxical as it may seem, the situation is not exceptional. It reveals the propensity of certain Black South Africans to draw a clear distinction between the ANC's "political brand," still bearing the laurels it earned from its feats of arms in the struggle against apartheid,[6] and its local representatives who, almost in spite of themselves, embody measures that are often defined by the government (see Tournadre 2018, 188–189). This distinction is above all a question of distance. More precisely, it reinforces or illustrates what Piven and Cloward wrote in their classic book *Poor People's Movements*:

> People experience deprivation and oppression within a concrete setting, not as the end product of large and abstract processes, and it is the concrete experience that molds their discontent into specific grievances against specific targets. . . . People on relief experience the shabby waiting room, the overseer or the caseworker, and the dole. They do not experience American social welfare policy. Tenants experience the leaking ceilings and cold radiators, and they recognize the landlord. They do not recognize the banking, real estate, and construction systems. No small wonder, therefore, that when the poor rebel they so often rebel against the overseer of the poor, or the slumlord, or the middling merchant, and not against the banks or the governing elites to whom the overseer, the slumlord, and the merchant also defer. In other words, it is the daily ex-

perience of people that shapes their grievances, establishes the measure of their demands, and points out the targets of their anger. (1977, 20–21)

In the present case, the daily and repeated experiences of water and electricity cuts, flooding, and a shortage of toilet facilities obviously crystallize around the ward councilor.[7] While these elected officials cannot be exempted from responsibilities, however, they should not be seen as holding too much power. Their room to maneuver is limited, first of all, by the intense centralization of power generally enjoyed by mayors and their close associates. Many of them are also handicapped in their work because of their very low level of education and training. It is not uncommon, for example, that some of them are simply not fluent in English and are thus unable to understand the documents that are handed to them at municipal meetings. They are therefore dependent on the instructions of their party. Be that as it may, the bad reputation of local councilors has been reinforced by the clientelist and plutocratic practices to which many of them resort and which do not escape anyone's notice. Conversely, decisions and positions within the governing party's ruling spheres appear to be more abstract, distant, unimaginable, or simply inaccessible to a population whose members may not necessarily have access to a television set, a radio, or newspapers.

Finally, we must certainly be careful not to ascribe too much political significance to the presence of clothes bearing the colors of the ANC at these meetings. This presence also has more prosaic roots, which lie as much in the destitution of certain residents as in the instrumentalization of this poverty by political parties. Electoral campaigns thus involve handouts, especially at meetings. These may be food parcels but also the well-known T-shirts. For particularly poor populations, these clothes mainly present a way of dressing for free. This anecdote underlines how much their living conditions place many township residents in a particular relationship to political parties and their representatives, whether local councilors or branch leaders: "The more one lives in the world of informality the closer one's day-to-day life intersects with—and even, in some cases, depends on—party structures" (Pithouse 2013, 101). Many ethnographic studies of these situations have been made since the 2000s. They have helped to better understand how, in the provocative formula of Dlamini, "a struggle for freedom" was thus transformed into "a struggle for stomach" (2010, 197). For some ordinary activists, the end of branch meetings can be an opportunity to "pull the councillor aside . . . to ask [for] food parcels, council services and such-like" (196). For residents in general, and especially individuals who have been forced out of the market, these branches often prove to be more effective channels of access to the state than those in which local government is ac-tively involved. It is partly on this type of relationship that the popularity of the ANC was maintained throughout the 2000s and 2010s, as such a re-lationship opportunely bolstered the effects of the imposing political capi-tal built up over the years of struggle against apartheid.

This omnipresence of the party in power makes criticism difficult. In ad-dition, those who indulge in this risky exercise are regularly exposed to sanctions. Many social activists, right across the country, have had bitter and painful experiences of this. Some have been regularly attacked by ANC activists, and some of them have even lost their lives.[8] Added to this, of course, is the threat of being sidelined from a whole part of the socioeco-nomic life of the neighborhood, as will be shown in more detail in Chap-ters 7 and 10. UPM members are perfectly aware of this, and some even claim to have been victims of the system where the attribution of certain jobs or certain goods is monopolized by the party's various local networks. This is particularly true of the man I first met in the city center in one of the res-taurants of a famous fried chicken franchise. At the age of thirty-four, Athandile lived with his mother and brother and was both a member of the UPM and the Economic Freedom Fighters (EFF),[9] a party that was openly active on the terrain of social protest. He told me:

> My name has disappeared from the lists for the RDP houses . . . because
> I am not a member of the ANC. If I don't go to the marches organized
> by the ANC, I won't have anything. If I am a member of the ANC, I will
> have any job. . . . You know, last year, when [the ANC activists and a con-
> tractor close to the municipality] saw me with the EFF T-shirt, they told
> me: "Go away! You can't have anything in Grahamstown!"

For a long time, therefore, any overly political criticism could not be ex-pressed at community meetings organized by social activists. Lungile, the young chairperson that the UPM had just selected during my first stay in Grahamstown in 2012, even admitted to me that he took care not to pro-nounce the name of the majority party at these gatherings. In other places, activists could sometimes seek to reassure people by explaining, right at the start of the meetings, that the talk would not be of "politics" but of "bread-

and-butter issues," all the themes (housing problems, the price of food, or the lack of work, and so on) that define the heart of living conditions. The discussion could thus focus on eminently concrete issues, such as allowing activists to confirm that previous protests had forced the municipality to tackle the bucket system. Things have nevertheless evolved since the mid-2010s. As is confirmed by Ayanda's words at tonight's rally, explicit attacks on the "betrayal" of the ANC elites now appear less risky than before. First, there were a few signs such as the contesting of the electoral hegemony of the African National Congress in the 2011 and 2014 polls, along with the rise of abstention even in its Eastern Cape bastions. A crucial line was crossed in the August 2016 elections, with the loss of Johannesburg, Tshwane (Pretoria), and Nelson Mandela Bay, the metropolitan area to which Port Elizabeth belongs. And on the national level, the ANC won 54 percent of the votes cast in this election, its lowest score since 1994. The scandals that punctuated the Zuma years, especially the issues of Nkandla[10] and the Gupta family,[11] have certainly contributed to these developments in the post-apartheid electoral order, even if the effects of national affairs on voters should not be overly homogenized. But it is mainly the persistence of the social and economic problems that shape the daily life of the poorest which has persuaded UPM activists that weariness, disappointment, and frustration were now sufficiently entrenched in the poor areas of South Africa that they could explicitly name their opponent without fear of alienating their audience.

Tonight, yet again, I also see how this type of moment offers the UPM a chance to display the diversity of its positions. The meeting is obviously dominated by this critical stance, which is expressed in the complaints and accusations leveled at the municipality and, more broadly, at political elites. But the protest leaders do not rule out the possibility of dialogue and negotiation with representatives of this same power, on behalf of and for the benefit of the poor of the city. At the end of the meeting, Ayanda announced that the movement was planning to convene a new rally and to invite the ward councilor to discuss crime in the neighborhood.

These meetings are of course vital for an organization which they provide with a regular presence in poor and working-class neighborhoods and the potential for gaining new members. Tonight a leaflet passes from hand to hand as speakers line up to denounce the lack of housing and the corruption that they claim is responsible. This leaflet bears the logo of the movement, a clenched fist circumscribed in a star with five branches, and contains a table with several columns for the names of those present to be recorded. The purpose of this maneuver is quite simple: it is meant to foster the ambition that almost continually drives the main UPM activists when they walk around the township "to recruit" new members. At the very least it is always possible, the day before a new meeting in the neighborhood, to knock on the doors of those who had attended the previous meeting so as to convince them to make the effort to come again. At first glance, it is indeed surprising that, year after year, so many people continue to attend these regular gatherings. A few months later, in the middle of the "freedom day"[12] and in the same place, a hundred or so people are there to answer the UPM call for yet more discussion of the housing problems. They gather together under a blazing sun, in this space without any shade.

What helps an activist maintain his or her long-term commitment is often a difficult puzzle for the social sciences to solve. The same is true of what causes "ordinary" women and men to drop what they are doing in order to attend another meeting, which they may quite reasonably imagine will not actually change their daily lives in any fundamental way. One initial explanation lies perhaps in the fact that there is nothing really difficult or constraining at work here. Most of those who swell the ranks of these meetings live not far away. The meeting point is usually chosen for its centrality in the neighborhood. When Ayanda arrived on the scene and noted the low attendance, he spent about ten minutes moving between the nearest shacks, a megaphone in hand, to convince latecomers or those who were still hesitant about coming. Another local woman took over. She dashed down the slope and into the area of shacks and small houses below, on the other side of the road. She emerged a quarter of an hour later at the head of a group of about ten people. This scene also highlights how the layout of these neighborhoods can affect the success of this type of mobilization. In the hours before a protest march, activists may rush through the narrow alleys that snake between the shacks, knocking on doors to summon people to attend. The cramped houses and the heat that, from the first days of spring, beats down on the tin roofs also play their part. They lead many people to spend long hours in the street or on their doorsteps. From this situation, logically enough, a certain neighborhood sociability comes into being: in addition to being cramped, the houses and shacks are often close to each other. The incentive to protest or simply to attend a meeting being held just a few hundred meters away becomes all the more obvious and compelling when you can see your neighbor going off to join the gathering. In a quite different context, that of the Paris Commune, Roger Gould has clearly demonstrated that these "neighborhood social ties" are often a "major element in mobilizing participation" (1995, 186). This can result in a mutual encouragement, which, in the case of South Africa, is reinforced by the fact that these meetings are presented and obviously experienced (both by their organizers and by those who attend) as in direct line with what has become an unquestioned tradition.

The outside observer must, however, be wary of overly idealizing what he or she may glimpse—an idealization found, for example, in the way some descriptions emphasize the "consensus" that, they say, inevitably characterizes decision-making at these meetings. For one thing, the whole "community" is not present. Tonight, it is true that dozens of people have answered the UPM call, but many have preferred to stay at home, even in this small area. After the meeting, Ayanda went to say hello to a woman who, although she lives just a hundred meters or so from the meeting place, had not turned up. For another thing, not all the people present take the floor: not

Informal settlement, Phaphamani

everyone dares or feels legitimized to do so. Even in this context, often presented as egalitarian, internal games of domination do, of course, exist. So there is no escape here from the gaps and deficiencies that characterize democratic places and structures as a whole.

More prosaically, the community meeting is obviously a good choice for a poor people's movement such as the UPM. It offers, with few resources, to foster a sense of roots and visibility in communities. It is possible that some of those gathered around us tonight have never heard of the organization before. It's something that often surprised me in my first few weeks in Grahamstown, almost as much as the women and men walking past a few feet away from such gatherings without even sparing them a glance. The brief remarks I exchanged with some of these residents occasionally left me at a loss. Those who agreed to reply—the ones who were not in such a hurry—did not conceal their mistrust of protest activists whom they associated with the world of political parties. But more generally, it was mainly a lack of interest that seemed to prevail. Influenced by those days spent in contact with activists, I certainly tended to think that the actions taken by the movement since the end of the 2000s had made it a sort of indispensable institution for poor neighborhoods. I was wrong, of course. Ethnography thus regularly showed me how many of those whom I observed had to make daily efforts to spread awareness of their organization in this city of less than 100,000 souls.

Even if the exchange of ideas for which it provides a forum can sometimes assume rather dramatic accents, the gathering in the community is basically quite an ordinary affair. It remains a relatively frequent framework for mobilization in South African poor and working-class neighborhoods. More precisely, this type of event is associated by a large number of people with a political form that mixes the tradition and culture inherent in lower-class social worlds. It seems to be one of the main moments when a politics of the immediate can emerge, quite basic in nature and foreign to those struggles "for top jobs" in which a "party politics" (insensitive to the most concrete aspects of the daily lives of the least well-off) exhausts itself. According to Ayanda, there is "nothing about electricity, nothing about water" in the debates and proposals of politics at its most official. Conversely, "popular politics" (since this is how it is often referred to in some activist and intellectual circles) goes straight to the essentials. According to its supporters, it is developed in close association with ordinary people and is the natural framework for action by all those acting on behalf of the community, be they community activists or community-based organizations. Popular politics fuels neighborhood meetings, peaceful marches against the low quality of life, and the activities of street committees and associations of concerned residents. It starts off with the *toyi toyi*, a mixture of dance and songs that has been part of the repertoire of discontent and resistance since the years of the struggle against apartheid. It is embodied in the actions of community leaders and, more generally, all those who tirelessly try to alert and guide the residents. Through this form of politics, it is the community that manifests itself and affirms a capacity to mobilize against what threatens it.

The very term "popular politics" is in fact little used by UPM activists, who sometimes even reject it quite categorically: "Popular politics? It means nothing. Popular politics is the ANC, because everyone knows the ANC. That's what's popular," one told me. However, we find some of its presuppositions in the way some of these activists detail what comprises the specificity of their approach, as Ayanda did:

> Between the politicians and a social movement, the difference should be . . . It's not community abstractly. It's not community in theory. . . . You are right there, on a daily basis, carrying out those struggles . . . for water, for housing, against rapes. You're asserting the humanity of that community. . . . The NGOs, they want to go in the communities and explain to the communities to care about these things . . . climate change and so on. Yes, we understand the climate crisis, but don't tell me that we must fight against climate change when we don't have water. I cannot wait for that. I cannot wait for people to sign petitions. I cannot wait for funding proposals for all that process. What we must do is to make sure that we fight for material things immediately! We give confidence in our people to struggle. We give hope in our people.

It is therefore the idea of a politics made *by* and *for* the people that prevails—a politics feeding on "what really hurts the people."[13] Once again, such trends are highlighted in the way UPM leaders describe what constitutes their daily work:

> We do interviews most of the time. In the township. That's how we get the mandate. That's how we know what to do. We do it every month. Interviews

on housing, rape, social grants, education. Every month . . . we go to the township and talk to people. Individual interviews. We go to the community and develop programs. . . . We don't develop our own programs. Our programs are influenced by the community.

Gathering together residents' experiences through interviews ("because we know that this or that person knows someone in their neighborhood who experienced this or that") should help to highlight what "hurts" the poorest. It then becomes possible to outline solutions, such as the curriculum on "sexism, patriarchy, and familyism" that activists managed, through contacts with school principals, to present in three of the township's high schools in May 2016. Seeking to assert itself as a lookout post for the township, the movement is then again perfectly in line with its claims to be a community-based organization. Its members no longer move in the protest context, strictly speaking. They act in accordance with what can be expected of community activists, those individuals who "take care" of the problems of their community. However, these actions directly feed into the structure of commitment that characterizes the UPM when it assumes the other side of its mission, that of being a social movement of the poor. Collecting data on sexual and domestic violence can indeed serve to consolidate the protest posture of the collective by reinforcing its critique of the living conditions of the poorer residents.

According to the activists, it is also a matter, through these interviews, of continuously taking the pulse of the poor districts. This is how they say they anticipated the xenophobic wave that hit the city in October 2015:

> The crime was on the peak . . . so we did interviews. Then we went to the police station to say, "The crime is on the rise and that people think that people who are responsible for the crime are our comrades from Bangladesh and Pakistan. The police need to dispel these rumors because these are the rumors that can lead to xenophobic attacks." . . . We had a discussion with the police. We picked up the issue with the magistrate. . . . But because it was coming from us, the police did nothing to dispel the rumors.

"Popular politics" is a privileged subject of studies of poor people's movements. The interest it can arouse in the case of South Africa is all the more understandable once we pick up the thread of this country's history. What this political form is usually associated with has origins that can be traced back to the vigilance and other residents' committees that emerged at the end of the nineteenth century in Black areas (Bundy 2000, 25–51). Beyond that, it is especially related to the decades of apartheid. By excluding "non-whites" from political representation, this regime has forced them to channel their political expression in other directions. A sort of political tradition was thus consolidated and developed *outside* and *against* classical parliamentary politics. In the 1970s and 1980s, "popular politics" could easily merge with the "township politics" (Mayekiso 1996) designed to circumvent the institutions imposed by racist power. It relied on a movement of committees active at the level of streets and neighborhoods, the civics,[14] and on the establishment of assemblies, forums, and people's courts. At the beginning of the twenty-first century, "popular politics" was partly transformed into the "living politics" (see Chance 2018) popularized by the activists of Abahlali baseMjondolo in Durban and Cape Town.

As well as being practical, the concept of "popular politics" is attractive. Indeed, it gives substance to an almost ideal democratic form by appearing entirely built around the agency of the weakest members of society, which has, among other things, justified part of the program of subaltern studies. Writing this, I obviously do not intend to question a certain reality. At first glance, what is presented as constitutive of a "popular politics" does indeed embrace an area with well-defined contours: frameworks for action and mobilization (such as community meetings), ways of doing things, specific discourses (extolling the "values of the community"), themes (the famous bread-and-butter issues), real emergencies and concerns, and so forth. However, its formalization in the form of a homogeneous category results mainly from sometimes rather distant and abstract academic work, which is not without effects on the way of thinking about the practices in question here.

In the 2000s and 2010s, many South African and foreign scholars and academics focused on postapartheid protest and affirmed the politically avant-garde nature of the protesters. Mixing references to the writings of Agamben, Rancière, Badiou, and Žižek, they sought to convince their readers that poor people's movements in South Africa were potential vectors of social and political change. Although they were relegated to the social margins, and thus systematically inferior in the balance of power throughout society, the poorest people would indeed share a conception of politics without artifice and therefore pure. Nevertheless, by amalgamating a little too quickly things that do not necessarily have a political meaning for those who carry them out, this argument tends to project into "the 'minds' of the agents a representation of their practices which is that of the expert studying them" (Bourdieu 2020, 48). The same goes for the notion of "agency": one sometimes wonders whether it does not reflect "the view of the observers, who recognize its existence only when practices meet their expectations of openly manifested resistance" (Fassin 2014, 431).

This does not mean, of course, that in order to be political everything must expressly be lived as such. To give it this dimension by authority and from the outset does however mean that we put to one side certain social realities that may seem more trivial but are equally important. The presence of some residents at a community meeting can simply be the result of social conformism. Many of my interlocutors, surprised to find me questioning them about what drives them to attend these gatherings, come out with the implacable formula, "everyone does it." In a similar vein, some are likely to attend these gatherings because they are impelled to do so by a form of habit, linked to the routinization of these moments, without any conviction needing to be displayed. Whatever the contexts, the localities and the social circles involved, such an attitude is indeed more frequent than one imagines: "One can participate without conviction, or even by thinking or doing something else, especially because these are acts that go without saying, that is, that are intended to be carried out without individuals having to justify themselves" (Mariot 2012, 196). For others, however, the fact of being present should allow them access to information that is not provided by elected officials, who are regularly accused of giving their party's activists exclusive rights to what they know or what they have learned. These people have all the more reason to be here tonight because UPM activists have reported in recent weeks that they were in possession of an important document on the allocation of RDP houses (see Chapter 7).

For these different reasons, then, it seems difficult to interpret upsurges of "popular politics" in terms of a voluntarism or democratism characteristic of the least well-off South Africans. Rather too often, these readings are marked by *exteriority* and objectivism. Above all, they reveal a propensity to endow with dignity, *on principle*, whatever is "popular," that is, belongs to the people. The criticism voiced by some intellectuals and activists over the publication of an article (Pointer 2004) pointing to the existence of overtly sexist practices in the activities of a poor people's movement in Cape Town may be the best illustration of this.

Logically enough, associating poor populations with a specific relationship to politics has sometimes led to "popular politics" becoming a separate and autonomous world. This perception of things partly echoes the influential theories developed by Partha Chatterjee from the end of the 1990s. Starting out from an analysis of the Indian situation, this significant figure of the subaltern studies collective focuses on "popular politics in most of the world" (2004, 3). His analysis is based first and foremost on questioning the classic opposition between the state and civil society, which he believes debars us from understanding the complexity of postcolonial societies. As a child of Western modernity, "civil society" is in fact the preserve of the "closed association of modern elite groups" (4). According to Chatterjee, civil society is indeed based on recognized rights and duties, equality, procedures of decision making, autonomy, and freedom: all of these are principles that define a citizenship to which the rest of humanity cannot lay claim. The "subaltern"—or the "governed"—therefore form heterogeneous "populations" that the state administers, protects, monitors, and controls but does not treat as a set of proper rights-bearing citizens. Strangers to civil society, these women and men move in a third section of the social and political order: political society. Far from being reduced to powerlessness, they develop an agency that serves as a foundation for an autonomous "popular politics." Chatterjee thus describes an area where the "governed" organize among themselves and bring their claims to the knowledge of the political and administrative power. This power can then be led to respond, but on the fringes of the formality and legality that characterize the political relationship it maintains in parallel with civil society. Chatterjee relies on the example, common to many societies in the Global South, of households illegally occupying land and also illegally using water and electricity connections. He observes that governmental authorities do not systematically clamp down on these practices. They sometimes recognize that "these populations serve necessary functions in the urban economy and that to forcibly remove them would involve huge political costs" (Chatterjee 2011, 14).

Points of convergence between this analysis and the situation in contemporary South Africa have often been highlighted (see Paret 2017). The creations of organizations such as the UPM seem by themselves to reinforce this reading. They explain those moments when "populations respond to the regime of governmentality by seeking to constitute themselves as groups that deserve the attention of government" (Chatterjee 2011, 15). Chatterjee's ideas about the place of the poor in relation to civil society can also help to explain the postapartheid era. After 1994, the establishment of democracy was in fact accompanied by various processes meant to bring the country into an era of "normalization." In addition to the guarantees given to international organizations and markets, this desire on the part of the new rulers facilitated the dissemination of a discourse calling for the emergence of a "civil society." Presented as the guarantee of a successful entry into the experience of liberal democracy, this process would more surely contribute to reshaping the social world by blotting out the memory of past antagonisms. During the 1980s, civic bodies and entities such as the United Democratic Front (UDF) had signed up to a highly polarized representation of society. This was summed up, schematically, as a simplistic contrast between the "communities" and the authoritarian state. The concern for national reconciliation in the post-1994 period obviously involved making the fighters of yesteryear evolve into a less sharply context, alongside religious structures, associations, and NGOs. The former spearheads of protest, already suffering from a loss of their social position after 1994, due to the attraction of a newly opened political world that offered various jobs and positions, were also neutralized by the invitation issued to them to adopt the sage demeanor of ordinary actors in a liberal democracy (Seekings 1996, 151). The repression and criminalization to which leaders and activists of social movements have been regularly exposed since the beginning of the twenty-first century, and their difficulty in gaining access to formal channels for criticism of the State, invalidate this quite loose definition of the social world. Conversely, like the squatters studied by Chatterjee, poor households sometimes obtain concessions from political representatives by following paths far removed from the official framework that characterizes the relations between the state and the constituents of civil society. In the first months of 2018, for example, many families settled illegally on a vacant lot north of Joza. They built shacks that might have been immediately threatened with destruction by the municipality. However, nothing happened. The construction of shacks continued; there was barely any response, as everyone understood that they were protected by the elections to be held the following year.

These different aspects of contemporary reality may thus be sufficient to justify a reading of South African society through the lens of Chatterjee's theses. It seems to me, however, that these theses fail to account for two essential things. They tend first of all to apprehend "official" political activity and the political activity which the poor practice as pure and finite forms, inscribed in hermetic spaces. Admittedly, the approach adopted by Chatterjee represents a new direction compared to the ideas put forward in the original form of subaltern studies, which suggested the existence of a split in the domain of politics between an "organized elite domain" and "an unorganized subaltern domain." The author of *Politics of the Governed* offers a more nuanced view, emphasizing the existence of "forms of the entanglement of elite and subaltern politics" (Chatterjee 2004, 39–40). These "forms of entanglement," however, do not seem to leave room for a sensitive analysis of possible circulations between spaces, hybridizations, and borrowings. The second limit is to consider only one aspect of what is presented as the "politics of the poor." Organizations such as the Unemployed People's Movement are not just asking for the people they represent to be protected by the state. On various occasions, as we will see, they also seek to exercise surveillance over political power, which is usually one of the functions of the "civil society" in its classical sense.

Let us first consider the relationship between "official" political activity and that of the poorest. I would like to adopt another logic here, drawing on the work of the historian Roger Chartier. Even if the contexts and objects studied are, to put it mildly, foreign to each other, the arguments put forward by Chartier against the idea that there was a "popular culture" totally distinct from "high culture" in the France of the ancien régime seem to open up an interesting perspective. More specifically, Chartier questions the existence of strict correspondences between cultural splits and social oppositions; he affirms, on the contrary, the presence of fluid circulations, shared practices, and blurred differences (Chartier 1987, 6–9). If we relate this analysis to the case that interests us, it makes it necessary to check whether the boundary between "popular politics" and liberal democracy is as watertight and clear as some say.

The postapartheid political and administrative system has thus regularly decked itself out with participatory trappings that directly echo the logics associated with "popular politics." This has been achieved through a search for legitimacy, but also in harmony with the international zeitgeist. The first implementations, observable since the mid-1990s with the establishment of forums for negotiating the transition in different sectors,[15] are reminiscent of the recommendations of some international institutions in favor of "good governance" in emerging countries. At the same time, Bolivia and India, to name just two countries, were following quite similar paths: one, via the passing of the Popular Participation Act; the other through different policies seeking to ensure minority representation and promote a more inclusive process in decision making at the local level (Cornwall 2002). Soon, the young South African democracy provided itself with various forums opening wider dialogue between the state and South Africans: ward committees, RDP forums, community policing forums, development forums, and so on. Officially, these mechanisms were intended to facilitate the more systematic involvement of residents in the definition or monitoring of public policies. Nevertheless, these places and instances have often proved to be spaces where participation is in fact only "invited" by the rulers because it is practiced according to their norms and criteria ("invited spaces"), unlike the participative spaces which invent themselves according to popular initiatives ("invented spaces") (Cornwall 2002; Sinwell 2010). Grahamstown's Integrated Development Plan (IDP), which all municipalities must have, illustrates this. Designed to heal the wounds opened by the management of urban space under apartheid, the IDP is a coordination and planning tool based on an inventory of development projects in the city. This inventory is based in particular on meetings to which representatives of the communities and all those who "fight for the rights of unorganized groups," such as "gender activists," are invited.[16] But, as a sign that it is above all a space deliberately designed by the political power, the main part of the discussion is directed and supervised by local elected officials and municipal figures. At the end of the meeting, the audience has only a few minutes to ask representatives of the municipality any questions (see Piper and von Lieres 2016). One day in July 2009, frustration with one of these meetings prompted several Grahamstown residents to step outside the imposed framework and arrange a meeting of their own, at which they decided to set up the Unemployed People's Movement.

This willingness to highlight the merits of a certain participation and, even more, to convince "communities" and individuals of their integration into the decision-making process has become more pronounced since the beginning of the twenty-first century. It has gradually crept into some corners of liberal and party political democracy. This is revealed by, among other things, the use of *imbizos*, assemblies that were originally intended to allow a population to discuss matters with traditional leaders.[17] Scarred by the relatively disappointing results of the December 2000 local elections, the ANC leaders decided to temporarily abandon a political strategy strictly focused on the media. It then seemed necessary to "go back to basics" in order to convince people that the party was sensitive to the needs of the residents. This traditional tool of the *imbizo* was thus presented as a perfect consultation channel. Its use mobilized municipal officials, senior party officials, and ministers and members of the South African presidency. Many community gatherings were held, with the stated goal of developing a new "social contract" with citizens (Kassner 2014, 151). The ANC's secure victory in the 2004 national elections was therefore attributed to a reestablishment of this link with communities, a link that years of bureaucratization had damaged. Mandela's party thus continued to "resemble a social movement rather than an electoral machine," according to one of South Africa's leading political analysts (Lodge 2006, 163). The years that followed confirmed this (re)positioning. At the 2007 ANC conference in Polokwane, where he also won the party presidency,[18] Jacob Zuma called for a focus on participatory and community structures in local districts. In the wake of this, activists and elected officials of the African National Congress engaged in the establishment or reactivation of the community policing forum and other branch executive committees (Meth 2013, 269–277). Having become president of the Republic of South Africa, Zuma also announced the revival of the residents' committees, which had once been the main spearheads of the internal struggle against apartheid governments. Meanwhile, however, the enemy had of course changed. These neighbors' associations were no longer expected to challenge an oppressive regime but to help its successor to fight crime.

These initiatives can obviously appear as attempts to instrumentalize and misuse "popular politics." Many analyses have carefully noted the flaws and the illusory nature of these participative arrangements (see Bénit-Gbaffou 2015). Nevertheless, we should at the same time remember that many leaders of the African National Congress were politically socialized by this "politics of the people." They grew up in communities marked by the presence of street committees, community leaders, and large public gatherings. Even today, a majority of ANC activists live in these neighborhoods. These women and men can therefore participate, as residents and members of the "community," in everything connected with "popular politics." The first consequence of this situation is to bring together the *activist styles* that characterize the contemporary spheres of party politics and protest (see Chapter 10).

These phenomena of borrowing, taking over, or simply using principles and tools from a supposedly foreign world can be observed working in the opposite sense, as we will see in more detail in the following chapters. In neighborhoods, for example, community leaders sometimes know how to profit from local power relations between political parties. By getting closer to one camp rather than another, they sometimes hope to strengthen their position or gain access more easily to certain goods (see Piper 2015). Party political struggles are therefore part of the competition between the influential figures of "popular politics." Protesting activists also tried, in the 2000s and 2010s, to find their place in the very official framework of local elections. They did so by claiming to import the values and principles of "popular politics."

This last example invites us to question more generally the diversity of positions that the South African poor people's movements adopt. In the specific case of the Unemployed People's Movement, everything leads us to think that its leaders and activists do not limit their ways of being and doing to a single register, a register deeply rooted in a space where the poor are merely the subjects of power. While many aspects of their action seem to verify the thesis of the "political society," several initiatives and positions also place the movement in a relationship with the state which could very well be the same as that enjoyed by the components of civil society. Thus, the UPM does not hesitate to adopt the formalism of its interlocutors when it addresses the administration officially. The memorandum delivered to the local authorities in November 2017, after the end of yet another demonstration denouncing the "corruption" of the municipality, shows this quite well. Throughout this three-page document, activists in fact provided many references to specific passages in the Constitution, and also to a report commissioned by the Eastern Cape Local Government. They quoted parliamentary documents reaffirming that "access to safe water and adequate sanitations is vital in reducing poverty, reducing diseases and saving lives." Thereby, UPM members directly claim rights and, more broadly, a citizenship that some authors of subaltern studies seemed to doubt applied to the poor of the Global South. At other times, this logic even goes a little further. In November 2018, UPM activists helped to gather more than twenty thousand signatures as part of a petition campaign to place the municipality under administration—a procedure strictly regulated by the South African Constitution. They did so alongside residents, mostly white, campaigning in two associations that continuously alerted people to the mismanagement of the municipality in the 2010s. A delegation including a representative of each of the three collectives was finally received in the offices of the provincial minister in charge of governance issues. At the end of this interview, where they were able to submit the petition, the three residents were invited by local media to summarize their expectations in front of a camera. All three then emerged as the official actors of a democratic counterpower. Sitting between his two current allies, the UPM activist did not appear as the representative of a "population" or the simple subject of Power, but as the concerned citizen of a city.

Perhaps it is not fundamentally necessary to describe what Ayanda, Dumisa, and the people of Phaphamani are doing on this rainy evening. It is indeed not so much the existence or the possibility of a "popular politics" that this chapter intended to question, but rather its homogeneity and what it was supposed to be organizing: a small, autonomous world protected from the eyes of elites for which it would remain a mystery. Certainly, the polity concerned by these ways of doing and these particular moments is the one formed by the residents of the township, especially the poorest of them. However, it seems fairer and more appropriate to consider "popular politics" as a common domain that nourishes, in varying degrees, the practices of various groups right across social boundaries. This domain is all the more subject to sharing in that it is anchored in the "community" and is therefore a source of legitimacy wherever one finds oneself in the South African social order.

7

LEADERS IN THE COMMUNITIES

Located at the edge of the city, the district of Vukani ("Wake Up") first saw the light in the early 2000s, thanks to a program that led to the construction of more than 1,000 RDP houses between 2003 and 2007 (Mukorombindo 2012, 62). The public authorities of the time intended to assert their prerogatives over land that had gradually become covered by squatter shacks. Built on a hillside at the end of a long strip of asphalt that was supposed to connect it to the main road between the city and the township, the place is among the poorest in Grahamstown. If other places can arouse a sense of emptiness in a stranger who visits them, it is mainly a certain incompleteness that predominates here. The workers who built this beige and grey landscape seem to have suddenly deserted it, leaving behind a few mounds of gravel to which no one now seems to pay any attention. The road surface is not completely tarmacked. It also has broad cracks across it that often damage the flat undercarriages of the few cars that venture into these streets.

Vukani looks like an island of cement all alone in the veld—a veld that, here and there, licks at the walls of the houses and pours its vegetation out on the pavement. Stuck halfway between confinement and extraterritoriality, the neighborhood mainly has a certain "out-place" air (Agier 2016, 35). Although legal, it seems perched on the edges or the limits of the normal order of things. For several days on end, for example, water may no longer flow through the pipes that run through the neighborhood, without the municipality notifying the residents. Taken by surprise, they have no choice but to load their wheelbarrows with plastic cans and buckets, and then head off to fetch some of the precious liquid from a neighboring district.

All this has not stopped Vukani from gaining a community, one in which Andiswa is now well known. The RDP home of this woman in her fifties has become a refuge for a handful of local children who have been orphaned by AIDS. The situation is far from isolated, as Leslie Bank found in his ethnographic study of the township of East London, 160 kilometers from Grahamstown (Bank 2011, 187). For a large number of women living alone or with an unemployed man, taking in orphans is a significant source of income insofar as it means they receive child benefits. Social workers are definitely overwhelmed by the ravages of AIDS in the townships, and they have also regularly permitted five or six children to be taken in per household, on the sole condition that they live in houses and not shacks.

In Vukani's early hours, and when she had just given birth to a boy with a mental disability, Andiswa also took part in the creation of a nursery for children with disabilities who had previously been abandoned to their fate by the public authorities. Despite the inertia of the municipality, she now plans to open the community hall to all the schoolchildren in the neighborhood to take them off the streets after school. With this in view she has formed many contacts and is trying to forge partnerships with various tradespeople and the social worker in charge of this zone.

Initially skeptical about my request, Andiswa finally agreed to tell me about her daily life. So we ended up at her place, in her living room. I sat not far from the front door, left open on this early autumn day; I could see the total lack of animation in the street, a situation for which my familiarity with other neighborhoods had not prepared me. With her hair covered by a cloth kerchief, as with many women of her age in the township, my hostess was sitting in a chair, with a three- or four-year-old child on her lap. Two others were playing not far from us. Her voice hinted at a real determination and a certain pride in describing her commitment, one that had every sign of altruism. After a few minutes, she even stood up to point out two frames in a corner of the living room. They contained the two "awards" for "community serving" that had been jointly awarded by the municipality and a bank a few years earlier. Listening to her describe the ceremony, I could easily imagine one of those moments where philanthropy comes together with an ode to the spirit of initiative.

Of course, it is first and foremost within her own neighborhood that her commitment has long been recognized. She has become a well-known figure. Opportunities to consolidate her status had not been lacking. Andiswa had regularly led the demonstrations that, at the end of the first decade of the twenty-first century, were launched in protest against the defects that had started to appear on RDP houses built less than five years previously: cracked walls, leaky roofs, doors that had come loose because of damp. At the time, these actions drew the attention of the leaders of the Unemployed People's Movement, which was then in the process of being set up.

Over the years, Andiswa has become a person relatively difficult to ignore in her neighborhood. In 2008, for example, a majority of the residents chose her to sit on the community policing forum, a structure where residents and police representatives discuss safety problems in the communities. Although her term of office ended five years later, she did not stop tackling the problems of insecurity and criminality afterward. It is not uncommon, she assures me, for her to get together with other residents and try to "find a solution when people behave badly." Indeed, it was to her home that, one morning in 2015, a shopkeeper rushed when the shop was being ransacked by a horde of young people. The intervention of Andiswa and a handful of neighbors finally stemmed the violence of these looters, some of whom had grown up in Vukani.

If we had to summarize the above, it would be sufficient to say that Andiswa is a "community leader," one of those central and almost banal figures in the poor and working-class neighborhoods in South Africa. This phenomenon is not specific to this country.[1] Indeed, it is one of the most common forms of "the informal politics of representation in poor, urban neighborhoods of the Global South" (Piper and Bénit-Gbaffou 2014, 39). The Unemployed People's Movement includes within its ranks a large number of individuals explicitly claiming this status within their neighborhood. By leaving the theater of protest operations and pushing open the doors that lead to ordinary life in the township, you really become aware of their presence and its importance for the movement. Community leaders active within the UPM are visible links between the political cause and the neighborhoods; they extend and reinforce the "attachments" which define the UPM's regime of the near. They are the first makers of the movement's politics of the near.

Studying the social and political life of a Brazilian slum, Martijn Koster and Pieter de Vries have aptly summarized the situation by explaining that the

term community leader "is not applied to individuals appointed to particular functions, but to persons with particular life histories and characteristics" (Koster and de Vries 2012, 88; see also Koster 2012). In the various
places where I conducted fieldwork, it is most often through an election (informal, because not officially validated by the public authorities) in which
residents of a street or a district vote, or even through being the head of an
association or a locally influential collective, that an individual can gain
such a position. This recognition can also reward someone who has led
social and community initiatives such as the development of vegetable
gardens or soup kitchens, involvement in the implementation of health
prevention programs, and so on. Regular and visible, these *gifts of oneself*
generate real "local meritocracies" (Retière 2003). In Durban, for example,
the woman who later became one of the first female faces of Abahlali base-
Mjondolo, the squatters' movement, helped to create a self-managed nursery
that opened in the middle of the Kennedy Road shack settlement in the
1990s. The gratitude she gained for this initiative led, at the beginning of
the next decade, to her being elected vice chair of the camp's development
committee, the body responsible for dealing with the problems faced on a
daily basis by residents, and for negotiating with the city council. In the
1980s, in Cape Town, Josette Cole also reported the very eloquent words of
a resident of the Crossroads neighborhood about the local rise of one of her
neighbors:

> We first noticed Ngxobongwana because he used to have a small bakkie
> and did odd jobs for people. One thing he did was to help take the school-
> children on outings. One day we asked him how much we should pay
> him for his help. But he refused. So we thought to ourselves, "Hey, this
> man can be useful to us." It was then that we elected onto the Noxolo
> School Committee. He wasn't elected. We just put him there. . . . Ngxo-
> bongwana was the person always around the community. Slowly lots of
> things, like the reports on things happening on our absence or messages
> from the authorities, used to get left with him. In this way Ngxobong-
> wana got to be more and more powerful. (Cole 1987, 44)

In the case of Andiswa, the popularity she enjoyed in her neighborhood
preceded her entry into the community policing forum. She has never sat
on a residents' committee. Her altruistic commitment and the fact that she
has regularly taken part in neighborhood affairs justify the fact that, ever

more naturally and systematically, people turn to her in case of problems. Perfectly logically, after all, these commitments also go hand in hand with one of the most salient features of life in society: the very presence of leaders is reinforced by the propensity of many residents to rely on those institutions, the "community," and its spokespersons. The example of a man who, in Thembelihle (Johannesburg), came knocking on the door of one of the district leaders to get fresh drinks on a very hot day proves as much, however absurd it may seem. Beyond the merely anecdotal level, however, it is obvious that to hold such a position within a more or less extended neighborhood exposes one to the expectations of those who populate it. The community leader is, among others, the person who is asked to obtain information or answers to the most mundane administrative questions. He or she is expected to intervene in disputes between neighbors, pay a visit in the aftermath of floods, or be able, in the middle of the night, to find a vehicle to take a woman going into labor to the hospital. She or he can also be called on to help when a family is struggling to collect money to pay for a funeral or, more prosaically, to help a resident replace electric cables stolen from his or her house overnight. These individualized relationships do not overshadow the missions that are supposedly in the collective interest. The community leaders are, above all, the people who are supposed to speak out when the neighborhood is going through a rough patch. They then organize the community against whatever is threatening it.

It can be deduced from these very specific social relations that community leadership certainly confers a social status, but that it may, even more, refer to a role in itself. It is indeed akin to "a set of behaviours related to the position that the person occupies and that allow this position to exist, consolidate it and, especially, make it perceptible to others" (Lagroye 1997, 8). The requests formulated by the locals are therefore so many reminders of how this role should be fulfilled. One might even be reminded of a kind of priesthood when listening to Lukulele complaining about the constraints and risks of a role that he nonetheless seems proud to fulfil. In addition to his activism in the UPM, this young thirty-something runs a "Bible society" and a circle of young Christians in his neighborhood, and he hosts a program devoted "to the community" on a small radio station that has been set up in the township. These multiple activities have attracted the attention of one of the members of the street committee of his district, he says, who asked him to join it:

It's a kind of risky. A kind of risk of life . . . 'cause the thugs, they will chase you. They think you are police. . . . So, there's no happiness at all. So be aware of that if you're getting in the street committee. [The people] will demand everything, as if you're a municipal official. And if there's a trouble, they quickly call you: "What are you going to do about that?" So people are after you, after you, after you . . . but it needs a strong person if you say "no."

Beyond their multiple interventions and actions, an important part of the legitimacy and authority of community leaders rests on their "ability to channel and redistribute resources to the community, according to some kind of local 'moral economy'" (Piper and Bénit-Gbaffou 2014, 38). The relationship thus established between the leader and the other residents gives us a glimpse of the contours of a system of obligations and expectations, respect for which is supposed to contribute to maintaining a certain balance within the community. The challenge then becomes knowing how to access the state, the main provider of these resources (jobs, project financing, etc.). When the ANC dominates local politics, as was generally the case in the 2000s and 2010s, the answer to such a question is obvious. Many studies have thus perfectly well demonstrated that it is easier for Black and poor communities to reach state institutions through the various networks based on this party than through formal channels (See Piper 2015; Dlamini 2010; Katsaura 2012). Proximity to these networks is therefore an advantage in the competition between local leaders. It explains, quite logically, how ANC activists and those of the South African National Civic Organization (SANCO), an organization often considered as the "little brother" of the majority party, can successfully lay claim to preeminent positions in many neighborhoods (see Piper and Anciano 2015).

What follows quite naturally from this type of situation is a certain clientelism that is regularly denounced by UPM activists. The literature in the social sciences, however, has shown how this phenomenon can be much more complex than it seems. Over and above any moral considerations, it first and foremost allows the poorest to access the distribution of public resources relatively efficiently. The relationship it establishes is far from being asymmetrical. Clientelism or patronage, whether practiced in Grahamstown or Mexico City (on these questions see, among others, Shefner 2008 and Holzner 2004), must indeed be apprehended as "poor people's problem-solving strategies" (Auyero 2012b, 99). It works "as webs of resource-distribution and protection against the risks of everyday life" (100). In addition, the subordinate position in which residents are apparently placed must be qualified since they can take advantage of certain local rivalries. Communities are indeed real political spaces where competition is all the more intense as contenders for positions of local leaders are not lacking. The reason is quite simple: in a context marked by poverty and unemployment, community leadership is regularly perceived as offering opportunities for social advancement through enrolment in "state-sanctioned projects by public-private players" (Piper and Bénit-Gbaffou 2014, 41) for example. The visibility of the leader, it is true, may make him or her a perfect intermediary in the eyes of the "outside" world. In the late 1990s, for example, the leaders of a civic affiliated with SANCO played an active part in a program for running the railway stations in Soweto, one of Johannesburg's townships. They took on in particular the task of selecting the individuals recruited for this job. Likewise, it was the leaders of the civics of Vosloorus (Gauteng Province) to whom the managers of a supermarket chain turned when plans were being made to open a store in the locality (Gervais-Lambony 2001b, 215). On a completely different scale, Andiswa was chosen by an NGO to disseminate health and nutrition information in her neighborhood. Another NGO used her as its "champion" to distribute seeds to develop the cultivation of individual vegetable gardens. One can easily imagine that her past initiatives, especially those on behalf of children with disabilities, persuaded and reassured the leaders of these organizations, always on the lookout for reliable partners in the field.

Such positions can also translate into promises of political advancement, as suggested by one UPM activist who presents himself as a community leader: "When you're in SANCO, you position yourself to be the next councilor in the area." These latter elements shed light on the sometimes tortuous nature of the relationships between community leaders and local councilors. More or less explicit partnerships rub shoulders with attempts at cooptation or, conversely, with exclusion. A few months before local elections in which she planned to stand, Andiswa was approached by the ward councilor, determined to lure her into the embrace of his party, the ANC. She finally gave up her candidacy (she was supposed to be standing for the United Front, a left-wing formation that some UPM activists were close to).

Andiswa, however, recalls with a smile the "visits" she has received and which, as she knows, attest to her position in the neighborhood.

To be identified like this by figures with political power can also expose you to more unpleasant treatment. Bongani is a UPM activist in his forties, with a fleshy physique. Jovial and speaking an English that is sometimes difficult to understand, he works for a shopkeeper in the town center who pays him to secure the area around his shop. Five days a week, he walks the street, wearing a high-visibility vest and armed with a stick meant to deter anyone who might be tempted to hassle his employer's customers. However, his aim is to set up a small agricultural cooperative with the help of two friends. This would be a chicken farm that would supply one of the supermarkets in the town. The idea came to them during their many domino games ("Because there is nothing else to do in the township"). As often, however, the lack of capital means that, for the moment, this project will remain a dream.

When not patrolling, Bongani is a community leader in Vukani. Unlike Andiswa, whom he knows well, the councilor and local ANC activists have made no attempt to lure him in. On the contrary, they often strive to marginalize him within the very community where his problem-solving qualities

"African supermarket"

have made him popular for many years. (In particular, it is to him that burglaries and fights in the neighborhood are usually reported, so that he can notify the police.) He is not always informed when neighborhood meetings are being held and he is sometimes the subject of gossip. He and his friends are also left out when the councilor or community leaders close to the ANC have a few jobs to "distribute" among the residents. This difference between his treatment and Andiswa's experience can be explained quite easily: in addition to being a UPM activist, Bongani is a very assiduous member of the Democratic Alliance, the main opposition to the ANC in the country and within the municipality. His status as a local leader makes his campaign work on behalf of his party all the more effective.

The majority of the local leaders who are activists within the UPM acquired this status well before joining the movement. This is the case of Andiswa, of course, but it is also true of Ayanda and Dumisa, and equally of Zache and Angela.

The former, Zache, is a man in his fifties who played an active part in founding the UPM. In the early 2010s, after spending much of his life in Joza, one of the oldest neighborhoods in the township, he moved into an RDP house in an area that the residents still call "Transit Camp." A few years ago, the place was a plain covered with shacks. The windows of the house today look out over a landscape still marked by this past: a vast wasteland covered with tall grass and bristling with looming electricity pylons. In places, as if emerging from the earth, ribbons of twisted barbed wire from which plastic bags dangle scratch the ground for a few meters before disappearing into mud puddles.

Zache became a well-known figure as a result of the years he spent in Joza. As a teenager, he attracted attention at the Congress of South African Students (COSAS), an anti-apartheid student organization of which he was one of the youngest members. Then, in the early 1990s, in a South Africa in the process of freeing itself, he joined the newly formed ANC local branch and actively campaigned within the Youth League of the party. But it was mainly with the Cosmos of Joza, the most famous amateur soccer team in the township at the end of the twentieth century, that he became a celebrity. Armed with this aura and his activism within the UPM, Zache soon stood out in his new community in the transit camp. Members of the residents' committee quite naturally proposed that he join them. He became the chairperson.

Tired of seeing "gossips" and "stories where a resident is bitten by his neighbor's dog" take precedence over "necessary things" ("houses and education") at committee meetings, he resigned after four years. Nevertheless, he remains sufficiently influential in his district to be associated with his old functions, so people regularly come to ask for his opinion or his intervention, as he told me in a conversation in 2017:

Saturday night, at about 3 in the morning, I had a knock:

"Hey, it's me . . ."

"What's the problem?"

"There's someone who has been stabbed so I report to you . . ."

"No, no, I'm no longer a member of the committee. I don't want to involve myself in these things . . ."

"So you see, Jérôme, I left the committee because it was all about things I wasn't interested in. . . . But even now, people come to me for that kind of things . . . "

Angela lives nearby. My first meeting with this woman in her mid-fifties took place at her home, in a recently built and modestly furnished RDP house. She was coming back from church. In our first conversations in 2012, she had told me that she had had to give up the community leadership a year ago: she was "ill." Over the course of the discussion, things had become clearer, which allowed me to better understand her obvious weariness. This "illness," she told me, was in fact a "depression." This was the first and last time that I heard this word in the postapartheid activist circles that I had been studying for several years.

Without even having to dissect Angela's private life, we can easily imagine how exhausting the two decades preceding our meeting had been. They boiled down to a series of battles for a "normal life" and tensions with the holders of political and administrative power. Angela spent part of the 1990s in the notorious transit camp, in the regularly renewed and then immediately disappointed expectation of seeing the shacks finally replaced by proper houses. Chosen by a majority of residents to be their leader at the beginning of the new century, she had the task of negotiating with the municipal team over the construction of "cement houses, with two rooms and a kitchen." The construction of the houses was finally agreed after some "very rough meetings" with the officials supervising the project. "People here know she's reliable," one of her UPM comrades explained to me one day as we walked through the neighborhood: "They know she didn't compromise herself during the discussions, even though it was very stressful. Blows were exchanged, verbally. And [the people of the municipality] were afraid of her. And she made it clear: 'We want this, this and this.'"

However, Angela's troubles were not yet over. The suspension of the work, provoked by the nonpayment of the workers, forced her to organize the community again, this time with the help of the UPM. The demonstration that followed, covered by some of the TV media, was intended to put the municipality "under pressure" on the eve of local elections.

The houses have now been built and do not seem to suffer too much from poor workmanship. Aware of the state of disrepair of some recent constructions in nearby neighborhoods, Angela and other leaders were vigilant during the construction work. Some of those to whom these dwellings had originally been allocated, however, soon left them. Often too poor to pay the expenses, they preferred to rent their property out to other households and return to the shacks in a camp built on top of a landfill. In any event, Angela, for her part, was psychologically damaged by those years of mobilization which also put paid to her ANC militancy. She was involved in local anti-apartheid demonstrations in the 1980s ("Of course I was involved. Everyone was. And you also, [in France] . . . you were involved?"), and joined the party the day after its unbanning, in 1990. She excelled, she told me, in the recruitment of new members, a task that had obviously allowed her to gradually get to know a significant proportion of the transit camp population. Disappointment finally overwhelmed her, however, and she finally left the party in the late 2000s ("I don't like crooks"). Her neighbors, and local people in general, nevertheless continued to come to her home with "personal problems, problems with crime, problems in the house . . ." Her social knowledge probably still set her apart in the local landscape:

If they needed something . . . for housing, electricity, water . . . they came to me because I knew who to see so they could get it. . . . And I saw the people suffering . . . they can't get the money for pensions . . . the old ladies . . . I like to help the people, you know? So they came. And they also knew I was a UPM activist. And . . . when there is a problem, I call [UPM leader] Kota and say: "Kota, I've got a problem here. Can you come and help me?"

The perseverance and firmness that Angela seems to have shown during the talks with the municipality also highlight what is certainly one of the main social effects of community leadership. Through what she or he is called to say and do, the leader contributes to objectifying the existence of the community and showing that it is endowed with a certain agency. A few days before I met her for the first time, Andiswa had received a visit from a group of residents bringing a highly specific request. The local school was about to close, and they had come to ask her to go to the information meeting organized by the local councilor. All of them, Andiswa told me, knew that she would not hesitate to approach the problem head on and publicly express the community's fears.

This outspokenness is obviously valued by the residents. The case of Dumisa, another community leader particularly active within the UPM, is a more than convincing example. Like many people in South African townships, Dumisa speaks only very basic English. She can therefore hardly converse in this language whose mastery is an essential resource for local leaders who are likely, among other things, to be in contact with the representatives of the administrations. However, this does not prevent her from enjoying a real local influence. The fact that she was among the first to settle in this part of Phaphamani in the early 1980s certainly plays a part in this situation. But if her opinion matters so much, it is also because people fear her outbursts of anger, her frankness, and her tendency to speak in community meetings where she never treats her interlocutors with kid gloves, whether they be weak or powerful. Ayanda experienced this when he was walking through the township to publicize the UPM cause at the end of the 2000s. He told me several times about the first meetings and the audiences who, exhausted by still having to wait for the changes promised in 1994, kept swinging between lassitude and distrust. He particularly remembered the stormy gatherings in the Phaphamani neighborhood. Dumisa, whom he did not know personally at that time, was a regular fixture in those small crowds, as he told me, determined to be a bulwark against any attempt to exploit the situation:

At all those meetings, there was this woman. And she was very very influential in the community. She was giving me bad time. . . . She spoke her mind and took up out on me: "We know people like you! We don't trust politicians!" So I had to explain that I was an activist, not a politician. She has such a good heart . . . but she can be so rough [*he laughs*].

The individuals we have just mentioned are quite often forced to contend with more or less intense hostility from ANC representatives in their neighborhood. Moreover, not all of them are (still) active within these structures, which may sometimes be treated as partners by the government authorities, whether they be residents' committees, area committees, and so on. It is therefore difficult for them to compete with their peers who are close to the majority party when it comes to accessing material resources. The (albeit somewhat unusual) case of Bongani shows this quite clearly. Their influence within their community is therefore based on other types of skill or other ways of distinguishing themselves. This is true, for example, of Joseph, whose knowledge of labor law regularly explains why his neighbors come knocking on his door, even late on Sunday evenings: "They come and say: 'I have this letter from my employer and I have to reply tomorrow.' It doesn't really please my wife." However, he fulfils without demur what he seems to consider as a form of responsibility and duty. The activists with whom I talked about it often explained to me, as if it were obvious, that only "volunteering" and selfless dedication allowed one to grasp the very essence of community leadership. As a UPM activist and community leader, Sibahle, told me, "You call the people, you sit with them, you talk to them, you talk about living conditions. Then you make decisions. . . . You go to the meeting, the public forum, and they recognize you as a leader."

The words most regularly used by my interlocutors—"vocation," "selflessness," "mentorship"—clearly express the ultimately highly moral dimension that they hope to associate with community leadership. The fact that some, like Andiswa, can draw a (very) meager profit from their work alongside the NGOs can sometimes irritate some of them:

In Extension 7, you could see that the community has confidence in Athandile. You could see that the community has confidence in Bheki. . . . In Phaphamani, you could see that the community has confidence in Dumisa. In Fingo, you could see that the community has confidence in Ayanda . . . I think it comes from selflessness. If you look at Thabang . . . the kind of work he's doing in soccer [as coach of a team of young players] and everything . . . not getting paid . . . dedicating his life . . . every day. . . . You don't have to be elected. You are influential outside the formal structures. Thabang is not accountable to any formal structures. He does what he does because he's passionate about it. He's not tied to any formal structure and UPM is like that. I'm not tied to any formal structure for anything that I do in the community.

I asked him to elaborate.

"When you walk down the street . . . the people come to you when they have a problem?"
"Yeah, yeah . . ."
"What kind of problems?"
"It's various. It could be related to school. It could be related to funerals. It's various . . ."
"And you have to find a solution?"
"Yeah."

One word in particular can be used to summarize this: reputation. It does indeed take shape in the repeated and visible gift of oneself that clearly characterizes each of these leaders, and in the assessment made by *others* of their ability to solve problems of various kinds. The activist quoted in the previous conversation mentioned the case of Thabang, whose self-presentation expresses this state of affairs quite well. This young man from the Zulu nobility has been unemployed for several years. He has actually worked for only two years since the end of his accountancy studies at college. This was as a service consultant in a bank in town. However, he has no trouble filling his days, which usually begin with discussions with his neighbors about "community problems." Later, he can, depending on the requirements of the day, go to the UPM office, devote himself to his position on the board of the school where his two daughters study, or make himself useful to the church of Zion, whose cap he sometimes wears. The late afternoon is regularly reserved for the team of young footballers he voluntarily coaches. He has also undertaken training to become a sports coach, but financial problems regularly prevent him from completing this. On an October afternoon, in a freezing wind, as we were watching some teenagers play on a football field with imaginary limits right in the middle of one of the plains surrounding the township, he first and foremost insisted on the importance of instilling "rules" into these young people and on the need to provide them with "role models and leaders." Then he came to speak more explicitly about himself, specifying and justifying his position within his community. He told me that if the neighborhood schoolteacher regularly asked for his help, as did the members of the community policing forum ("which is ineffective"), this was because he was known and recognized for certain qualities in his community: "People knew that I was an obedient child. Always ready to help. If anyone needed me to get something from the other end of the township, I would do it. They knew about it. Afterwards, when I became an adult, they realized that I could always find solutions. You see? It's quite simple [*laughs*]."

"Find a solution." This was, for example, the task he was entrusted with by a couple of neighbors who came knocking on his door one morning. Both expected him to give their son a talking-to when he was on the point of succumbing to the lure of drugs. Thabang thinks that he completely fulfilled this role. He took the time to talk to the young man and make him understand "the damage it would do to his brain." In doing so, he believes, he also defended the cohesion of his community by opposing this "capitalist" scourge of drugs spreading through the poor neighborhoods of Grahamstown. Thabang also assumes this position in the exercise of his function as a sports coach. He feels empowered to act as a "moral leader" to help his young footballers find "an alternative to drugs." This young man feels rela-

Training on the plains around the township

tively unconstrained by the boundaries of the intimate and the private spheres, and he also organizes meetings with their parents at which he tries, in his own words, "to convince them to respect their children": "When they come home from school with a poem to learn or an essay to write, parents say, 'Leave it and clean the house.' I can understand that, but they must also be aware of the interests of the children. My role is to convince them that the most important thing is the homework. You see?"

The example of Thabang tends to show that what can be interpreted as reputation or local notoriety generally convinces the leaders themselves of their authority. At the very start of the xenophobic violence, such a conviction very probably impelled Onke to try and intervene between the looters and the shop owned by Sherif and Omar, two Bangladeshi brothers who had settled in Grahamstown over ten years previously. This shop is contained within the four walls of a room without windows, over about thirty square meters. The predominant impression is one of profusion. The shelves are tidy but overflow with vegetables, heavy bags of sugar, boxes of tea, tin cans, sweets, soft drinks, and shampoo. Business seems pretty good, and the two men even opened four other shops here in the 2010s. The place is also kept lively thanks to the regular presence of customers and the conversations of the three Bangladeshi employees responsible for shelving the goods and performing various operations. One of them also sits at the till, behind a security grille and an iron door. Onke has known these people for years. Her daughter worked a few hours a week for Sherif and Omar when she was a high school student.

Onke, a woman in her fifties, is both discreet and energetic. She lives in the Joza neighborhood, where she has also worked as a teacher for a few years after having had a succession of different small jobs. I often see her talking to her neighbors on the doorstep or in the street. On occasion, she does not hesitate to emerge from her reserve to engage in long arguments with those she wants to convince. One can certainly see the influence here of her long-standing and almost visceral commitment to the Azanian People's Organization (AZAPO). She also says, not without pride, that most of her neighbors vote for this small party even though it has been relegated to the margins of the political space since the early 2000s. These same neighbors know that, in the last years of apartheid, she was extremely active in the underground networks of this pan-Africanist formation linked to Steve Biko's Black Consciousness Movement. According to her, her youth and her smallness of stature regularly allowed her to evade the notice of the regime's police, unlike her husband, who was imprisoned for the same activities in the mid-1980s. At that time, Onke's house was also the rallying point for the children, now in their thirties, who came to play and sing after school while listening to her talk about the "Struggle" and the pride that came with being Black. This same house has since been transformed into a little HQ for the AZAPO in election periods. Candidates' posters are stored there, and activists stick them on pieces of cardboard and fix them on the traffic lights and lampposts in the city.

Onke's notoriety in her neighborhood is also closely linked to her continuous and varied commitment within the community. For example, she never misses a community meeting, even those organized by the local ANC councilor: "When the meeting is about the residents, I have to go," she told me. "I'm not going for myself, but for all the people I represent. Because . . . other people cannot talk. So I talk on their behalf sometimes."

Onke has also been a regular member of residents' committees since the end of apartheid, as well as sitting on school boards in the surrounding area. More recently, the residents of Joza elected her secretary of the clinic committee, the body in charge of relations between the community and the hospital. What problems do Joza residents face when they are hospitalized? How are they treated? How can medical staff and the community work together to improve things? Aware of the lack of space in the hospital, Onke and the other members of the committee fought for the municipality to give it a police precinct that had been abandoned for years. They later negotiated so that this office would not need to close on weekends.

The meeting at which Onke was elected secretary of this committee was organized by the elected ANC official of the ward. In any event, and like Andiswa, the seniority and visibility of her commitment protect Onke against any attempt at exclusion that other influential people in her neighborhood might make. She says she maintains "good relations" with this councilor so long as they do not talk about "ANC things" but focus instead on local problems. When she thinks that the municipality is not fulfilling its mission, however, Onke does not hesitate to speak "as a UPM activist" and to contradict the elected official: "I do attack and he knows that."

But let's go back to that October afternoon in 2015. On learning that the downtown shops were being vandalized, Onke soon realized that the violence would spread very quickly through the township. She immediately went to the shop owned by the Bangladeshi brothers, a hundred meters from where she lived. The point was simple: to dissuade any neighbors who might be tempted to loot. So, strengthened by its status as a community leader, Onke took up a position in front of the brothers' shop. Her daughter, Sherif, and Onke alike told me that she had spent several minutes reminding those who faced her how well the two brothers had been integrated into the community: they could speak a few words of Xhosa, regularly extended credit, and participated in the collections organized for the funerals of the poorest people. These arguments, legitimized by her authority, seem to have finally borne fruit. The residents gradually returned to their homes, removing the imminent threat to the shop.

This example suggests how much the notoriety enjoyed by these individuals is a resource that requires both time and direct and regular interactions with the residents. This is obviously the price to be paid if personal qualities are to be perceived and valued by the rest of the community. What followed mainly confirms the strictly localized efficacity of such qualities: while she thought she had saved the shop, Onke finally had to leave when a determined group of looters arrived. In fact, they came from other districts and did not know her.

A significant proportion of the resources available to the Unemployed People's Movement is therefore based on the local popularity that these women and men brought with them when they joined it. They have become established in the neighborhoods, most often before the birth of the organization, and this has given them visibility and a settled status over the years. The notion of capital is definitely the most appropriate for talking about the credit they enjoy with many of their neighbors. We can, more precisely, speak of a "capital of autochthony" (Retière 2003): a popular and local social capital based on neighborly, kinship and friendship relations, and a local reputation. They have gradually accumulated it and made it grow as they invest in the life of the community, and can transfer some of its benefits to their protest collective.

Originally, it was also community leaders who introduced the small founding group of the UPM into neighborhoods where there was nobody to foster their cause. They did so by organizing meetings to present the cause of a movement that was still in the making. Some even directly approached activists, as in one informal settlement where the invitation came from the members of a street committee tired of the "broken promises" of their successive local councilors.

However, we should not deduce that a unilateral relationship is at work here—as many of these activists explicitly agree. If "people [from their neighborhoods] come to see [them]," they often tell me, this is also because their membership in the UPM is known. To put it another way, the recognition that their organization has come to enjoy now helps them, in part (and in return) to stay in the game. Many residents value the arts of protest in which the community leaders associated with the UPM are masters. They still nurse other needs and other expectations on a daily basis. As will be shown in Chapter 9, the organization has been able to adjust to this by relying in particular on links formed with the organizations of "civil society." Its proximity to an association of jurists gives it, for example, access to an expertise for which its activists work as intermediaries with the poor people of the area, often in ignorance of their rights. The requests made of these same activists tend to show that a proportion of the population has clearly incorporated this dimension. From a more general point of view, the fact of mastering different forms of information (legal, administrative, etc.) and being able to share it constitutes a significant resource on which local leaders in the ranks of the UPM can count.

One episode in particular is a good illustration of the reality of this triangular structure formed by the movement, the residents and their leaders. In autumn 2016, members of the Unemployed People's Movement took advantage of rallies at various points of the township to announce that they had obtained a document of major importance in the housing crisis: the official list of Grahamstown households selected to receive a grant (R15,000) to finance the purchase of an RDP home. This file, obtained from the provincial ministry after they had cited a law facilitating access to administrative documents, very clearly showed the extent of corruption in municipal management: there was a significant number of residents whose names were on this list but had never been informed that this might enable them at last to move into an RDP house. The municipality had simply placed the file under "embargo," to use the words of the activists. According to the latter, the elected officials thus reserved the freedom to allocate new housing to the households of their choice, in most cases supporters of the ANC and their relatives. At the end of UPM meetings, the residents present were invited to check if their names were in the document. Those who had not attended the meetings addressed the movement's representatives in their neighborhoods, who could then go directly with them to the offices of the organization to have their identity papers photocopied. The UPM's objective was to send a delegation to Port Elizabeth to assert the rights of these households before the provincial housing administration. During this period, which lasted for several months, a stack of photocopies regularly piled up on the corner of the desk, waiting for a sympathizer of goodwill to transport the activists to the main conurbation of the Eastern Cape.

The place these women and men occupy in their neighborhoods has given them a local fame or notoriety (even a notability) from which the UPM opportunistically derives part of its own legitimacy. As a first step, the organization was indeed able to aggregate various types of "good reputation" (Bourdieu 1991, 194) that were clearly the products, in the main, of the reconversion of a capital of autochthony accumulated in different domains. The relationship thus shaped was largely the opposite of what often characterizes party or trade union organizations, where elected officials and leaders owe their authority, in principle, to the fact they have a proper mandate.

The relationship between the UPM and "its" community leaders does, however, go both ways. Indeed, everything leads us to believe that, in a second phase, the fact of belonging to this collective with its growing notoriety has strengthened the position of the activists in their neighborhoods by allowing them to respond to some of the requests made by residents. This all entails a form of circularity or, more exactly, a continuous and mutual reinforcement of the positions of individuals and the position of the collective.

INTERLUDE 3: BREAKUPS

It is a July morning, and a dozen of us, women and men, are sitting on uncomfortable benches in one of the rooms of the High Court in Grahamstown. It is a dark, somewhat narrow room; its walls are covered with dark brown wood. Caught up in the silence that the place imposes, we are awaiting the verdict in a case that has deeply affected most UPM activists.

One of the four young men sitting in the dock is Andie. A former journalist and anthropology student in his thirties, Andie has long been one of the movement's driving forces. Two years ago, he and four accomplices were arrested for the murder of a young man. The judge, whose words are simultaneously translated into Xhosa by a clerk, describes it as "one of the worst murders one can imagine." Therefore, he adds, this is one of the most difficult decisions that he has ever had to take during his whole career. Then, at length, he reads out the biographies of the accused, whom he simply designates by a number: "accused 1, accused 2 . . ." Fragments of their lives pass before us. We learn without surprise how much each of these young men has been plunged into poverty since birth. The youngest, twenty-four, earned a few rands thanks to a donkey cart that he made available to neighbors. Another worked on a farm for less than half the minimum wage. Their family situations are also mentioned. One of them was supporting his grandmother and two younger sisters before the murder, while another had a child with a high school girl who is "obviously not in a situation to take care of him," says the judge.

The judge finally returns in some detail to the tortures suffered by the deceased, who, he reminds us, was "a pillar of strength in the family." In particular, the young man was helping to build a family house, now left unfinished. Andie's laptop is believed to have triggered the onslaught of violence, since the victim was suspected of stealing it. The machine contained a collection of poems on which Andie had been working.

I watch Ayanda, sitting by my side. Before we entered the courthouse, I asked him if he was nervous. "I hope the best, but I don't know what it means," he told me.

After a twenty-minute monologue, the judge finally hands down a life sentence for the four defendants. Ayanda cannot conceal his despondency. Amanda, an activist I have met regularly in recent years, is at one end of our row. The victim was one of her cousins. Sitting next to her mother, she shows no emotion as the sentence is passed.

As we return to the UPM office, a few hundred meters from the court, Ayanda breaks the silence he has observed since the verdict. "You know, it's not the first time I've been in this courtroom and heard that kind of things," he says. "All this cruelty. All those crimes . . . torture for hours. It means the township no longer exists. There's no longer a sense of township, no longer a sense of community. All this violence. . . . Our township is a concentration camp now."

Andie used to portray himself as a poet, playwright, and activist. In the early 2010s he founded a circle of poets, all from the poor and Black communities of Grahamstown. At the same time, he put on his own play at the National Art Festival, which attracts thousands of visitors each year to Grahamstown. It was the "political and social story" of a soldier involved in World War III. There are also several videos online showing him declaiming texts in different areas of the township. Usually dressed in clothes cut from traditional Xhosa fabrics, he talks of the lives "chosen by fate" for those who, like him, live in "hunger and poverty" and have "pain written in [their] eyes." Like other young activists, he also evokes the need to return to one's roots in a South African society overly fascinated by the West. In the mid-2010s, Andie also made a name for himself in the "decolonization" movement that was causing tremors in the South African university system. He even appeared regularly as one of the main spokespersons for the mobilization of Black students at Rhodes University.

Andie was also a well-known community activist in Extension 9, his neighborhood: "He was very respected because he had been a very disciplined child. And he always consulted people," one local woman had told me. And yet it was his neighbors who, in the days following his arrest, showed their anger. An outbreak of "mob justice" even drove his grandmother out of her house. The old woman was suspected of having witnessed some of the victim's ordeal but subsequently remaining silent.

I know very little about this period of unrest at Extension 9. Activists generally avoid talking about it or downplay its importance. The organization was, however, forced to reduce its activities in this district for many months. According to Tshepo, a twenty-year-old activist, "the people of Extension 9 were very angry with the UPM because, in South Africa, people charge an organization because of one person." At first, though, it seems that Andie's neighbors in fact expected activists to organize a demonstration to denounce the murder, just as they had previously done in another neighborhood, when an alleged rapist had been allowed to go free.

The dissensions spread to the organization. A few people, including activists living on Extension 9 (certainly pressurized by their neighbors), openly asserted the need to condemn Andie's act. In fact, even in other neighborhoods, people were taking UPM members aside and expressing their surprise at the organization's "silence." In contrast, other members of the movement wanted to remember that Andie had been a "comrade." The split was not fatal to the UPM, but it did lead to the departure of Amanda, a full-time activist.

On the outskirts of the township

Manise, a researcher at Rhodes University who knew the young man well, told me that several times she had suggested driving to the prison with the activists so that they could see Andie. She had met with nothing but embarrassed refusals.

The last time I saw Amanda was at home, two days after sentence had been passed on her cousin's killers. She had left the movement almost a year before. We were actually at her mother's house, where she lives with her three sons. Amanda, forty-three, has been out of work for several years and does not live with the father of her children.

My arrival did not seem to disturb her habits or her schedule. She was sitting in the living room, obviously without much to do. I found her sitting on a sofa, a little tired, wearing a bathrobe. We stayed in the room for just under an hour, regularly interrupted by the comings and goings of her mother, busily tidying things. I used the moments when Amanda was trying to think how to answer my questions to try to remember a few details about the room: the statue of the Blessed Virgin placed on a table, the small display case filled with glass objects, the table covered with a well-ironed tablecloth, the brightly colored painting hanging not far from the crucifix. What met my eyes was the clean and sober interior of a house in which the fate of its five occupants depended on the payment of three child support grants and an old age pension, altogether R2,700 per month, R800 less than the minimum wage set by the government at that time.

I had known Amanda, a former ANC Youth League activist, when she busied herself all day long in the UPM offices, welcoming activists and residents and informing them of when community meetings were to be held. If I had not known that she was exerting herself every day on the government bodies of her children's schools, I would certainly have thought that few things now met with much of a resonance within her. The most surprising thing, in fact, was what she said about the UPM, the organization that she had left in painful circumstances. In her view, the movement was still "very democratic" and above all concerned with the "needs of the people." Conversely, ANC members only ever talked about their "benefits." Amanda, who distributed party posters and held meetings in her neighborhood during her teenage years, now has an intense grudge against the African National Congress. Her resentment seems all the stronger since she feels the party owes her "something." "I worked very hard for the ANC, but the ANC didn't work for me."

Amanda escorted me to my car, where three activists were waiting. On seeing her, one of them lowered the window and started chatting with her while I took a few photographs of the neighborhood. I did not hear their conversation. It would have been difficult, however, not to see the reserve that sprang up between these former comrades who, obviously, had not spoken for several months. After a few minutes, Amanda returned to her house. She had just promised to go to the offices of the movement before the end of the week to talk things over and, perhaps, to return to the ranks of a collective that, just a few months ago, had occupied most of her days.

8

LOST IN TRANSITION?

Autumn 2016. Every morning, Mark's job is to open the door and unlock the padlock on the gate that protects the small white house where the offices of the UPM are located. At the same time, the Nigerian shopkeeper, who has come physically closer to the organization since the xenophobic attacks of October 2015, generally finishes setting out his merchandise under the windows of the premises. Mark was born in Johannesburg in the early 1990s. He arrived in Grahamstown two decades years later to study at Rhodes University's Department of Political Science and International Relations. Unable to afford the rents in the university dormitories, he first rented a room in Fingo Village, one of the Black neighborhoods in Grahamstown, before getting permission from UPM leaders to move into one of the four rooms on the organization's premises.

Our first conversations allowed me to see that Mark differed from the other young activists in the organization by the nature of his politicization. A few allusions he dropped in the course of our discussions had suggested a family environment that was marked by the memory of the fight against apartheid as much as by the struggles relating to environmental issues and in favor of sexual minorities. Our first long conversation, one afternoon in the kitchen of the UPM office, confirmed my impressions. Throughout the day, I had been able to observe him busying himself, as usual, in the main room, which houses the computer on which the movement's press releases and official letters are written. He had slipped away for a few hours in the middle of the day to attend his classes at university, and then returned, bringing with him the megaphone to be used the next day to round people up for a community meeting.

On this quiet late afternoon, when most of the activists had already left, I finally had a little more time to ask him for some further details about his commitment. Answering my first questions, which were fairly conventional ones about his background, he quickly moved on to paint a portrait of his mother, telling me what a tutelary figure she still was for him. She had been reluctant to marry and brought up her three children alone, raising their awareness of feminism and inculcating in them a "critical" relationship to authority. She herself had her first political experiences during the 1970s, a period of many transformations.[1] In particular, she discovered the Black Consciousness Movement, which at that time was enjoying a high profile at the expense of the African National Congress; the latter was affected by the fact that its cadres and militants had gone underground or were in exile. In addition to the ferment of the times, it was the murder of her brother by the police that drove her into defiance of the apartheid regime. One of her main feats was the time she burned that regime's flag at a demonstration organized in her community. I could easily imagine, as I listened to Mark relate this episode with obvious pride, how many times he must have heard the tale from his mother's lips as a child.

Such a background certainly helps one to understand why this young activist was so involved in student struggles from the time he arrived in Grahamstown. During his first months in the city, he was the main organizer of a protest on the part of poor students who requested financial help from the university president to pay for their food and received a refusal they deemed "contemptuous," whereupon they invaded one of the dining halls of the university restaurant at lunchtime and simply helped themselves. It is also significant that he joined the UPM; we can find the basis of an explanation for this in the young man's years of political apprenticeship. He feels that he learned a lot from his uncle by marriage, one of the main media figures in the postapartheid social movement. This uncle, who had been a leading cadre in the Young Communists before he was expelled for criticizing the party's support for Jacob Zuma, was mainly distinguished by his commitment to the rights of homosexuals and the fight against AIDS. So Mark's first political memory is associated with his participation in a Pride march partly organized by his uncle in 1995. Also, uncle and nephew were close enough for the latter to become the former's assistant for a few months, working for a "sustainable and democratic development" program set up in a small rural community in the Eastern Cape in 2013. The aim of this, under the guise of raising people's awareness of ecological issues, was to question the power of traditional chiefs, a power that is still significant in several rural areas. Thanks to his uncle, Mark was able in particular to catch a glimpse of this sphere where the nongovernmental Left had come together since the beginning of the twenty-first century, at the interface of the intellectual, political, and trade union worlds. The young man regularly accompanied his uncle to various meetings and political actions in the early 2010s. It was on one such occasion that he met some of the leaders of the Unemployed People's Movement.

Mark's relatively sophisticated political socialization is not the norm among young UPM activists, those between eighteen and thirty. For one thing, not everyone comes from politicized family backgrounds. At most, the youngest of them know whether their parents vote or not. When this is the case, they most often cast their vote for the ANC—which represents a rather commonplace, distant reality that they now take for granted. It's how it is. No more than that. "They voted for ANC, if I can remember." Siphokazi, aged twenty-two, was not the only one to give me this kind of answer, in a rather apathetic, monotonous tone of voice. Thus trivialized and rid of its ideological trappings, this vote amounted to an obvious choice that history, at a given moment, had justified, as twenty-eight-year-old Bheki told me:

> I can still remember the election day, in 1994 . . . even though I was young. I was six. I remember very, very . . . because in my house, there were stickers of the ANC. Everywhere. It was basically yellow and green [the ANC colors]. In my family. In my street. Everywhere in Joza. Everywhere . . . politics was life.

For those whom the media regularly call the "born free" (because they were born after the first democratic elections of 1994), the ANC is mostly the party they have always known in power. Its past role as a liberator is therefore not the first thing that comes to their minds. The situation of their young elders, those who were barely thirty in the early 2010s, is not very different (Mattes 2012). They were children in the last years of apartheid, and they indeed came of age politically in the late 1990s. Their first political experience was therefore with a relatively normal political system. This reality can also result in misunderstandings or differences of opinion within families, as we can sense from the remarks of Arthur, a young thirty-something:

The whole family is ANC ... with ANC members. My mother votes for ANC. She would kill you if we talked bad about ANC. [*Laughs*] You know ... that mentality. There's a tendency in the old South African people ... that ... the ANC fought for freedom. The old people, they're talking about Mandela, and the ANC, and stuff, you see? So the whole family is ANC ... and I grew up in it like that. The whole family is ANC ... because of the liberation.

I asked him to elaborate.

> "*Your mother still votes for the ANC because of the liberation?*"
> "Yes, yes. [*Laughs*] So when I am talking about the PAC [Pan Africanist Congress], everyone is against me."
> "*But why the PAC?*"
> "I like the PAC principles ... and I knew someone from PAC and he explained to me and I Googled."

Surprisingly, it is common for those who grew up in more militant families to tend to qualify the idea of any strong political socialization. Thabang, thirty-one, told me that his parents, "active in the Struggle" against apartheid, did not talk much about politics when he was a child and teenager. Whether they were close to the ANC or another party during these years is not really important, he says. What matters most is their resistance to power. He remembers well the way the police brutally burst into the house of his uncle, a police officer imprisoned on Robben Island for helping communist activists: "I was very young, but I could see them coming inside, killing the dog ... putting tear gas in the house. They were harassing my family all the time."

Thabang can also remember the traces left by torture on the hands of a friend of the family. It is quite likely that these experiences exposed him to a specific conception of commitment. They also made him more receptive to the modes of action proper to protest and, in particular, to the possibilities of breaking the rules of a political order considered as unjust. This form of sensibility also crops up fairly regularly in interviews conducted with the young activists of the UPM who grew up listening to the stories of a parent's or a relative's fight against apartheid.

Before going further, let me add a few words about these "young activists" who are going to occupy the following pages. According to the famous formula, youth would be "just a word" (Bourdieu 1993b, 94–102), that is, the product of always relative and artificial boundaries between age groups. More exactly, youth is a historical, cultural, and institutional production whose contours vary with national and cultural borders (Galland 2009). For reasons that will appear quite explicitly throughout the text, I will rely, for my part, on the definition given to the word by the African Union, which defines as "young" the population aged between fifteen and thirty-five years old (African Union 2006).

Now back to Mark.

Every morning, at about nine o'clock, once the door of the premises is open, Mark usually starts to heat the water that the activists, who are gradually arriving, will use to make their tea or coffee. Some of them will then settle on the threshold of the little white house and watch the animated life on this very busy road. On McDonald Street, where the UPM's offices were located in the mid-2010s, there are only a dozen "one door, two windows" buildings, those ground-floor, single-story houses built in the pioneer era, but it still constitutes a daily crossing for dozens of women and men. The street is located on the outskirts of the city center, in a former white working-class district that the fall of apartheid has gradually opened up to a Black petty bourgeoisie eager to move out of the township. It mainly connects the area to Shoprite, a shopping center mainly frequented by a clientele of Black workers and employees. More generally, McDonald Street is at the heart of a border zone separating two facets of the city. Not only are the UPM offices just a few minutes' walk from the neighborhoods in which whites live and work, which also contain the Town Hall, the administrative buildings, and Rhodes University, they are also just a short distance from the pavements of Beaufort Street and those dozens of street vendors who, every morning, set up their motley stalls outside a handful of modest grocery stores run by Pakistani or Bangladeshi shopkeepers. It was here that the looting began in October 2015.

Most of the time, the door of the house occupied by the UPM is ostentatiously open. The day is in any case punctuated by the almost continuous arrivals and departures of activists. Some come to get the latest news from the leaders who, most often, are busy in the office housing the computer. Others sit in the central room, which serves in turn as a living room and meeting room, and chatter about this and that before finally leaving. Every day, the premises seem to be a point of passage for many activists, even if just for a few minutes. The majority of them, who do not necessarily belong to the "cadres,"[2] obviously come without always having any definite purpose and thus make the movement a space of sociability like any another, or almost. The agitation of protest thus becomes the exception rather than the rule. It really lives on just in the daily life of the first circle of activists, busy writing leaflets and press releases. Conversely, the most common *militant time* resembles a kind of floating, or something a little indecisive. It is woven of moments where nothing really happens, without the boredom weighing down too heavily. Discussions begun in the living room sometimes continue in the kitchen or in the corridor, while some activists, sitting on the threshold of the house, swap remarks and jokes with the street vendors. This is often true of one group of three or four teenage girls—its actual composition changes—that takes shape in the course of these days. They have come along with their mothers, and stick together, away from other people. All these activists are far from being useless to the movement of the unemployed. Their presence, especially on the pavement that borders the house, contributes to the apparent vitality of the organization in these moments of "latency" (Melucci 1996). It is not uncommon, in fact, for this bustle to attract attention and arouse a certain curiosity among passers-by.

Things developed in the last months of 2017. The rent of the house on McDonald Street was too high, and this forced the organization to relocate its offices. The activists moved into a small room in a set of community premises located behind the Day Hospital. Here they rub shoulders with the employees of an association for the disabled and those of a federation of South African families. This solution should only be temporary, to be followed by a move to the township that has been planned for several years. Indeed, the UPM activists have not really settled down here. The walls are still covered with posters put up by the previous occupants, members of an association supporting development projects in rural areas. No phones or computers. Although it is not too far from the city center, this transitional office is far removed from the hustle and bustle of the one on McDonald Street: it lies a little away from the main streets and shops. Activists who pass during the day are relatively rare. Those who do so meet Simthandile and Siphokazi, two twenty-two-year-old women. They are on duty, in exchange for the promise of a weekly stipend of R200 (US $15) financed by the funds donated by a European foundation. The two activists arrive every morning at about ten o'clock, having walked from the township. They will close the doors of the premises six hours later. In the meantime, they will most often have tried to kill time by playing with their mobile phones and talking to each other. Sometimes Ayanda, who also spends part of the day in the vicinity, sends one of them off on an errand. This may, for example, consist of going to the university—more specifically, the sociology department—to make a few photocopies for free.

Simthandile and Siphokazi have been waiting for three years to retake some of the subjects that make it possible to obtain the matriculation ("matric") certificate (or National Senior Certificate, NSC), the high school diploma in South Africa. The former did not obtain this certificate at her first attempt. The results of the latter were not good enough for her to get into university. The delay in taking the exam again, in fact, is related to financial issues: their parents are unemployed and do not have the money to finance their studies. While the level of education among the younger generation of Blacks has increased since the Liberation, only a certain minority manage to pass the NSC: for example, only 41 percent of the 2015 matric cohort (i.e., the 1,118,690 second graders enrolled in 2005) passed this exam.[3] The stakes are quite high since not having this certificate exposes you to a higher risk of unemployment. In 2017, the official unemployment rate was over 33 percent for individuals without the NSC, compared with 28 percent for the entire working-age population.[4]

UPM activists aged between twenty and thirty-five in the mid-2010s often passed their matriculation. Few, however, went on to higher education, either for lack of money or because their results did not meet the minimum university entrance requirements. This situation is in fact quite symptomatic of the state of education in South African townships. The question has even become central to the contemporary public debate insofar as it confirms a duality within the national school system that quite closely reflects the general state of society. The media frequently highlight the "dysfunctionality" of primary and high schools in these neighborhoods.[5] As well as the teachers' lack of the right qualifications, another major problem is the insalubrity of the premises and the general lack of equipment. In Grahamstown, such a situation largely explains the increasing exodus of Black middle-class children to city center schools.

It is thus perfectly logical that Simthandile and Siphokazi should have had to postpone the realization of certain life projects. Their dreams of independence, in particular, have been put on a back burner, as Simthandile notes regretfully—she is eager to free herself from a mother whom she criticizes, among other things, for being "too lazy." The two women live with the young activist's grandmother, in a house that is also at the heart of a family conflict: one of Simthandile's uncle claims ownership and seems bent on having his sister and niece evicted. Siphokazi and Simthandile mostly went through a period of idleness in the months following the exam results. "I was doing nothing. I was sitting at home. I got bored," Simthandile told me. In fact, the French term *désoeuvrement* seems more appropriate here than "idleness," inasmuch as it more accurately reflects those feelings of discomfort and depression that accompany a lack of activity. It therefore manages, as Adeline Masquelier notes (2013, 483), to bring together in one word boredom, frustration, dullness, and dread. It is this emotional state that seems to have assailed Thando, a young man of twenty-three who visited the UPM office one afternoon in October. Unable to find work after studies in public administration, he admits to having led a "lazy," doubt-filled life for several months. In order to escape the lassitude that was beginning to overwhelm him, he finally decided to follow the example of his best friend, who had joined the UPM the previous winter.

The *désoeuvrement* expressed or manifested by these unemployed young people echoes the accounts given in many contemporary sociological and anthropological studies of the younger generation in the Global South (see Mains 2012; Masquelier 2013; Jeffrey 2010). They depict young people reduced to a state of waiting in the face of an uncertain future that they suspect will be filled with the same boredom they are already experiencing. In a study of unemployed young Ethiopians, Daniel Mains described a daily life in which there was an abundance of "unstructured time in which introspective thoughts about their future became a source of unease" (Mains 2007, 660).

In principle, it seems quite logical to transpose these analyses into the context of South Africa, especially if we remember that at the beginning of 2010, "half of South Africans under 24 looking for work [had] none. Of those who have jobs, a third [earned] less than $2 a day" (quoted in Hickel 2014, 106). As the years have gone by, the situation has not improved much. In May 2018, the National Statistical Institute, StatsSA, confirmed that the 15–24 age group was highly likely to be jobless: the unemployment rate in this group exceeded 52 percent.[6] In her survey of young men living in an informal settlement in the Johannesburg area who took part in violent protests in 2011, sociologist Hannah Dawson (2014) clearly saw signs of this distress. She describes young adults seeking to kill time by gathering at street corners. For hours on end, they play cards, talk, listen to music, and watch the neighborhood go by, including the various interactions that structure the exercise of local political power. As so often, the interpretation of such situations as these turns out to be relatively ambiguous, or at least more complex than a first reading might suggest. Because they allow young people to momentarily escape their frustrations and organize a sociality, these shared moments are part of a certain "productive idleness," in the phrase used by Craig Jeffrey to refer to unemployed young people in India (2010, 101). What they offer, perhaps above all, is a way of temporarily dealing with the feeling of "exclusion from the 'new' South Africa" (Dawson 2014, 870) that strips these young people of any illusions about their future.

Whether they deal with South Africa, India, or any other part of the Global South, these studies describe a period of suspension between childhood and adulthood: these young people are, as it were, stuck in a "prolonged adolescence" (Masquelier 2013, 475). Certain authors have called this a period of "waithood" ("waiting" for "adulthood") (Dhillon and Youssef 2009), arguing that it was now the social condition of a majority of young people in the developing world. It was even, in their view, gradually replacing conventional adulthood (Honwana 2014, 26) by pushing the boundary of youth up to thirty-five years (Abbink 2006, 6), an option, as we may recall, validated by the African Union in 2006. Lack of jobs, insecurity, and shortage of money is preventing them from crossing the social thresholds that enable them to settle into their roles as responsible adults: economic independence, a home of one's own, becoming part of a couple, parenthood, and so on. In South Africa, waithood also has a perfect ally in the shape of *isishumane*: this is the fear, present in the imaginations of the young men of the township, of their manhood being diminished because they are too poor to have a girlfriend.

However, waithood may foster the emergence of subcultures or alternative forms of livelihood (Honwana 2014, 26) and would not necessarily involve total renunciation. Living in uncertainty can make it possible for people to hope that something might happen, as the uprisings of an educated younger generation trapped in unemployment during the Arab Spring of the early 2010s clearly showed.

Even a schematic account of the living conditions of several UPM activists aged from twenty to a little over thirty seems, at first glance, to give a good overview of these postulates. Just consider the case of Arthur who, at age thirty-one, still lives with his mother, a pensioner. The little money he earns in a community program prevents him gaining any real emancipation. The same is true of Thabo, twenty-eight, who, like hundreds of thousands of young South Africans, lives under the same roof as his parents and grandparents. We could continue this list, adding in particular the name of Zandile. The thirty-year-old lives with her baby and two unemployed sisters in the bond house of her father, a retired policeman. However, several things suggest that we should nuance the straightforward reading we might give of these few fragments of existence.

First, the oldest of these young activists, those who are approaching their thirties and would therefore seem to be the privileged targets of waithood, occupy other social roles than that of prisoners of waiting (even if they are that too, of course). As Marco Di Nunzio notes from his contacts with young urban Ethiopians, they are not "centred around transitioning to adulthood, as the literature on youth in Africa has often assumed" (2015, 159). Zandile, as we have just seen, is also a single mother who manages to get her child looked after during the day so that she can perform the duties of UPM administrator paid by a European foundation. She is also very involved in the issues of sexual violence, parenting, and women's empowerment, issues she seeks to promote in the Young Women's Forum, an association affiliated to the UPM. Bheki is a husband and a young father who, after giving up his schoolteacher training, worries about the future of his family but has finally found a job in the construction sector thanks to the support of his movement.

Second, the apparent indecision of these lives is not systematically synonymous with an absence of projects. Lungile's case is, to say the least, evocative. When I met him for the first time, Lungile was twenty-one and had just been elected chairperson of the Unemployed People's Movement. Silent and reserved, he was still struggling to fully enter this role but seemed anxious to take advantage of the experience (especially the political experience) of other leaders, mainly older than him. Four years later, the transformation is quite striking. Far from the seemingly anonymous appearance of his former tracksuit and cap, Lungile has opted for a Rastafarian style that sets him apart in the township. More voluble than before, he has above all gained a certain emancipation by settling in a shack of a little less than ten square meters, a few steps from the dried earth dwelling in which his parents and his grandparents live. When you push open the door, you discover what now takes up a large part of his time. The walls are covered with the "revolutionary" stencils that decorate the T-shirts he has been making for a few months. There are portraits of anti-apartheid activists such as Chris Hani and Robert Sobukwe alongside those of African nationalist leaders of the 1960s and 1970s, but one can also see the faces of self-proclaimed champions of "anti-imperialism" such as Hugo Chavez and Muammar Gaddafi.[7] Forced to leave law school at the end of his first year, Lungile is seeking to raise capital to buy enough blank T-shirts to launch his business. He has developed various projects, such as selling his creations at the annual National Arts Festival in Grahamstown. At the same time, he has gradually moved closer to local artistic circles and their various activities. This occupation has not totally removed him from the protest cause. I continue to run into him in the UPM offices, even though his visits are obviously less frequent. His activism is now mainly expressed in his neighborhood, especially during the community meetings where he always appears, in the eyes of his neighbors, as one of the main representatives of his organization. If his existence is still rather insecure, being largely reliant on the sale of a few T-shirts and the jewelry that he makes, Lungile feels he has the right to believe in a better future than his current condition. This is, in any case, a feeling that I have regularly observed when talking with other young activists who I knew were finding life difficult. With all the wisdom of her twenty-two years, Siphokazi describes it in a very explicit way: "For my future? I want a lot. . . . A lot, a lot. I want to go back to school, first. . . . I want to go to the university. I want my own house, my own car . . . have money . . . be able to help people. I want a lot for myself."

This hope, which at first glance contrasts with what day-to-day life is like, has already been noted in other research on the township youth (see Swartz 2010). It expresses a desire to belong to the "South African social body" despite adversity. Such confidence in the future seems to reflect the desire to cheat fate by exercising the control over one's own life that poor people cannot always aspire to (Swartz, Harding, and De Lannoy 2013, 32).

While a degree of optimism about what postapartheid society can offer is found relatively often in the lives of these young people, it is by no means naive. Most young UPM activists say, for example, that they do not recognize

A young resident of the Fingo Village neighborhood

themselves in the "cosmopolitan Johannesburg" image broadcast by the main media, especially in fictional depictions and TV shows that spotlight "Black middle-classes living happily." The more politicized of them interpret this type of situation in the light of a certain fascination for the West evinced by the South African media, to the detriment of an "African culture" despised by the elites.

At twenty-three, Ndisa, who studies human resources management at Port Elizabeth University (although his first wish was to be accepted in business management at Rhodes University, in Grahamstown), is also particularly eloquent on the "nepotism" and "corruption" that, she claims, foster incompetence in postapartheid society: "If you're educated, you won't have key positions because people know that you will see things and that you won't be a puppet," she told me in 2018. If she also believes it is difficult for a young Black woman to find a good job without having to rely on her charms, Ndisa still hopes to find a company, perhaps an international one, powerful enough to resist these contemporary problems. Perhaps she also needs to convince herself that uncertainty does not close off all possibilities. And isn't this what Bheki suggests when he tells me he is "still young" at twenty-eight, an age when he can see that things might yet improve?

Whether they are at university or college or enrolled in one of the high schools in the township, many of these young activists clearly place some of their expectations in study. Indeed, study seems to play a central role, even though the young people interviewed by Dawson were under no illusions and felt there was not even any point in obtaining the matriculation qualification in a context of high unemployment (2014, 870). Apart from potential family pressures, the importance given to education is certainly reinforced by the language used by several leaders of the movement who are always quick to encourage their young comrades to persevere on this path. The daughter of an activist who wants to get involved when she is only sixteen years old is told that she must first of all focus on her studies. The organization can sometimes suffer somewhat from these principled positions, as is highlighted by this brief anecdote that is supposed to convince me of the intransigence of Dumisa, the "granny" who led the movement in the middle of the 2010s. Ayanda recalled, "We had a meeting of youngsters from Phaphamani . . . in political education. And she arrived . . . and she told them to go back to school. She said: 'Stop with this political education, you must go back to school.' They were so offended [*laughs*] . . . and many youngsters have never returned."

The links that the organization maintains with Rhodes University teachers have sometimes helped young activists in their search for scholarships. The financial help of a professor close to the UPM even allowed one of them to improve the results of his "matric" in order to study philosophy at the university. The young man, who later benefited from a government loan and a room on campus, had lived until then in a shack without water or electricity, and thought that his poverty would make it impossible for him to pursue his studies.

In addition to these refusals to abandon certain aspirations, there is an element that should, in principle, protect the young UPM troops from the specter of waithood and the sense of social uselessness that accompanies it. First and foremost, the *désoeuvrement* sometimes felt by these young people seems to have dissipated as they decided in favor of full-time activism. The latter is indeed experienced as a structuring activity: "It's like a job . . . other than sitting at home. I took it as a job because it's better than sitting at home," Simthandile said. This situation sometimes means they can earn a few rand when the organization manages to attract funding. Simthandile and Siphokazi were able to glimpse this just before the European foundation stopped its funding and deprived them of the promised weekly stipend. Sometimes, too, a close acquaintance with certain researchers and teachers working on issues related to life in the township can result in small temporary salaries for assistants. Most of the time, this work is to help academics in conducting interviews or collecting data.

Beyond these legitimate pecuniary considerations, the choice of full-time activism obviously offers a purposeful temporality to those who embrace it. It seems to convince them that they are doing something, even if this "something" can take the form of days spent discussing many subjects other than the cause.[8] But—and perhaps most important—commitment can be especially meaningful to the extent that it allows these young people to experience (or, at least, to glimpse the possibility of) a type of responsibility specific to adulthood. Some of those who have just joined the movement are obviously already aware of this. While she had only really been active for six or seven months, Simthandile told to me one day that her membership in the protest movement was beginning to be known within her neighborhood, where she was already carrying out her first missions:

> "I do tell people about the meetings," she said.
> *"You do a report?"*
> "I do a report, yeah."
> *"Do your neighbors come to you when they have a problem?"*
> "No . . . not yet. In the future, maybe they will come . . . because I am planning to bring them. It's important to be that kind of people . . ."
> *"Why?"*
> "It's important because I'll be very useful . . . and helpful. I'll try to help them with . . . whatever they're facing challenges in the area."

In the same way, while Tshepo recognized that the youthful ages (twenty and sixteen, respectively) of his friend Luntu and himself meant they would not be taken seriously by their neighbors, he confided in me:

> People think we're children. That's normal. But come back in a year and you'll see . . . You'll see. People will change their minds . . . because the young

people in the community, they see that we are active . . . because we help them. Their parents . . . and the people in the community, they will know about it and they will come to us. They will change their minds. You'll see!

Tshepo went on to detail their various interventions in the life of the neighborhood: his plea on behalf of a comrade threatened with expulsion from school after losing his books, his friend's involvement in the fight against drugs, alcohol and cigarettes in his high school, their involvement in street cleaning "because the municipality does not do it," and so forth.

What Tshepo looks forward to—his forthcoming recognition as a "young pillar of the community"—is perfectly exemplified by Thabo. Perhaps, indeed, it was while I was first listening to this twenty-eight-year-old activist that I became aware of the impact that commitment could have on the daily lives of these young people. Late one afternoon in April, when we were in the city center, Thabo had asked me to take him home so he could pick up his jacket, which was essential for the part-time job he had just started. For a few weeks, and for just a few hours per week, he had been on night duty at the reception desk of one of the hotels in Grahamstown. Ten minutes later, I parked my car in front of the cinderblock house in which he lived with his parents and grandparents. It was built on the slopes of a tree-covered hill, Makana's Kop, just under two kilometers from the city center. This area, which some also refer to as Mount Zion, is regularly the scene of processions led by the many churches found in South Africa. One private foundation even considered building a statue of a gigantic Christ figure similar to the one that dominates Rio de Janeiro in Brazil. When I discovered this neighborhood of small houses with flat roofs, separated by iron wire fences, I questioned Thabo on the way he thought he was perceived here since he had joined the UPM two or three years earlier. His answer took the form of two short stories.

A few months earlier, a delegation of neighbors had knocked on his door. Several houses in the neighborhood had been deprived of water for a few weeks due to a failure in the hydraulic pumping device:

> They came to get me because they would never have complained to the municipality. They came to see me because they know that I am a member of the UPM and that I know how to talk with the municipality. They know that I will be listened to because I am educated and I know how to organize a march or a demonstration. And people know that I will make a report to the community.

A few "old women in tears" also came looking for him a few weeks later. In the absence of adequate sanitation, the municipality had installed mobile toilets in his neighborhood, which the technical teams were regularly late in emptying. Once again, members of the community decided to entrust him with the resolution of a problem which affected them and involved negotiating with the local political and administrative authorities. A public meeting was hurriedly organized. The ward councilor was invited. During the discussions, it was decided to call for a march on the town hall. On the day, dozens of people would take part in it. But above all, the young UPM activist and other residents had managed to convince their neighbors not to stop there. Arriving in front of the city's technical services department in central Grahamstown, the protesters managed to enter the building and occupied several offices. They came armed with a simple and unambiguous threat: they would leave the scene only once the authorities had made a commitment to remedy the problem that had brought them here. The technical services did indeed subsequently intervene.

These two episodes give some idea of the activist reputation of this young cadre from the Unemployed People's Movement. They say a lot about how he is perceived in his community and, more generally, what can be expected of him. His case is actually far from isolated and shows how commitment within a poor people's movement like the UPM can allow young activists to find a place in their neighborhood. For some, entry into the movement may also be accompanied by a form of education in the community and its values. Siphokazi acknowledges that before joining the UPM, she did not really listen to what was being said at community meetings. She just did not care. But things changed. She says she now needs "to know how things work in [her] community. Who's doing what? When?" For, she adds, "when you're with the UPM, you need to be aware of what's happening in the community in order to help people." The same goes for Thando, who adopted a rhythm of activity close to full-time activism as soon as he joined the organization:

Now . . . I pay more attention to my neighbors. It gives me another perspective. People come to me and now I can see that they do not have the same problems when they live in a shack or in a house. It makes you more conscious of what's going on, and I like that. I see things differently now.

Commitment can therefore be very revealing: it reveals the individual to himself or herself as needing to adopt new forms of behavior, but it also reveals the need for another relationship to the world, via the "discovery" of the community.

The case of Likhaya offers perhaps the best illustration of these transformations. He joined the UPM at twenty-one, just weeks after the murder of his older sister, and quickly became an assiduous activist. The murderer was actually a young man whom Likhaya and his sister had regularly met during their childhood and adolescence. The criminal investigation had been botched and the killer, just a few months after his crime, was about to be released on bail. This seemed to be the end of the matter, since Likhaya's mother did not have the money to pay for a lawyer who could appeal. The family was then approached by UPM activists and some members of Students for Social Justice who were soon able to mobilize opinion in the surrounding communities. They also tried to draw the attention of journalists from the local weekly newspaper to a situation that was sadly commonplace. A demonstration was finally organized outside the courthouse, just as magistrates were preparing to rule on the terms of bail. It is difficult to explain the turnaround that occurred then. According to Likhaya, the noise produced by the protesters was such that the lawyers were prevented from bringing the case to a conclusion.

Likhaya was not especially predisposed to join a protest collective. He himself said he had never been involved in political discussions during his teenage years, and his parents kept him away from them "for religious reasons." Most of his time was devoted to the Adventist Church at which he belonged. However, an emotional bond quickly developed between him and the leaders of the UPM, the only ones to have shown any concern for the fate of his family. One year after the events described, while we were talking in the premises of the movement, he returned in particular to the phase of the preparations for the demonstration in court. This time spent with activists had, according to him, gradually changed his vision of things. These women and men, whom he had only known for a few days, had convinced him that the murder of his sister was, above all, a symptom: the painful symptom of sexism, underdevelopment, and the persistence of poverty in some areas of the city. He had subsequently turned some of his anger on the living conditions in Zolani, the neighborhood where the shack without electricity and water that he had shared until then with his mother and two sisters was located:

> After the UPM came to me and helped me, my mind was open to see how important it is to work for the community. . . . I told myself that I should join this movement . . . to fight for the rights of those who are suffering . . . those who are affected by these afflictions . . . poverty, crime . . . all these problems in society.

Time has certainly helped Likhaya to rewrite his story a bit and to make his commitment seem consistent, even if this has happened unconsciously. We can also detect in these remarks the traces of a discourse of conversion, as the convergence between his deeply religious upbringing and his way of conceiving militancy seems obvious. As a devoutly practicing Adventist Christian, he claimed to see no difference between the social movement and the church: "They all do help people."

The weeks and months that followed this meeting with the collective seemed to reinforce this presentation of things: the young man quickly became a full-time activist and the main representative of the UPM in his community, as an organizer. His enthusiasm, however, could not hide certain dissonances. The fact that he rubbed shoulders daily with the most politicized members of a collective also fighting against sexism did not dissuade him, for example, from making openly homophobic remarks. At various times during our first conversations, he criticized "the State" for spreading "homosexuality and abortion."[9] He also showed no hostility to the African National Congress and never referred to the "socialism" and "anticapitalism" that so many of his comrades use to justify their commitment.

This tendency to ignore the more political and even ideological aspects of the UPM can probably be explained by a very religious education, marked by a drastic distance from politics. The changes that took place at the very heart of his life also probably played a part. On his own admission, Likhaya spent three years following the death of his sister wandering through a world without landmarks, losing sight of the importance of his studies. In these moments of deep doubt and uncertainty, the only stability seems to have come from his loyal commitment to the UPM and the role he subsequently played in his neighborhood. In a few months, he had become the go-to person during the floods that follow the heavy rains, when "water is coming into the houses and the houses are leaking." It is then necessary, with the "comrades," to make up for the weak responsiveness on the part of the municipality by evacuating the residents to a community hall, where "blankets, soup, and bread" are distributed to them. In the same way as Thabo, Likhaya has gradually taken on new responsibilities and, more generally, a new role within his community. These facts are a reminder that any institution—and the organizations of protest are no exception to this rule—largely draws "its 'power' from its ability to manage [the] identity constructions of [its members] with the help of more or less explicit models" (Dubar 1994, 227). In this case, this young member of the UPM has been invited to adjust to a role that is both rewarding and valued by local social life: that of "community activist." In some respects, what is at stake is nothing less than a social status in the informal neighborhood hierarchy. This status, like that of community leader (see Chapter 7), can be accompanied by a certain authority and recognition at the local level, while generating a certain responsibility for the expectations of the residents.

Another transformation has taken place over the years. At first, the young man merely wanted to see the community dimension of the Unemployed People's Movement, to the detriment of its more political charge. However, things have gradually evolved, in particular through the strengthening of his links with the movement's leaders. The discussions that we had five years after our first meeting are, on this point, quite convincing. Making many references to national political life and now presenting himself as a "socialist," Likhaya drew on a very precise and sophisticated discourse that allowed him to establish logical sequences and chains of meaning between the present living conditions of the poor, apartheid, and colonization. Surrounded by his "best friends" within the movement, the young man also felt that, without the UPM, he would certainly have been "singing in [his] church" and not "doing anything with [his] life."

The way Likhaya has changed in less than five years might seem surprising. It is not an exception, however. I can also observe it in other young activists, to varying degrees. In the first months of their commitment, almost all were reluctant to talk about politics and refused more generally to include the social movement in this register. Most of them, in fact, did not vote: "I was not a political person, I didn't do politics," Siphokazi felt obliged to point out. A few years later, however, we find that they show a greater ease in the handling of these issues and themes. In conversations, some even claim to support the Economic Freedom Fighters (EFF), a party created in

2013 and particularly popular with the youth of poor Black neighborhoods. Led by Julius Malema, a former leader of the ANC Youth League, the EFF has been able to develop in the social and symbolic field occupied by protest organizations since the end of the 1990s. They have developed a discourse that combines a call for an "economic war" against white capital with a demand for the right of Blacks to luxury and consumerist abundance historically reserved for the descendants of Europeans (see Posel 2010). A few months before the local elections of 2016, Thabo was, for his part, on his way to represent the United Front, the organization created two years earlier to embody a left-wing opposition to the ANC.

These cases confirm an obvious fact that it is always worth remembering: rubbing shoulders with politically well-trained activists (this is the case of certain leaders) places individuals in a privileged context of politicization. The daily activism characterizing this situation is also a way to access new skills, such as the ability to speak in public, to organize one's work or to speak to certain types of interlocutors: "I helped write letters to the municipality and other important places. Now I know how to do it," as Ndisa notes.

In a movement that is both politicized and rooted in the regime of the near, it also becomes more obvious that people will connect their daily lives

Sunday in the township

and those of their friends and relatives to a more general context, even to a worldview, as we can see from the example of Likhaya. Because it allows them to isolate possible causes, such a situation can give activists the feeling of better understanding their condition and thus being less passive in the face of events that threaten to overwhelm them. Social activism (practiced at different intensities) can therefore "change people" (Giugni and Grasso 2016, 100) somewhat or, at the very least, help to change certain attitudes and perceptions of things (on the biographical consequences of activism, see Fillieule and Neveu 2019).

Sometimes, too, activism plays a part in consolidating people's vocations. This is relatively obvious for Tshepo, Ndisa's brother. Raised in a family of ardent activists in AZAPO, a small pan-Africanist party, this young man of barely twenty, with a youthful and almost frail appearance, impresses with his determination and the seriousness with which he approaches and justifies his commitment.

When he was only ten years old, Tshepo was practically able to observe the birth of the movement in the living room of his house. As his mother was part of the UPM's first circle, it was indeed often at his home that the activists met to discuss the cause and the means of making it known in the township. Although, in the early years, his youthfulness limited his commitment to accompanying his mother and older sister to demonstrations, he subsequently asserted himself more individually in the UPM, attending political education workshops, for example, or spending time in the offices of the organization.

It was obviously not in the movement that this son of seasoned activists (his father was imprisoned under apartheid, and his mother was active in the AZAPO underground during the same period) encountered politics. Joining the UPM, however, allowed him to put his convictions into practice and give them shape, while adding a subversive dimension specific to the protest movement. He clearly states his desire to become a "fully revolutionary activist" after the studies he would like to undertake in political science ("because politics is my life"): "I want to continue helping people and . . . conscientizing people, solving their problems, showing them where to go . . . because a lot of people here are lost."

The process in which Salinda is engaged is a little different but suggests similar logics, including her way of assuming a vocation as "leader." Barely older than Tshepo, Salinda has thrown herself into UPM activities for almost three years. Still a high-school student during the first months of her membership, she went into the offices every afternoon after class. Obtaining her matriculation, however, allowed her to devote herself fully to it "from the morning to the afternoon."

Although originally from Grahamstown, Salinda spent part of her childhood and adolescence in Western Cape. As is sometimes the case in South Africa (Seekings 2008), her mother, without work and without a husband, entrusted her to her sister, who was financially better off. Her aunt's husband was a "big politician" in the small town where she lived then, so Salinda grew up in a more politicized environment than most young South Africans:

> He would take me to meetings, you know . . . to familiarize myself with the environment of a politician. . . . So he would take me there. I would never say that I am an ANC member but . . . I would listen as they talk. I would try to get into the conversations. . . . How the "big men" talk. . . . And I remember my aunt's husband read a book about how leaders have to be. When he was not at home, I would read it.

This relatively early exposure to politics shaped her desire to become committed. Returning to Grahamstown in her early teens, she first put it into practice in her school, as a student representative, and then in her community in Vukani, where she spent a while providing school support.

Her path crossed that of the UPM during her high school years, at a meeting organized by the movement a few months after the tragedy of Marikana. In August 2012, thirty-four striking miners were shot dead by police in the Pretoria region. The investigation that followed, though not without difficulty, had succeeded in bringing to light the economic interests of Cyril Ramaphosa, then vice president of the Republic of South Africa, in the company that owned these mines. This episode has had a lasting impact on the nongovernmental Left, which saw in it the most significant sign of the collusion between political elites and the most powerful economic interests. Spotted by the leaders of the movement when she contributed to the discussion, Salinda joined the UPM shortly after this information and discussion meeting.

Even though it ended in a brutal departure three years later, her time in the ranks of the protest organization seems to have served as an apprenticeship and a source of revelations for the young woman.

"As much as I left the UPM with . . . bitterness . . . but at the end of the day, UPM brought up another Salinda that, I didn't know, was there, in me. 'Cause when I joined the UPM, I didn't know there was . . . feminism. I didn't know that the power of men was also called patriarchy. I was just protesting but the idea of . . . of . . ."

She paused for a moment.

"Why they protest, what rights they have, why it is important for citizens to advocate for themselves . . . I didn't know and I thought: 'Okay, they're doing this because they don't like something.' But each and every day, within the UPM, we ever had meetings. Our minds were open. We talked about the political context, about what was happening in South Africa. . . . So I did learn something else. . . . Whatever I said, the UPM contributed to what I am," she said.

"You became more politicized?" I asked.

"More conscious . . ." she replied.

"And it helps you today?" I posited.

"Yes, 'cause today I'm able to lead people. Today I'm able to advocate for people. I remember . . . at one meeting of the movement that I joined [after I left the UPM] . . . the secretary was unavailable for that meeting, so I had to step in as the secretary. And when I took control, when the leaders like old people listened to me, I realized. I had to take leadership. I had to be a leader."

She paused again.

"As the meeting ended, a comrade came to me and said: 'You know, the kind of leader you are . . . imposing respect, fearless. It's a good thing. You're going somewhere.' It's what I learnt from the UPM: that you have to stand up for yourself. You can't sit in a meeting and let men talk about issues that affect women and let them decide, and just keep quiet. You have to say something," she added.

The presumably formative years that Salinda spent in the UPM also strengthened what is now her main ambition: to become a "professional activist." But her life has been turned upside down since she came of age. She gave birth to a little girl the year she turned nineteen and is raising her alone: "I am a mother and a father to my daughter. Her father is around, a student at a university, but yet there is not much that he is doing."

Although she can sometimes count on the help of her mother, with whom she still lives (with her younger sister), Salinda was thus soon forced to face the main inequalities that activism instils between the sexes. Admittedly, the UPM, which has a large number of female activists in its ranks, does not hold meetings after 5:00 p.m. A day in the life of a female resident in a poor South African neighborhood, however, does not start when she has to cook the meals. Most of these women are obviously in charge of household maintenance: childcare and cooking, of course, but also cleaning and gardening. Moreover, as Sarah Mosoetsa has very clearly shown, in social contexts strongly marked by AIDS, poverty and unemployment, they are also "seen as mothers of the community as well as of the household" (2011, 63). In many cases, they take care of older neighbors, help friends and relatives with money they receive from social grants, look after children other than their own, especially those who have been orphaned by the AIDS epidemic, and more. This may be especially true for UPM activists, who are often very active in their neighborhood, even when they are not community leaders. As a result, mothers are far less free to be activists than are men, even if the latter are fathers, though some women activists may take their children or young teenagers into offices and to public gatherings in the township. Conversely, I have never seen a male activist do the same. The various domestic burdens that these women regularly bear generally keep them away from the movement's premises. Few say they are full-time activists, and their number among UPM spokespersons is small, even if not totally nil. The profiles of those women who can claim such a status are still rather out of the ordinary. There is obviously the case of Gladys, the sexagenarian who lives alone, or Linda, who lives at her mother's with her children and can therefore break free of some of the constraints on her peers. The movement also officially follows a resolutely antisexist line, which is reflected in particular by the organization of public meetings to denounce patriarchy, sexual violence, and discrimination against LGBT people. The UPM is thus different from other South African protest organizations, which were sometimes accused of considering gender issues as a "Western import" (Pointer 2004, 277). None of this prevents the persistence of certain patriarchal representations in the functioning of the protest collective. This is true of the association between the feminine and the "private" space, the space of the home and the family—witness the fact that the women of the organization prepare the food at the meals that sometimes close the main internal meetings. Inequalities between the sexes also regularly overlap with other forms of domination, such as those characterizing the relationships between generations and between classes. When they proposed organizing workshops on the most political dimensions of feminism, Salinda and two other young women activists were belittled in no uncertain terms by one of the male leaders. In his view, it went without saying that only academics close to the movement could discuss such topics with seriousness and competence. It is not unlikely that this rejection was also used to bully young women who were sometimes viewed as too independent.

The presence of several young mothers, often single, has led to ways being found to accommodate these inequalities. These young female activists, including Salinda, joined the Women's Forum of the UPM that had somewhat fallen into abeyance when its main organizer suffered a nervous breakdown in the early 2010s. Renamed the Young Women's Forum, the structure has gradually evolved into a separate space within the Grahamstown unemployed movement: "a safe space where women could discuss anything," as Salinda, who became one of its main organizers, calls it. I myself have witnessed this atmosphere of camaraderie and trust. On two occasions, arriving at the UPM premises at the end of a meeting, I was able to observe the laughter, the sharing of the dishes of meat and potatoes prepared by a few women, and the songs sung by the fifteen or so women at the gathering.

Initially conceived to promote initiatives for the benefit of the township female residents, the forum quickly became a place of learning, exchange, and support between activists. Said one:

> I remember our first rape case. We had no idea what to do or how to respond. . . . We took that as a learning method where we went all out to make sure the women who come to us for support would receive the best support from people who are trained for such incidents. We partnered up with relevant stakeholders to make sure everyone would be supported emotionally. We would go to police station to make sure such cases are followed up and the perpetrators are punished.

As happened at other times in women's movements (Staggenborg 1998, 127–130), a kind of "caring community" was gradually created, whose task was as much to enable everyone to get involved as to provide collective support to the female inhabitants of the township. The meetings, open only to women in the movement, were opportunities to reflect, among other things, on what it meant to be a twenty-year-old mother in the township. The female participants were most often accompanied by their children so that, as one of them said, they could be "mothers while being activists at the same time." Indeed, Salinda soon decided to keep her daughter at her side at these meetings and various workshops "as a way of teaching her." Such intimacy between women inevitably liberated speech, whether on the sexual harassment that some of them experienced in their private lives or the sexist remarks and attitudes of certain male comrades within the movement itself. This group made it possible to collectively grasp the gap, long since demonstrated by the social sciences (see, among others, Evans 1979), between the egalitarian ideals of an organization and the reality of its internal relations. It was also in this forum that Salinda first heard about feminism and patriarchy, terms that, she recalled, were new to her, even though she "knew exactly what they meant in reality." A few months after our first meeting, I began to exchange a few emails with her in order to keep abreast of her progress. One of her first messages told me that she had just become the youngest local councilor in the country. She now represented the Economic Freedom Fighters on the city's municipal council. Since the beginning of the 2020s, each of her emails had under its signature a sentence from Thomas Sankara, the socialist and pan-Africanist president of Burkina Faso, assassinated in 1987: "There's no true social revolution without the liberation of women; the revolution and women's liberation go together." These few words quite perfectly capture the approach of Salinda and her female comrades within the Forum: what they defended in it should not be dissociated from the more general fight of the UPM against poor living conditions in the township. As Salinda recalled in an email to me:

[The forum] taught me that being a women is everyday activism where you constantly have to fight to be recognized and heard. Feminist struggle can be linked against the poor living conditions, you find that those who suffer from the poor living conditions are women that are oppressed by society where they are limited to live and sustain their livelihoods. A woman will be expected to stay at home, give birth and do chores because as a woman you are expected to create a home for a man/family, because of our society which prefers a man to bring about change undermining a woman. Even when you identify yourself as a Feminist, the community will say you are not respecting culture which puts men first, the same culture that will promote decision makers as men.

What Salinda says goes to confirm how poverty is both a total and a relatively multiple experience. Beyond lack and need, common to all, what the women of the forum endure, just like those of the township, is rather different from what someone like Arthur, for example, experiences. The daily life of the latter is, in fact, above all marked by this crisis of social reproduction to which young Black men in poor neighborhoods are said to be exposed. The same difference could be observed with the situation of a father like Melekile, who seems above all to experience poverty as a threat to his masculinity: he remains convinced he will lose the respect of his wife and children if he is not able to "put something on the table" (see Chapter 4). Approaching the protest by examining "the near" therefore highlights the fact that one and the same cause aggregates ways of knowing and incorporating the social world that are significantly different from each other because they are shaped by the dynamics of gender and/or generation.

I have already had occasion to discuss Salinda's departure after a dispute over the interruption of a stipend (see Chapter 3). However, it is not certain that this arbitrary decision, taken by one of the leaders, was the main cause of the break between the young woman and the rest of the organization. The qualities that Salinda recognizes in herself ("imposing respect," "fearless," and so on), qualities that those familiar with her can quite easily confirm, had probably irritated some within the movement. One of her former comrades had described her to me as a "problem person." It seems to me that her commitment mainly highlighted character traits that neutralized traditional assignments of gender and age. The activity of older women is frequently appreciated in light of qualities attached to their gendered role in the domestic sphere. More specifically, it is maternal qualities that are often highlighted, as when I am told that one woman is "very kind-hearted" and another is "gentle and knows how to listen to people." It is different for many female activists of Salinda's generation, determined to challenge the norms and constraints weighing on women. Thus, while deploying many glamorous poses in the photos of her Facebook profile, Salinda has shown entrepreneurial qualities in her daily life and within the movement; qualities usually associated with the masculine, far removed from the stereotypes that crush poor single mothers. These characteristics, but also her outspokenness, her ambition and, more generally, the fact she was not intimidated by men despite her youthful age likely set her at odds in a collective where sexism was not totally eliminated by an official discourse denouncing patriarchy.

Her departure from the UPM, however, did not undermine Salinda's taste for activism. It is easy to understand, while listening to her, how much activism is now part of a carefully considered project to which most of her energy is devoted. She has also put her studies on a back burner; in any case, they are mortgaged by medium-term financial imperatives. Recognizing that legitimacy within the world of social activism depends first and foremost on a "local background," she and two other former UPM activists have set about founding an association to help Black women in Grahamstown. The project has been compelling enough to grab the attention of a structure that gives financial support to South African social activists. At the same time, Salinda has taken on responsibilities in a nationwide collective specializing in land claims, an issue that has become increasingly central to political debate in the 2010s. Salinda's commitment to professionalization, which she fully assumes in an environment that still swears by volunteering, has in particular led her to apply—successfully—for a training program for promising social activists. The organization in charge of it aims to foster the emergence of a "network of young leaders" in South Africa. Salinda expects this experience, which will involve her staying in Johannesburg, far from her daughter, to "build [her] as a leader," as she says. She can, more concretely, hope to acquire more formal skills in setting up projects and to be offered the opportunity to develop her social capital by approaching new activist circles.

In a context marked by high unemployment and often difficult living conditions, the examples of Salinda, Likhaya, Thabo, Simthandile, and their peers suggest that commitment to a movement like the UPM can help people escape boredom and helplessness. It is not limited to that, however. It also has socializing and educational effects, and can give rise to a certain self-esteem. These benefits are in fact relatively frequent in the movements of the "poor," the "subaltern" or the "dominated" (see, among others, Lazar

2017; Fernandes 2010). These rewards of activism (Gaxie 1977) therefore enable the organization, be it a political, trade union, or protest movement, to assert itself as a place of sociability and inclusion.

If we outline an anthropology of youth activism by apprehending it in some of the nodes of social relations that extend across neighborhoods, however, we can go a little further. This approach highlights how these phenomena can go beyond the organizational framework and influence other segments of social life. The commitment of young activists of the UPM allows them to find a place they consider useful, valued, and valorizing in that social order in itself, the community.

Finally, the example of Thabo makes it possible to show that the tasks which the activist performs at the heart of his or her community are frequently supplemented by mediations with groups and institutions that do not belong to the worlds of the township. Far from the "radical" posture with which it is often associated by some observers, the movement maintains relatively diverse relations with the "outside." This is explored in more detail in Chapter 9.

9

THE COMMUNITY, THE MOVEMENT, AND THE "OUTSIDE WORLD"

"Hurry up!" This morning, yet again, I am hot on the heels of Ayanda without really understanding what his plans are. We met in the UPM offices and then walked straight to the city hall. On the way, he tells me about the organization of a meeting dedicated to the fight against sexism and cases of rape—those rapes perpetrated both in the township and on campus, and which students have been demonstrating about for almost a week now. As always, the trip, which lasts less than five minutes, is punctuated by handshakes and greetings exchanged across the road. We finally arrive at the city hall, and I realize that he wants to reserve one of the rooms in the building so that the Young Women's Forum, the women's organization affiliated to the UPM, and a group of female students can hold a workshop on sexual violence open to all women in the town. We pass one counter, then another. We go through a few rooms whose rather denuded aesthetic reminds me of a series of photographs taken by David Goldblatt in the early 2000s (2005). After photographing apartheid for nearly four decades, Goldblatt undertook to explore the "new" South Africa. An abandoned mill and mineshaft, stacks of cement slabs destined to become townhouses in a suburb of Johannesburg, an isolated billboard stuck in the middle of a vacant lot but announcing the construction of "Tuscan styled villas"—the images of this odyssey testified to a transition whose shape was as yet uncertain. Some pictures also displayed local government in all its banality. Subtitled "Municipal People," these photos showed almost empty offices, floors covered with dingy carpets, walls that were bare or decorated with nothing other than a portrait of the South African President. The furniture was kept to a strict minimum.

A table and some chairs. A rack cabinet, sometimes. At the heart of this destitution, there were mostly women and men who, frozen at their posts behind a desk or in the middle of a room, gazed at the lens with cautious restraint.

Ayanda speaks to his interlocutors in a mixture of Xhosa and English. Room reservations are actually made in another building, a hundred meters away. On leaving, we meet Thabo, who is deep in discussion with a group of about fifteen individuals. They are gathered on the pavement, not far from the main entrance to the city hall. The young activist goes into more detail with two of these people, who have left the group so that their discussion won't be completely drowned out by the songs that their friends have started singing. Two or three of them also strike up a rather static *toyi toyi*. Ayanda's attention is clearly captured. He walks over to the group and tries to understand what's going on. Thabo yields his place to him and comes across to me. He tells me what the problem is. These women and men are workers who have been hired by a local company to work on a stretch of the N2 road that runs past Grahamstown. They were due to start work in a week, but they have just learned that their contracts have been cancelled, the company having enlisted the services of other residents. The explanation for this turnaround is quite simple: the municipality had apparently forced the contractor, deemed to be close to the ANC, to engage party activists. I am already aware how commonplace this practice has become, and I have no trouble believing Thabo, who also tells me that he does not know these people personally ("A few, by sight, maybe"). These women and men seem, however, to be totally relying on Ayanda. The latter is determined to take matters into his own hands: he invites some demonstrators to follow him into the UPM offices. He plans to telephone the local councilor who announced the cancellation of their contracts and presumably supervised the selection of the new workers. After a few minutes on the phone, the activist is forced to admit that the elected representative is unreachable. There follow exchanges with the man leading the delegation of the ex-contractual workers. A solution seems to be found: advice will be sought from the legal center whose offices are not far away. So we set off. On the way, Ayanda even believes he is in a position to say that "the center will take care of the case."

The days that followed this meeting were marked by regular round trips between McDonald Street, where the UPM offices are located, and High Street, which the house containing the legal center looks onto. I would learn later that lawyers from this structure eventually telephoned the contractor to remind him of his contractual obligations. Fearing prosecution, he preferred to engage again the women and men whose services had initially been retained.

We find, in this example, the way the movement claims to take in hand a range of the community's interests. In seeking to help the workers cheated of a job, the UPM activists were mainly attacking a system they consider a threat to community cohesion—a socioeconomic system built on nepotism and patronage, which excludes those who have not gained access to the circles that form around local political leaders.

Opportunities to denounce this system and expose it in broad daylight are not lacking. One afternoon two years later, the UPM gathered more than fifty people to prevent work being carried out on the highway in the town center. At first, the rumor had been that the jobs generated by such a project had been given to residents of Port Elizabeth. The reality, however, had become clearer as the hours passed. The workers were indeed from Grahamstown, but their recruitment had been entrusted to councilors and members of ward committees who were obviously inclined to favor their relatives. "That's why the same people get employed on projects every time," said one of the spokespersons of the UPM to local journalists who had come to see the demonstration.

The UPM favored the path of protest in this case by organizing a noisy demonstration that delayed the completion of work expected by a majority of Grahamstown residents, as a lawyer close to the movement told me. While the Unemployed People's Movement has cordial relations with other local associations, such as that of the predominantly white residents who regularly alert the public and the provincial government to the mismanagement of the town, it often tends to be perceived as too "radical" by some actors of "civil society." Jim, for example, is a fifty-something Coloured man employed by an organization that in the 1970s brought together white citizens opposed to the apartheid regime. Now transformed into a foundation, this structure has set up various social and educational programs that Jim is in charge of monitoring for the Grahamstown area. He helped create an ephemeral "civic forum" in which the UPM participated, and he also provides training for elected officials of the municipality. It is precisely this inability to compromise for which he criticizes the activists of the movement of the unemployed. In his view, they are too inclined to systematically denigrate the initiatives of the administrative and political authorities.

The observation of the edges of protest, however, suggests a more nuanced reality than that which Jim seems to perceive. The activists themselves seem anxious not to appear solely as expressing opposition and critique. The consequences of the demonstration against the roadworks have also confirmed the nuanced positioning of the movement. The success of the event, images of which were used by the local newspaper, forced the municipality to negotiate directly with the protesters. The next day, the interim municipal manager, renowned for his independence from the local interests of the ANC, went to the movement's offices to hear their demands and to insure, in return, that the demonstrations were suspended. The informal and improvised nature of the encounter, but also its outcome, thus seemed to test Chatterjee's analysis according to which rulers and marginalized populations can sometimes negotiate "not within the framework of stable constitutionally defined rights and laws, but rather through temporary, contextual and unstable arrangements" (Chatterjee 2008, 57). The official promised to return the following week with specific information on how the workers had been recruited. For their part, the activists mainly won the chance to go back to the communities to establish a list of unemployed residents ready to work on the site.

The jobs in question are actually pretty basic. They involve taking up positions at either end of the construction site and waving red flags to warn motorists to slow down. The presence of workers and their machines is also indicated by safety signs, so these jobs may appear relatively superfluous. The leaders of the movement are not totally fooled: most concede that these jobs are neither "very useful" nor fulfilling. They do not require any special skills: "Everyone can wave a flag." It is likely that some of them also see it as a form of compensation, conceded by governments who have bid farewell to a society built on wage employment (see Ferguson 2015). These jobs, lasting a few weeks or a few months, seem to suggest a form of "redistribution by stealth."[1]

I was not in South Africa during these negotiations. Several activists simply explained to me that the list they gave to the municipal official was based on names provided by community leaders and also included those of the "ordinary people" who had taken part in the demonstration. Gradually, I realized that the relatives of some activists had also been employed, a situation that I had already observed two years before, after learning that Bheki had been hired by a construction company.

The movement, then, does not systematically adopt a contentious posture, even when faced with political or administrative authority. That it can become a negotiator is quite logical in that its primary objective is to obtain something from its interlocutors. It can also become an intermediary, as it has in fact done by going back to communities to propose candidates for jobs. This principle of intermediation, which accords here with the desire to set the UPM up as a "community-based organization," can be observed on a daily basis. It can take the form of the aid that activists provide for households intimidated by the language used by the administration, or with too incomplete a grasp of English to understand any kind of invoice or mail. Joseph, as we have seen, does not hesitate to accompany some of these people to the offices of the South Africa Social Security Agency (SASSA). He then helps them fill in the application forms for social grants and tries to negotiate with the agents of this organization when a problem arises. On these various occasions, the activists show an aptitude for dealing with the "outside," relying most often on knowledge and information (legal, administrative, etc.) that poor households rarely have access to. The knowledge mobilized can come from regular delving into the mysteries of the administration. Since 2009, the leaders of the UPM have learned to interact with the various departments of the municipality and to locate the office or the appropriate counter for an authorization to stage a demonstration or to call on these authorities to assume their responsibilities in a particular neighborhood plagued by lack of housing, water, and electricity. Some have also been able to attend workshops organized to this end by NGOs or foundations. Ndisa, for example, learned in them to "write letters to important places." So activists have assimilated certain rudiments of the language and logic of bureaucracy, and this can be made to bear fruit. Such knowledge can also come from the relationships, or even partnerships, that the organization forms with structures often identified with "civil society." One example is the well-known legal center to which Ayanda led the ousted workers. But we will come back to this.

On the occasions I have just mentioned, members of the Unemployed People's Movement thus come into contact with individuals, groups and institutions that appear to lie outside the township and its social life. However, it is necessary to use quotation marks when mentioning this "outside world." The formula would not make much sense if it only served to reinforce the representation of a completely hermetic separation between the Black lower-income neighborhoods and the rest of the world or, at least, the town. The township is not a closed universe. The "informal" economy that is developing there maintains relations with its formal counterpart. It would in fact be more accurate to write that "'formal' and 'informal' need to be seen as part of a continuum, or as interacting sets, each with high levels of heterogeneity in the nature of economic activity" (Valodia and Devey 2010, 22). Similarly, liberal democracy and the "popular politics" practiced by some people in the Black neighborhoods do not form two worlds that are all that foreign to each other (see Chapter 6). More generally, the collective isolation of many of the poorest residents does not prevent them from being in contact with certain segments of the state.

The idea that there may be an "outside world" beyond the township, however, has solid foundations. It feeds in particular on the representation of the world shared by many of its residents, a representation based on the aforementioned split between "them and us." I sometimes witness it directly when, in some Black neighborhoods, children begin to chant "*umlungu*"—"white person"—when they see me, and feign panic if I approach them. This division of the social world is partly sustained by the discourse on the "community"

Shop, Fingo Village neighborhood

that its self-proclaimed guardians deploy. It is obviously reinforced by the claim of collectives such as the UPM to be the spokespersons of the residents of the township vis-à-vis . . . the outside world.

However, as we have just briefly seen, these relations with the "outside" are far from homogeneous. Protest may leave room for negotiation or intermediation. Sometimes, too, the movement adapts its protest to the norms and practices of its adversary and/or interlocutor. The mobilization that took shape in Extension 7, in 2017, is quite a clear example of this.

Athandile lives in Extension 7. Originally from the Western Cape Province, this man in his thirties who most often conceals his dreadlocks under a cap, moved to Grahamstown in 2012, after the closure of the construction company for which he had worked until then. When he is not involved in activism, Athandile tries, year in, year out, to sell his skills as a "self-employed builder" to neighbors who want to build a wall around their house or add a new room. This will be an opportunity to enlist his brother and various unemployed relatives. Athandile's professional life is somewhat unpredictable. In particular, he feels that he is suffering from competition from foreigners, who are cheaper than their counterparts in South Africa.

Athandile joined the UPM in the months following his arrival in the town, after seeing the "adverts" put up by activists in various points of the township. He quickly became the main UPM representative in his neighborhood. His neighbors later chose him as a community leader, at a large gathering in the community hall. With this status, he was one of those who was quick to denounce the "lies" of the ward councilor. The latter had announced the destruction of an entire area of shacks prior—he had claimed—to their replacement by RDP houses. Habitually wary of the words of the elected official, Athandile undertook to discuss matters with the members of the ten or so residents' committees of Ward 11, where Extension 7 is located. According to him, the large number of ANC activists and supporters on these committees was not a problem, most of them being "tired" of broken promises. Some residents then decided to check up on the councilor's comments by directly consulting the municipality's IDP, the official document listing the town's development plans. They found that no such program was envisaged in their neighborhood.

Several community meetings, announced at door-to-door encounters, were then organized by Athandile and other community leaders. The aim was, of course, to explain to the population that it had, once again, been deceived by the councilor. The instigators of this nascent mobilization also went to the only meeting convened by the local politician, who was being increasingly pressed by the "ordinary" residents to explain himself. Athandile and his allies hoped to force him to recognize his contradictions; and, as the UPM activist acknowledges, they also sought to "disrupt" the rally. The councilor, however, had grown suspicious and saw to it that police officers were present.

After a mass meeting held in the lobby of a community clinic, and faced with a new refusal on the part of the elected official to come and take part in a debate, it was finally decided that the "community" would turn directly to the Speaker of the municipal council. The letter written on this occasion called for the organizing of a vote of no confidence in the ward councilor.

Athandile built his own house with his own hands. He lives there with his brother and mother, his young children having stayed with his ex-partner in the Western Cape. The building comprises two rooms made of cement blocks with rather summary cement joints. In one of these rooms, there is a cupboard in which the activist keeps the bundle of documents that this case produced over a few months. The cardboard folder he showed me one day contains a letter headed "Residents of ward 11" addressed to the speaker of the municipal council. The letter begins by noting the repeated requests of the residents to get the local councilor to come and explain himself. There follows a list of about ten grievances which, according to the writers of the letter, justify the way people have "overwhelmingly voted against [him] continuing to [their] ward councillor." As might well be expected, this list gives pride of place to the corruption apparently demonstrated by this official, by reserving jobs, food parcels, scholarships, and "so forth" to "his twin brother and those close to [him]." But it is above all a defense of the representative function that is outlined in the course of this letter. This man is mainly reproached for his "general incapacity to carry out his responsibility as a ward councillor." He is accused, for example, of having failed in his duty to inform and consult the residents. He also failed to respect the commitments made under the IDP (including the suppression of the bucket system in some neighborhoods), accentuating the "lack of development in the ward." Finally, his "inability to interact with people" apparently led him to hit or insult those who challenged him.

Athandile has also kept the letter acknowledging receipt of the previous letter by the Office of the Speaker. Subsequently, the latter said he had never received anything. He never came to talk with the residents anyway, even though he promised to do so three times. After describing the growing discontent of his neighbors, Athandile finally handed me a form that he had completed a few months before to organize a demonstration in the town center. Noting the lack of reaction from the municipality, the "community" had decided to go directly to the mayor with a petition asking for the dismissal of the local politician. As he had done in writing his letter to the speaker, Athandile had taken care to respect the proprieties. The form clearly indicated the route, the names of the organizers ("Ext. 7 residents + UPM"), as well as the sequence of operations ("We meet at 11.00. We hand over memorandum at 14.00"). To the question "What steps will be taken by the applicant(s) to ensure an orderly and peaceful gathering/procession?" he had laconically answered, "Training of marshals," visibly trusting to the experience of his UPM comrades.

The waves of protest experienced by South Africa since the beginning of the twenty-first century have often led to the demand for a "recall," which makes it possible for voters to oblige a local elected official to renounce his mandate. However, South Africa does not have this kind of legal mechanism. On the other hand, parties such as the ANC have occasionally withdrawn their mandates from councilors—sometimes because the latter were contested by the people, most often in order to suppress dissent. In this case, things are different in that Athandile and the community leaders of Ward 11 adjusted to the legal framework: the vote of no confidence they requested is an institutionalized option. They cast their protest in a mold, so to speak, shaped by law. Their criticisms of the local councilor's failures to meet his obligations even made them the unexpected defenders of representative institutions.

Adaptation to a legal and normative framework, as was the case in Extension 7 and on many other occasions in the history of the UPM, means there is no need to be limited to a protest register that the authorities have, in general, little difficulty in condemning and delegitimizing. This presence on the very ground of the adversary and/or interlocutor has sometimes been facilitated by outside support. Since the end of the 1990s, individuals and groups at the confluence of the academic, intellectual, and activist worlds have in fact been involved in the postapartheid social movement, providing it in turn with highly political arguments, material aid and social capital allowing them, among other things, to gain access to the pages of daily newspapers or money from foreign donors.[2] Committed in the early 2000s to a fight against the power cuts then affecting thousands of households in the great township of Johannesburg, the activists of the Soweto Electricity Crisis Committee (SECC) drew over a long period of time on work by a small group of experts, lawyers, academics, and independent researchers. Combining expert knowledge, statistics, and feedback collected by activists, the Municipal Services Project aimed to work toward the emergence of "alternatives to privatization and commodification" in the most essential public services (Fill-Flynn 2001). The studies conducted under its auspices thus pointed to the financial inability of a large number of households in Soweto to pay their electricity bills. By revealing how much these people were imprisoned in a spiral of arrears, these data thwarted criticism of the "bad payers" voiced by the authorities. In addition, they served to answer those who claimed there was a persistent "culture of nonpayment" inherited from the apartheid years, as Trevor Ngwane, one of the SECC figures, noted:

> It was immensely useful. In a number of ways. . . . It consolidated the allegiance, loyalty and commitment of SECC comrades who conducted the research. . . . And they would speak at mass meetings: "I thought I was poor but when I went house to house I knew I was a privileged person." . . . But it also authenticated our argument. . . . It helped to turn the SECC into a mass organisation. Because the first real mass meeting that we held was a report back on the research. You know usually we would hold meetings in different townships, and with the research we called the whole community to a meeting. And said "Hey, we have just done some research. Look, they are lying when they are saying we don't want to pay . . ." And from that day the SECC has never been the same. (Quoted in McInnes 2006, 84)

Of the various bodies working regularly alongside the protest collectives, the group composed by legal specialists was among the most active from the middle of the 2000s onward. In parallel with the carrying out of more or less subversive and illegal actions by the organizations, the help of these experts consisted in a *judicialization* of the case (when it is shaped in the language of law) leading quite frequently to its *juridicalization* (when it comes to court). In Johannesburg, Cape Town, and Durban, activists and lawyers collaborated to bring before the courts such matters as evictions, destruction of encampments, forced installation of prepaid water meters, and delays in construction of homes for disadvantaged households. The challenge, in the medium term, lay in contributing to the formulation of a jurisprudence likely to reveal and to affirm, with the force of res judicata, the Constitution's potential in terms of social and economic rights (see Tournadre 2018, 132–141). This rapprochement has not been self-evident, however: many activists consider the law as an instrument of oppression in the service of the powerful—a "paper apartheid," to use the explicit formula of one of the protest leaders in Cape Town. In their eyes, it was synonymous with eviction orders or the payment of bail to free their comrades after demonstrations.

The relationship between the governed and the law is, to be sure, a fundamental question, one that goes beyond South Africa alone. It is certainly just as fundamental as the question of political representation. The way it is treated also contributes to assessing the "success" of a young democracy. It sanctions the entry into a state respectful of the law in general and of the rights of citizens in particular. The relationship of the poorest to the law or, more generally, to the legal system, has a history. In his discussion of the Black Act passed in 1723 by the British Parliament to fight poachers, the historian Edward P. Thompson, for example, clearly showed how much the law was subsequently both an instrument for the defense of private property and a means to mediate existent class relations "through legal forms, which imposed, again and again, inhibitions upon the actions of the rulers" (1975, 264). If we follow Thompson's demonstration, the so-called subaltern, the dominated, or, more simply, the poor, can potentially take advantage of the law, even in the face of the body that uses that law as its privileged language, that is, the State. The development of what has been called "cause lawyering" (see Sarrat and Scheingold 1998) tends to confirm this. This use of legal skills, which seeks to promote social change by supporting the poorest and the oppressed, has often turned the power of the law against the dominant. This was, for example, the case of the fight against racial segregation in the United States, as crystallized in particular by the Supreme Court's judgment in *Brown v. Board of Education* (1954). In South Africa, there was no lack of legal professionals working alongside the weakest, before and after the end of apartheid. It is to this category that the legal center to which Ayanda led the workers of the N2 belongs.

Founded in the late 1970s by a handful of white lawyers opposed to the regime's racist policy, this independent center is a nonprofit public interest law clinic with representation in several South African cities. It is part of a galaxy of associations and organizations that emerged under apartheid or in the early days of democracy, working for the development of human and social-economic rights. In everyday life, the employees of this legal center, as one lawyer told me, intervene on "basic issues," in order to "force the administration to do what it is supposed to do." Among other things, they can be asked to help when schools—most often located in townships or in rural areas—do not have the most essential supplies or when the government is slow to replace an absent teacher.

In Grahamstown, these jurists have settled in a small Victorian-style house, equidistant from the Cathedral and the buildings of the university presidency. The long entrance hall serves as a waiting room and is almost always occupied by Black and visibly poor women and men. They come to seek help when their benefit has been suspended or to obtain legal advice, as the posters on the walls invite them to do. UPM activists have gotten into the habit of crossing this hall without delay, in order to directly knock on the door of the officials responsible for Grahamstown. They do so whenever a legal problem arises. This was the case when the workers were sacked or, a few weeks later, when three Black students were threatened with exclusion by the university presidency for their participation in violent protests against rape on campus. At the end of the 2010s, in a national context marked by the land redistribution debate, I also regularly saw two or three of the activists accompany farm workers in conflict with their employers, or families in the process of being expelled from the farm where they had been living, sometimes for years. On these occasions, the members of the UPM fully assume their role as intermediaries between the Black and poor people seeking their help (whether they live in the township or in the surrounding farms) and lawyers and legal experts. The Centre is thus useful to the cause and to the high profile of the protest movement in the Grahamstown social landscape: it provides access to free information and support (especially when activists are arrested by the police) and allows the movement to provide a service to those populations which it is constantly seeking to address.

Activists are not present only when a connection is being made with the center. They also follow developments in the case. When it came to the three female students, UPM members, some of the youngest who had participated in the protest against sexual violence, accompanied the young women to the Centre. They then facilitated the organization of a meeting at which the students were able to explain their situation to lawyers. In the days that followed, the relationships between the lawyers and the students were literally mediated by the UPM leaders. Since they went several times a day to the premises of the Centre, it was they who transmitted the lawyers' advice to the three young women, still busy with their action; and it was they too who kept the legal professionals informed of developments by providing copies of the summonses sent by the university presidency.

Beyond these "ad hoc cases," the UPM has also collaborated with the Centre in broader ways. Noting that the demonstrations were not enough to get the municipality to grant what they were demanding, the activists entrusted the lawyers with the development of a "legal strategy" that could eventually lead them to defend their case before the High Court. Originally supporters of a "blowing all up strategy," as one lawyer put it, they were persuaded by legal experts to adopt a more modest but no less effective ambition: to attack the local government on specific points that laid bare its shortcomings, namely the regular overflowing of sewers, the lack of collection of household waste in certain neighborhoods, and so on.

The relation that UPM members may have with those who, outside the community, allow them to access certain resources is not, however, unilateral. An exchange is sometimes explicitly shaped. The movement can indeed appear as a point of entry or a guide to the "ground." This is true for a researcher such as myself, of course, but also for the members of the legal center. On several occasions, these lawyers have expected activists to assert themselves as "facilitators" by playing their role of "in-between." This happened, for example, in a case in line with the Centre's "cause lawyering" principles. It involved defending thirty poor households, the construction of whose houses had been suspended by the discovery of burials there. Activists had been tasked with calling a large public meeting to allow the jurists to share information and collect feedback. Even if it is organized at the request of a third party, such an event obviously serves the cause of the UPM, by giving it a chance to promote its proximity to a group of legal experts. This is all the truer in the face of populations that are very often unable to defend their rights due to lack of money or, more simply, because they do not know that they can at any time benefit from the advice of this legal clinic by going to the town center. One of the lawyers present at this meeting remembers having to deal with a large audience, asking him about problems that went beyond the scope of this single case. The members of the legal center needed the UPM again in the days that followed. Indeed, they entrusted activists with the responsibility of checking "on the ground" the veracity of the information collected. The women and men of the movement were mainly to visit those who, although concerned, had not bothered to go to the meeting. It was impossible for lawyers to reach these households by any other means.

This "give and take" relationship suggests that the protest movement's actions since 2009 have not frozen it into the image of a troublemaker or of radicalism. While it is not particularly representative of the links between the UPM and the legal center, one case helps to make this clear. The last months of the Zuma presidency were marked by the political opposition's desire to pass a motion of no confidence in this power weakened by corruption scandals. Faced with the refusal of the speaker of the National Assembly to organize a secret ballot, which would have meant ANC deputies hostile to the president need not fear reprisals, a parliamentary group took its case to court. This raised the possibility that individuals or groups would join the case, not as parties but as *amici curiae*. This procedure allows you to place yourself "on the court side" by providing information or expertise. Those in charge of the legal center saw this as an opportunity to intervene on a problem close to their hearts. However, they had to find a "front man" who could bring their arguments to the judge. They then thought of the UPM activists, who immediately agreed: "It was good for their profile. It didn't cost them anything. And they were in the newspaper," as one of these legal professionals concluded.

More generally, the UPM very often appears as a legitimate interlocutor in the eyes of those who are interested in the social worlds composing the township. One example is the center affiliated with the university and specializing in the assessment of public services. Its researchers have established partnerships on several occasions with the Unemployed People's Movement, most often to highlight the inconsistencies of municipal power. In the mid-2010s, the two organizations signed an open letter requesting the intervention of the Provincial Government. A few months later, the center's management sought to implement a project more directly oriented

A resident of Fingo Village neighborhood

toward the population of the township. The aim was mainly to teach the residents, especially the poorest, to exercise their right to "social account-ability." This project needed to be extended into the Black neighborhoods, and so the UPM quickly emerged as an ideal partner. Its members had to organize mass meetings delivering a certain amount of information on pub-lic services, and to collect, through questionnaires, residents' feedback in order to transmit it to the researchers. After training a small team of activ-ists in data collection, the program manager was able to access information that might well have been inaccessible to her in other circumstances. As for the protest movement, its role as the "voice" of the community, to use the formula in one of the documents produced by the university-based organization, was reinforced.[3] For a certain period of time, the UPM also had access to resources that may have seemed meager but were essential to the regular functioning of such a movement. The research center thus paid for the food shared at the end of the working meetings, but also certain transport costs, as well as the vouchers for the cell phones of the activists involved in the research. The UPM leaders also seized the opportunity of this rapprochement to relieve their movement of certain expenses, in particular those related to the printing of flyers announcing their own community meetings. However, their frequent visits for the sole purpose of using the photocopiers forced their partner to compose a memorandum of understanding setting precise limits to these requests.

The previous example highlights how links with relatively privileged individuals or groups can sometimes be a means to access resources that are more material, and thus more directly assimilated by the movement. The financial fragility of the organization requires its members to seize on if not create such opportunities. A few weeks after the closing of the National Arts Festival, Ayanda had asked me to accompany him to the Settlers Monument, where the organizers of the event have offices. As often, he left his intentions somewhat in the dark, until I realized that he was hoping to meet the main person in charge of the festival. For some reason that I still do not know, the latter had promised to pay the sum of R500 to the movement. Back in the car, and after having left his contact information with the assistant of the man he was in the end unable to meet, Ayanda had told me that this capital should allow the UPM to register with the administration and thus have a status facilitating the collection of donations and various sources of funding. The fact he had asked me for the same amount, and for the same reasons, a few days earlier, obviously did not seem to worry him.

These forms of imposed or constrained opportunism often give rise to a certain mistrust among those whom such opportunism targets. On a number of occasions, links with individuals or institutions seem to have been disrupted by overly regular requests, whether for money or repeated and free access to certain goods (computer equipment, photocopiers, etc.). This was the case with several researchers from the university-based organization, who became very annoyed at activists bursting into their offices, "without warning" and "often without much tact," as a center researcher told me, in order to make some photocopies or get money for a survey they did not always actually participate in. Perhaps I myself felt somewhat forced on the defensive when I was urged to invite two activists to France for the "launching of [my] book" or, on another occasion, when the question was raised whether "[my] students [were] from the middle class" and, therefore, likely to "fund a movement in South Africa." I know that the expectation of some form of compensation was being expressed here: I owe my thanks to the movement for the help I have received in conducting my research. I have no doubt, however, that I also appear as the representative of a "world of power and money, from which one can reap some advantages" (Cefaï 2003, 566). Without it being explicitly reported back to me, I also know that my closeness to certain people is interpreted by others as the result of cash donations of which the organization and these same people have obviously been deprived. The diverse nature of these requests (giving a few rand to pay for the bus, buying small pieces of equipment for the office, "lending" money to buy medicine, etc.) and their repetition over time suggest that every opportunity must be seized, even if it causes discomfort or arouses forms of exasperation among those who have to respond.

Such demands are a very simple way of underlining how activism has a financial cost, especially when it stems from a poor people's movement. The leaders of the UPM devote a significant part of their activity to raising money. The movement's inclusion in activist networks and a certain amount of friendly or political support have allowed its members to get in touch with Western foundations or NGOs wishing to finance the conduct of development projects "in communities." The protest movement then makes way for the community-based organization. The point is to prove that the presence of the collective in poor neighborhoods makes it the best way to encourage more widespread cultivation of individual vegetable gardens or to lead a campaign against domestic violence. Regularly, leaders also turn to individuals they know to be likely supporters of their cause. Emails are then sent out, describing the movement's latest disappointments, the cost of the actions envisaged and, inevitably, its compelling need for money. Some requests may obviously seem suspicious to people who are not familiar with life in the township. It is indeed sometimes difficult to know if they reflect the needs of the organization or those of the individuals who express them. There is nothing surprising about this, however, since activism in a poor people's movement like the UPM is constantly caught between these two worlds: that of the cause and that created by individual living conditions. One type of situation, which I have already mentioned, is quite revealing: if you live in the township, then attending a meeting organized on the campus, for example for the delivery of the results of a survey on which the movement has collaborated, usually involves traveling by minibus taxi. However, these transport costs are relatively high for people who sometimes have only a few dozen rand to ensure their daily existence. The equation we have already encountered resurfaces: "Do I use these R20 to take the taxi to the office, or do I use these R20 for bread?" It is understandable that activists are often concerned about who will defray these costs, which seem insignificant to some of their interlocutors.

In 2012, the mayor of Grahamstown suggested that UPM activists join certain ward committees, those structures designed to maintain contact between the population of a ward and the councilor. The offer had been rejected on the grounds that these bodies had been infiltrated by ANC activists, with the risk of "cooptation" by the authorities. The fact that the mayor actually made this suggestion and that the leaders of the movement studied it, however briefly, nevertheless underlines the diversity of positions within the protest collective. Far from being a permanent embodiment of popular discontent, its activists are involved in daily negotiations and intermediation *for* or *on behalf of* poor and Black households. This situation results in a twofold responsibility (toward the township residents on the one hand, and toward institutions and groups outside the life of the township on the other) and a regular testing of the UPM's claim to represent the poor in the town. It is also in this context that certain gaps become particularly visible between the needs and concerns of activists, who are, above all, the residents of deprived neighborhoods, and the way in which their interlocutors perceive them. Perhaps we can see this as the mark, among other things, of a broader phenomenon: the transformation of yesterday's racial segregation into social exclusion.

10

"YES, WE DO THE SAME THING"

The group of young people burst into the main room in Noluthando Hall, interrupting the man on the platform who was giving details of the water crisis that had been affecting different neighborhoods for several weeks to an audience of a few dozen people. What was originally meant to be an information meeting turned to fisticuffs. The police were slow to intervene and, amid insults, cries, and threats of blows, a familiar theme resurfaced: that of the "counterrevolutionary plot." At first the disrupters, members of the ANC Youth League, took to task the UPM activists who had called this rally. Their hostility was particularly focused on Lizeka, who a few minutes previously had been describing her daily life in Vukani, a poor neighborhood where water cuts are commonplace: "Lies!"

Then it was the turn of academics, invited by the unemployed to share their expertise. The director of the Rhodes University Water Research Centre was the first in line, with young activists presenting him as a member of the Democratic Alliance and, above all, as one of the donors of the Afrikaner Weerstandsbeweging (AWB), a white neo-Nazi supremacist group. Also in the room, another professor, notoriously close to the UPM, was accused of paying no less than R15 million to one of the leaders of the movement. More serious was the accusation that all of them, organizers as well as guests, were pursuing a single goal through this meeting, that of destabilizing the Black neighborhoods a few months before local elections. And the young people from the African National Congress claimed that *they* were "community members" able to provide solutions to the lack of water in poor neighborhoods.

Such an episode is not isolated in the recent history of the UPM, nor in that of postapartheid social protest. At other times, in other neighborhoods, in other cities, ruling party members have sought to intimidate protest activists or dissuade residents from following them. This hostility, however, has not always been appropriate in Grahamstown. In the first months, the creation of an association based on the fight against poor living conditions had not seemed to attract the attention of local ANC leaders. Some ANC activists were, it is true, among the founding members of the Unemployed People's Movement and had taken care to reassure them. Zache, one of the first to foster the idea of such an organization, had been active in the ANC since his teens. He remembers going to talk to his party mates to explain what the UPM would be like and suggest that they "work together": "Some of them were part of our meetings . . . and they approved the UPM."

However, things changed rapidly. The breaking point seems to have been the invitation sent by UPM members to some of the figures of postapartheid social protest. In the early 2010s, one of the leaders of the Soweto Electricity Crisis Committee (SECC, Johannesburg) and those of Abahlali baseMjondolo (Durban) came to Grahamstown to share their experiences, including resistance to the measures decided by the government. In the eyes of the ANC members, the Unemployed People's Movement then became "problematic," according to Zache: "They started to say, 'No, no, no . . . we don't want those social movements. They're coming with problems. We won't accept a social movement.' That's what they said . . . but we decided to continue."

The intimidation of UPM activists probably reflects much of the ANC's relationship to contemporary South African society. The anthropologist Judith Hayem has offered a compelling analysis of this in an article about the tragedy of Marikana (2014), which saw thirty-six striking miners fall beneath the bullets of the police in August 2012 (see Alexander et al. 2012; Sinwell 2016). Contrary to readings that locate this repression at the convergence of political and capitalistic interests (the then–vice president of the republic, Cyril Ramaphosa, had invested in the mining consortium and is said to have personally requested the intervention of the police), Hayem argues that the government first intervened to overcome "the refusal of the miners to be represented by official intermediaries." These workers had emancipated themselves from the leaders of the National Union of Mineworkers

(NUM). In doing so, they had broken with one of the components of the Congress of South African Trade Unions (COSATU), the main ally of the ANC from the mid-1980s. The strikers thus decided to go for an "autonomous but organized expression," addressing the management of the mine in their own name (Hayem 2014, 128). According to Hayem, this event, far from being isolated, provides us with information on a broader phenomenon: the emergence, in different contexts, of "alternative political forms to institutionalized and parliamentary representation." They express a protest that leaves "the authorities no more indifferent today than under apartheid" (129–130).

A number of things argue in favor of such an analysis. The regular criminalization of protest activists and the stifling of discordant voices in the government alliance confirm how much the majority party's leaders have often favored the erasure of dissent and anything that could give rise to competing options. In the early years of the twenty-first century, for example, some national ANC leaders took an active part in the creation of the National Association of People Living with HIV and AIDS (NAPWA). Such an undertaking probably had an ulterior motive: to diminish the influence of the Treatment Action Campaign (TAC), an organization that was highly critical of the management of the AIDS epidemic by President Mbeki. A few years later, UPM activists were able to witness this type of logic: they were approached by an emissary of Jacob Zuma, who suggested that they organize "events where Zuma could meet with the unemployed," as Lungile recalled. In particular, the meeting meant that activists learned about the imminent creation of a national unemployed organization to marginalize protest movements perceived as a "threat" by the ruling party.

The altercation at Grahamstown's Noluthando Hall, however, allows for other, more localized readings—though these do not contradict Judith Hayem's thesis. This moment of tension is indeed indicative of the rivalry between two groups regularly involved in the same segments of local social life—a rivalry that takes shape within the "community." As I have tried to show in the preceding pages, maintaining a presence in the neighborhoods is obviously the raison d'être of the activism deployed by members of the Unemployed People's Movement. It alone justifies their claim to form a "community-based organization" and largely forges their modes of action. But this connection with working-class and poor neighborhoods is also a component of party political activism, and even more so of the activism characteristic of the ANC. There is nothing illogical about this: many of the

"Do not throw away waste. Vote ANC."

ruling party's activists live in the Black lower-income districts and are involved in local social life. It is on this objective reality that their leaders have relied when emphasizing, from the first years of the democracy onward, the need to put down sustainable roots in communities. This strategy has justified the inclusion of local activists in the various community bodies created or desired by the state: community policing forums, ward committees, and those residents' committees to which the Zuma presidency has sought to give a new impetus. All in all, these orientations have often been read as attempts, often successful, to monitor communities: once one has become part of these bodies, it is undeniably easier to explain and justify the measures taken by the political authorities, to identify all those who could criticize them, and, more simply, to stifle any discussion. The activists who most regularly go to these meetings all describe the same situation. Said Tshepo, "It's always the same. When the ANC people are there, they don't stop talking. And when you want to ask a question or say something, they tell you 'No, no, this question doesn't interest the community, let's talk about this or that instead.' They neutralize people who want to be critical."

The 2010s saw these approaches become more diverse and nuanced. From the middle of this decade, the party also sought to capture community approval as an actual part of recruiting its own local cadres. In 2015, the *Mail & Guardian* revealed the development of a strategy to arrest the decline of the ANC vote in urban areas.[1] The journalists of this weekly paper mentioned the existence of an internal document suggesting that candidates be selected for local elections based on their "skills in local government," of course, but also on their "community popularity." By adopting such an approach, the ANC therefore allowed itself to recruit outside its organizational boundaries. One of the aims of such an option was, according to these well-informed journalists, to thwart the increasingly virulent criticism directed at ANC ward councilors in lower-income neighborhoods. They were regularly accused of incompetence and ignorance of the problems facing the residents they were supposed to represent. The approach described in this document certainly involved establishing, at the level of each ward, a committee for choosing the candidates finally selected, but it also meant organizing a confrontation with the population at a "community hall meeting." On the occasion of this gathering, and under the eyes of the residents, the applicants would be asked a question deemed essential by the authors of the document: "What do you do for this community?"

This search for a form of approval had actually been latent since the beginning of the 2010s. In April 2011, for example, just weeks before a relatively unpredictable municipal election, local leaders of the African National Congress organized a meeting in Grahamstown's Ward 10. It was the party's job to "present" to the population the candidate who would be standing under its aegis in this ward that its leaders thought seemed safe. Speaking to some forty residents, the candidate was quickly forced to respond to the distrust of his audience:

> We are not sending you to the council to sleep there. Councillors should not work for themselves and their families, but should understand that they were employed to work for the people. We will recall you if you do not do what we ask you to do.

He could not, at the same time, evade certain explicit requests:

> We have been complaining about houses for many years now. I have been living in a shack for 17 years. We'll be happy if you can look at this issue.[2]

It was therefore up to him to convince them that he would obviously act in the interests of the community, among other things by presenting it with the budget of the municipal council. This is not just a trivial matter: these few exchanges between the residents and the person who at that time appeared to them as their future elected representative shed light on two points. The first relates directly to the contrast previously mentioned between "invited space" and "invented space" (see Chapter 6). While this is an interesting contrast, especially for interpreting the motivations of the rulers when they accept the participation of the governed in a framework that they themselves have determined, it does not always reflect the complexity of the power relations that then take form. In any case, the course of this meeting convened by the ANC did not fully correspond to what its organizers had planned. They had obviously not anticipated the criticisms and unrest within the public—or not enough. This was a finding already established by Gillian Hart after observing open budget meetings in the city of Ladysmith:

> From one perspective these encounters between township residents and local state officials could be seen as key sites for the production of consent. Yet the critical intensity with which participants in the meetings held local officials' feet to the fire suggests that consent is conditional,

precarious, and must be constantly renewed and recreated. . . . What was happening in the Ladysmith open budget meetings, I suggest, was not just the production of trust or even consent, but intense plays of power in which the terms of consent were being renegotiated, along with a recreation of township dwellers' sense of themselves as political actors in relationship to elected officials as well as to local bureaucrats. (Hart 2002, 285)

The requests voiced by the residents in this ward of Grahamstown give us yet another glimpse into a very particular aspect of the way the African National Congress puts down roots in the communities. On a daily basis, this presence manifests itself through the informal socioeconomic system that ANC representatives have fashioned in the municipalities held by the party, that is, in most localities in the 2010s.[3] The local elections of August 2016 confirmed the electoral supremacy of "Mandela's party" in Grahamstown. Of the fourteen wards that make up the electoral territory of the Makana municipality, of which Grahamstown is the main locality, ten are held by the ANC, with the remaining four returning to the Democratic Alliance.[4] Such a situation naturally places these elected representatives, and sometimes even the representative branches, at the heart of a system of resources that is both connected with and parallel to the official exercise of power. The case of the residents who were recruited to work on the renovation of National Highway 2 and then dismissed after the intervention of a local elected representative in favor of his relatives, shows this clearly (see Chapter 9): proximity to the local representatives of the party in power facilitates access to certain goods, and in the first place to housing and jobs more or less under the influence of the sphere of local power. The functioning of municipalities is also affected by such a system. It is well established that the poor performance of many of them, especially in terms of service delivery, is the result of party political appointments made in disregard of the skills actually required (Powell 2012).

These relatively common situations show clearly how in many poor and working-class neighborhoods, the ANC can rightly claim to occupy an almost central position in local life, in close proximity to the residents. Several UPM activists, drawing on the idea that the townships remain loyal to those who have emancipated them, have often felt that this situation was more pronounced in the older neighborhoods of Grahamstown, where the party can count on the presence and unconditional support of older people.

ANC activists are said to be more active there than elsewhere, and they frequently resort to action to channel any discontent and ward off any hint of criticism leveled at the municipality. The misadventure met with by some UPM activists at the water briefing is now almost commonplace. According to some people, meetings of political parties other than the ANC are even unthinkable in certain neighborhoods. These meetings are systematically held under the threat of a noisy irruption of activists from the ruling party. Other means exist, more insidious and less frontal than the use of physical threats or insults. One need merely, for example, impose a prohibitive price on protesting activists who seek to obtain a meeting room within a community hall when such a place can usually be hired almost for free. Over the years, the leaders of the Unemployed People's Movement have learned from these various skirmishes and outbreaks of bullying. Bheki borrowed my notebook to sketch a map of the balance of power within the township. According to him, the actions of the unemployed movement were less common as they were more difficult to implement in Extension 6 or Joza. On the other hand, Phaphamani, Zolani, Xolani, Extension 10, Vukani, and Extension 7 were among the places where the UPM could "intervene" because the organization could count on the support of community leaders.

There is no lack of stories to illustrate this positional warfare. Some activists recount, often with amusement, the incredible conditions in which the first UPM meeting in Vukani took place in the early 2010s. On that day, the organization managed to attract a large number of residents from this outlying neighborhood. Standing in front of the crowd, the activists had taken it in turns to narrate the birth of the movement, the cause it represented and its first achievements. Very soon, however, they had to stop. As Ayanda told me:

The ANC planned to come and disrupt [the meeting]. We knew that. They tried to physically assault us. So we had to pretend as if we had guns [*laughs*]. But the community defended us. And the ANC people were chased from the meeting. The other meetings, they tried again to disrupt us. They came in numbers . . . from different parts of Grahamstown. But the community was standing with us.

There is, however, nothing stable or immutable about this division of the territory. Bheki, for example, lives with his partner and their baby in a relatively "young" (i.e., recently built) neighborhood, where the ANC local councilor has already been attacked by unhappy residents. If the young activist's community involvement in this area of some sixty households or so gives his organization a higher profile, he also knows that "women from the ANC" are increasingly seeking to gain a foothold there. Coming from neighboring districts, they "discreetly" invite women residents to meetings on topics they describe as "nonpolitical." The agenda is probably just as full as the gatherings organized by the UPM, as it discusses living conditions in this limbo of poverty. Only the conclusions differ, of course.

Whether through moving into committees and other community forums, or through the search for new "grassroots leaders," the African National Congress confirms that the "community" is a major context of legitimation—a legitimation that is, of course, based on *proximity*. It is difficult, obviously, not to see this as the mark of political strategies imposed by electoral competition. On the other hand, there are more objective realities that once again underline the link between this party and Black lower-income neighborhoods. The main factor ultimately involves the very nature of contemporary party political activism. The latter really took shape in the 1990s, following the legalization of parties that had been banned under apartheid. As the traces of this regime faded away from the country's legal and political landscape, ANC leaders regularly emphasized the importance of activist mobilizations, even claiming that the party was "a mass-based movement, responsible for mobilising all sectors of society and members of all communities to participate in a process of fundamental social change through self-emancipation."[5] Over the 2000s and 2010s, they regularly claimed they had between 500,000 and more than a million activists.

According to Kgalema Motlanthe, secretary general of the party at the beginning of the twenty-first century, the branch was to be "the primary vehicle for maintaining and enhancing the mass character of [the] movement."[6] The appeal to activists thus became a leitmotif. This was of course connected to election periods, when these women and men alternated community meetings and door-to-door encounters, but also to more targeted campaigns where they are called to take up community issues. Problem-solving can be as much about school renewal and waste collection as the fight against gentrification threatening the poorest residents of a Cape Town neighborhood. The topics discussed in the discussions within the branches also reflect this involvement in the daily life of the community, as shown by the survey conducted by Jacob Dlamini in one of the eleven ANC branches of Katlehong, near Johannesburg: "long-lasting bulbs, the Society for the Prevention of Cruelty to Animals, rubbish collection, rubble removal, [and] title deeds" provide the main themes for the discussions (Dlamini 2010, 194). ANC activists are also invited to help their neighbors on a daily basis, for instance in their administrative procedures. The party's local representations must thus become "centres of information for [the] people."[7] These injunctions and incentives have obviously not been without effect. They have gradually shaped activists' *ways of doing* and *ways of being*, although, at the same time, many internal reports have deplored the sluggishness of many branches.

Perhaps one can indeed perceive in these trends the persistent gleam of the heroic years of the United Democratic Front (UDF). This organization, some of whose leaders made their mark as those who would create the "new" South Africa from 1994 onward, orchestrated large swathes of the internal resistance to apartheid during the 1980s. It did so mainly through local activism and repeated demonstrations in communities. If the legacy of the UDF is only one aspect of the political culture associated with the ANC, this mixture of daily protest activities on "bread-and-butter issues" endowed a whole activist generation with certain dispositions and reflexes. It also marked the minds of the following generations. Fragments of this can be found at the very heart of the internal life of the party. In 2011, for example, this aspect of the ANC's political culture was perhaps not unrelated to the reaction to the decision of local leaders to dismiss an outgoing woman councilor in favor of another candidate in Ward 5 of Grahamstown. A petition was circulated, but the main opposition to this decision took the form of a march to Church Square in the city center. For this occasion, about sixty people, activists and residents, alternated *toyi toyi*, slogans denouncing oppression and freedom songs from the years of the fight against apartheid.[8] Such an episode certainly does not sum up contemporary political activism in South Africa, any more than that of the ANC. It does however show that the singularity of this activism lies in the way it is caught in a sort of tension between the current issues imposed by the exercise of liberal democracy and the persistence of *ways of doing* inherited from a time when "popular politics" limited the horizon of nonwhite populations.

Party political activism tackles issues that its counterpart in the protest movement is unfamiliar with, especially because the latter does not in principle aim at gaining access to political and/or administrative positions. However, the two forms of activism often overlap and compare themselves with each other. Also, many of the women and men who joined the Unemployed People's Movement did so after serving in a local chapter of the African National Congress, the Azanian People's Organization, or the Pan Africanist Congress.[9] A synchronicity of commitment can also be observed: several activists of the UPM, who admittedly do not always seem to be the most committed, also belong to the Congress of the People, the Democratic Alliance, or the Economic Freedom Fighters. Bongani talked about this in conversation with me:

> *"So you were a party activist?"*
> "No, no, I am still a party activist. I'm a DA activist."
> *"What are you doing as a DA activist? How would you define what you do?"*
> "Well . . . I try to organize people . . ."
> *"You call meetings?"*
> "Yes, I call meetings. I organize people . . . because I know how to. I go door-to-door. I try to explain . . . to explain to people why they have problems, you see? Because sometimes they don't know or they don't understand what's going on. Actually, that's it: I try to help people. I also have to be there when there's a problem," he said pensively.
> *"And . . . as a UPM activist? What do you do as a UPM activist?"*
> "Actually, it's kind of the same thing. You have to be with the people. Listen to them. Help them. Explain to them. You have to know how to organize them. Yeah, it's pretty much the same thing. I do the same."

These are questions that I systematically ask activists as soon as I learn about their past or current membership in the local branch of a political party. The answers are almost always the same. Like Bongani, most do not seem to see any significant differences between the tasks performed and the roles assumed within the district as a representative of a party or of the protest organization.

These answers help to explain the shifts from one activist world to another. Even if he does not use this term, Bongani is actually telling me about his "activist capital," that is, about those "apprenticeships conferred by activism . . . skills imported from outside, as well as those which are learned 'on the job.' . . . In other words, an activist capital that can be acquired—for the most part in the political field, where it is enhanced—but also transferred elsewhere in the case of an exit" (Matonti and Poupeau 2004, 7). It becomes conceivable and indeed easy to cross the borders separating the local party political world from that of the social movement, since the activist capital constituted in one is only subjected to a low exchange rate when it is converted into the other. This is clearly the case in South Africa, if you listen to Bongani and his comrades. The "exchange rate" is all the lower there since the *activist styles* (those sets of discourses, of ways of acting and of perceiving oneself) peculiar to each of these two worlds are very similar. In both cases (party political activism and the protest movement), the basic thing is that you stand out in your neighborhood as a partner likely to provide solutions to disputes between residents. It is also important to know how to unravel those "personal problems, problems with crime, problems in the house" that neighbors can bring to you, as Angela, a former ANC activist now working for the UPM, told me (see Chapter 7). Finally, you need to show that you can put the community on the alert. Therefore, moving from party political activism to the form of activism practiced in an organization like the UPM does not require relearning or acquiring new skills.

This is also true in other variations of local activism, and particularly in the activism embodied by the civics, those residents' associations that were particularly active in the last years of the apartheid regime. The Unemployed People's Movement, indeed, is not the only organization to claim the title of "watchdog" of the community. The Black neighborhoods of Grahamstown are also the theater of operations for activists from the South African National Civic Organization (SANCO), which has brought together a large number of civics across the country since 1992.

Because the civics sparked and then monitored much of the anti-apartheid protest at community level, and because they included a large number of ANC activists in their ranks, their national association emerged as "the little brother of the ANC" (Piper and Anciano 2015, 83). SANCO, however, fell apart in the 2000s, swept away by the twofold phenomenon of neutralization and downgrading that affected the world of protest as soon as democracy was established.[10] However, the organization can count on a few troops in Grahamstown which, like those of the UPM, operate in the same social environments as the majority of the city's Black residents.

This copresence and the way the causes defended by the two organizations map onto each other almost inevitably leads to rivalry—albeit one that social activists tend to deny. Some residents do, however, seem to perceive this competitiveness. For example, in June 2015, during the National Arts Festival, which annually attracts several thousand visitors to Grahamstown, a group of about thirty unemployed people threatened to disrupt cultural events if the organizers did not decide to hire local workers.[11] These unemployed women and men then met with SANCO and UPM officials in parallel, as if they wanted to exploit a competition that in fact led to two separate plans for demonstrations. However, a comparison between the two collectives is distorted by the closeness between the members and leaders of SANCO and those of the ANC. This proximity is perfectly summarized by the frequent situations in which a person may belong to the two organizations, both at national and local levels. The representatives of the political power have also regularly used the civics against those people active in social protest throughout the 2000s. In Cape Town, one of the ANC elected officials of Mandela Park acknowledged as much quite bluntly:

> [In] Mandela Park we managed to [launch] a structure of SANCO, which did not exist before. . . . Previously, they [didn't] want to see any structure, which is active in that particular area, except the anti-eviction.[12] But right now, we launched SANCO, and each and every weekend call mass meetings [that] a lot of people do attend. (Quoted in McKinley and Veriava 2005, 55)

In August 2014, making the most of this relationship, the chairman of the civics of Grahamstown could thus boast, in less than two weeks, of having obliged the town hall and its disaster management unit to relocate a bereaved, homeless family after their house had gone up in flames.

Municipalities and provincial executives have also regularly decided to legitimize this partner, for example by inviting its representatives to meetings related to living conditions in the poorest areas of the country, with a very high profile and a lot of publicity. The most egregious example remains, to date, the negotiations that led Eskom, the national electricity company, to clear the arrears of poor households in the Johannesburg area. In May 2003, representatives from this company, the Commission for Human Rights and SANCO reached an agreement under the auspices of the Minister of Public Enterprises, also a member of the SANCO management team. It was the spokesperson of the civics to whom the other parties gave the essential role in carrying out the arrangement, thus strengthening the organization in its self-proclaimed status of community advocate. As would be recognized later by some of those who took part in this setup, this was primarily meant to weaken the influence of two protest organizations then active in the townships of Johannesburg, the Soweto Electricity Crisis Committee (SECC) and the Anti-Privatisation Forum (APF). One provincial SANCO official was quite open about it:

> Credit goes to SANCO. . . . As a civic movement we grab those people that support Trevor [Ngwane, of the SECC], look at their issues, and actually change them. We can strategize. . . . Let the credit come to SANCO, and then SANCO will take the credit back to government. It is quite a nice ball game. . . . Whilst now we confront, they deliver. . . . You call a mass meeting, address the people, and say government has delivered. . . . That is how you deal with it. You actually strategically try to isolate them [SECC and others]. (Quoted in Zuern 2011, 155)

Such strategies, of course, are implemented in Grahamstown. A few months after the help given to the stricken family just mentioned, the municipal team asked local SANCO officials to join them at a meeting with officials from the provincial ministry in charge of informal housing areas. At the end of this meeting, ministry officials began to visit one of the city's shantytowns. This visit, in the presence of local journalists, was of course at the invitation of civic activists, and alongside them.

This type of situation is obviously not unambiguous. It places SANCO in a very difficult intermediate position: while the organization can point to its links with political power (and can thus emphasize the potential effectiveness of its interventions), the civics are still well established in communities whose poverty fills them with bitterness toward the ANC municipality. These awkward situations seem inevitably to be solved, it appears, by the regular presence of activists from the civic leading the protests, as in June 2015, in the Hlalani district. For a whole day, dozens of residents managed to block the main road through this area with burning tires. The SANCO activists present in the district, however, thought they had a solution likely to prevent the situation degenerating into a confrontation with the police. They called for a "peaceful" march to take them to the gates of the town hall. The demonstration, however, needed to be apolitical: "You can't politicize issues like water and sanitation" warned one of their leaders. He also took care to state that, if the need arose, the members of the civic

"A better life for all."

stood ready to help the municipality conduct an audit on the allocation of housing in the neighborhood.[13]

Whether or not they result from a form of ambiguity, these frequent stances inevitably expose themselves to criticism and some aspersions. "SANCO," one UPM activist told me one day, "they do their work, we do our work. We work for the community. They try to discipline the community."

Whatever the social activists say, the forms of activism of the civics and the UPM, like that of the ANC, are clearly not so compartmentalized at the local level. They take place along a continuum of collective commitments, alongside forms of action and intervention specific to community leaders. All these commitments are experienced as related to the community, a whole world of reference points, roles, and social landmarks. Perhaps it is this essential characteristic that, as the example of the Unemployed People's Movement strongly suggests, makes activism *in the community* both a set of activities and practices and a *social relation*. This relation is built on the sociability of daily life with all its vicissitudes, and on the repetition of common everyday interactions and experiences, far removed from the buzz of demonstrations. Thus, the activism of the unemployed and what it is supposed to produce—protest—are affected not only by the constraints and adjustments imposed by confrontation with the political authorities, but also by their most immediate social and physical environment. The activist style of UPM members is shaped by a cloud of relationships and expectations (and by the history of these relationships and expectations) that develop on the periphery of the space of protest in the strict sense of the term, that is, at a distance from the place where political power is encountered face to face. The activist's ways of being in his or her neighborhood are thus deeply marked by the models of the community activist. These are things that can be seen a little better when you walk along the edges of the protest.

EPILOGUE

He wasn't able to speak for long: just long enough, after he had pointed out the gap between the reality and the promises made regularly since 1994, to compare the ANC to a "gang of thieves" and to call on people to vote for the United Front (UF). Prevented from continuing by boos and insults from ANC and DA activists, Ayanda preferred to leave the platform set up in Zondani Hall. Five more debates followed, organized by local media as part of the 2016 municipal elections campaign.

Launched a few months earlier, the United Front was largely the creature of the National Union of Metalworkers of South Africa (NUMSA), excluded from the Congress of South African Trade Unions (COSATU) because of the growing hostility of its leaders to the ANC.[1] In the run-up to the elections, a handful of the most politically minded Unemployed People's Movement activists considered standing on the ticket of this "united front" which was then trying to bring the nongovernmental left together. Thabo thought about it, as did Andiswa in his neighborhood of Vukani. Ayanda certainly hesitated for a while, before finally abandoning the idea of launching himself into an election campaign. He was well aware of the divisions that, in previous elections, had split the movement. At the time, some activists had indeed believed they could be accepted as the candidates of parties opposed to the ANC in return for the votes that their membership of the UPM would bring in. Stormy internal debates had followed.

The risk was still there in 2016. In a second debate, Thabo had to defend the UF's proposals despite the whistles and boos of supporters of the Democratic Alliance (DA). Among the latter, dressed in the blue T-shirt of the opposition party, was a "granny" whose particular characteristic was that she was an activist in the ranks of the Unemployed People's Movement while also standing for the DA in Ward 10, in the very heart of the township.

These experiences reflect a more general movement, observable since the end of the 2000s, when some on the postapartheid social protest scene felt it necessary to breathe new life into the movement by venturing into the electoral arena. In Johannesburg, activists of the Soweto Electricity Crisis Committee took the plunge in the second half of the decade, while claiming to be operating in accordance with the values of the social movement (Tournadre 2018, 242–245). However, the structure created for this purpose, Operation Khanyisa Movement (OKM),[2] obtained only one seat on the municipal council in 2006. Admittedly, it kept this seat in 2011 but lost it five years later. It met with varying fortunes in other parts of South Africa. In East Rand, one of the regions comprising Gauteng Province, a handful of Anti-Privatisation Forum activists who had come together in an ad hoc structure, the Displaced Residents Association, had also stood for election in 2006, sending three of their members to the municipal council after the election. In Balfour, a small municipality in Mpumalanga province shaken by violent social conflicts, several social activists, defectors from the African National Congress (ANC) and the Pan Africanist Congress (PAC), as well as various religious leaders who had taken part in demonstrations, joined forces within the Socialist Civic Movement in 2011 and won two seats out of the twelve constituting the municipal council. The same year, the Mpumalanga Party won three of the thirty-two seats in the municipality of Marble Hall and, above all, twelve of the sixty seats in Groblersdal. The organization had emerged from the impetus created when the administrative attachment of certain communities to the poverty-stricken Limpopo Province was questioned.

Apart from this widely diverse spectrum of results, such initiatives gave rise to lively debate within the South African social movement, with some seeing them as a hijacking of the cause or as the risk of damaging the protest and its actors with practices and behaviors hitherto abhorred. Indeed, in 2012, one of the UPM's leaders summed up quite clearly what he thought was a "problem":

> You see, I met the people of the Mpumalanga Party. I have nothing against them but the problem is that they go to see people saying that if they vote for them, they'll build houses and roads. . . . But it's not true.

They won't be able to do it. . . . In the UPM, we try to make a politics of honesty. We expose, we show the limits.

The movements' leaders may be thinking, however, about a particular pitfall that it is less easy to admit. Shifts from the world of protest to the world of party politics are quite possible to envisage at the local level. On the other hand, converting the legitimacy achieved by the social movement into electoral terms is obviously less *mechanical*, as suggested by those mixed results. It is not self-evident that the capital of autochthony can bear fruit in the official political sphere, especially when the main adversary, the ANC, has privileged access to essential resources and long-term political capital.

At all events, the 2016 elections did not make it possible to verify this hypothesis in Grahamstown. The lack of financial means and the fear of splits ultimately forced prospective candidates to abstain from standing. What they preferred to remember from these weeks of aborted campaigning was that they had at least helped to allow the cause of the poorest to be heard in a slightly different way—by relieving it of the (sometimes divisive) noise of demonstrations.

It is time to put an end to this wandering on the edges of protest. Over the course of this journey, some elements of the regime of commitment typical of a movement such as the UPM have become clear. These elements, as we have noted, are hardly discernible for those who choose to endow the world of protest with stable and impassable borders. However, they are essential for a better understanding of the dynamics and some of the logic of this type of movement. These daily, ever-renewed relations (between community leaders and residents, for example), mundane forms of sociability (like the world of amateur football, in the case that interests us), routine events (such as community meetings), and profoundly localized initiatives (encouraging the residents of the township to cultivate vegetable gardens, etc.) are not unrelated to the visibility and legitimacy of the protest collective and, more simply, to its ability to mobilize people in its immediate environment. By taking them into account, an analysis of protest that might otherwise be too exclusively focused on questions of the political socialization of individuals and their experience of activism can be made richer and more precise. In the present case, it helps explain how the notion of "community," although it is not much in evidence in the moments of expression of anger, is a bearer of representations and "values" that may affect individual perceptions. As we have seen, these representations and values enable some people, for whom "politics" and "ideology" act as foils, to find their place within a movement that they may conceive as being solely "in the service of the community." Because it broadly contextualizes the grievances, such an approach also helps one go beyond mere slogans and claims, which sometimes tend to standardize things and strip them of some of their complexity. In the present case, the denunciation of the poverty that is eroding the townships gains in prominence and significance if we immerse ourselves in the lived experiences of the residents and show sensitivity to the ways in which they live them on a daily basis. The discontent leading to protest then unveils what it owes to ordinary phenomena of relegation and domination. The influence of gender and generational dynamics found across the township and, more broadly, South African society, is here revealed. We are thus given more evidence of the "experiences of precarity that go beyond material scarcity" (Das and Randeria 2015, S3) and that, above all, give another depth to the expectations of activists.

The last few pages of this book have also shown the resurgent figure of a politics that could be described as official. Politics, however, has not been totally absent from the previous chapters. To a certain extent, this book speaks of nothing else—of almost nothing *but* politics, but without ever really naming it, or trying to isolate it in the landscape of gestures, roles and words that is being described. It is indeed a *politics of the near* that is sometimes perceived in the multiple frictions between the ordinary aspects of existence and activist life. As I mentioned in the introduction, the politics of the near derives from the commitments of the Unemployed People's Movement. It emerges from the balance that the collective is permanently endeavoring to maintain between an engagement to follow the will of the residents on the one hand, and the claim to represent them on the other. It also lies at the heart of the work of strengthening the profile of the group, whether it be the protest movement or the community. It also springs from the effort of generalization provided by activists when they incorporate individual destinies into the more general framework of the contempt suffered by the weakest. More broadly, this politics arises from the critique of the order of things, a critique that these women and men formulate on the basis of what comprises their everyday lives. The politics of the near engendered by a movement of the poor is therefore not confined, as "popular politics" is in the various definitions that have been given of it. The fact that it is rooted in what are sometimes the most material or intimate details of existences does not prevent it from carrying within itself a more symbolic and political critique. By entering the public space, the mobilizations of the poor remind governments of their part in the contradictions characterizing a society. This dimension is particularly strong in postapartheid South Africa, where the expression of discontent is unlikely to be aimed at overthrowing the social order. It is a question, more surely, of giving content to the "better life for all" that the ANC has regularly promised since 1994 in exchange for unwavering electoral support. When one observes, as I have tried to do, the daily life of UPM activists and their families, one sees that it is often dominated by the conviction of an inevitable confinement to a "raw life." Even those among the youngest who often say they hope for something from their future are not totally immune. This perception of things is obviously rooted in deplorable living conditions. More generally, however, it is the result of the persistence of forms of segregation that liberal democracy was supposed to put an end to. In any event, the rulers did not create the conditions for what would have reduced the "inequality of lives" (Fassin 2018) and marked the entry into a "Rainbow Nation" with a solid foundation: a large disentanglement of race and class. The success of the Economic Freedom Fighters in the poorest Black neighborhoods of the country largely confirms this. By addressing the inequalities and poverty that almost invariably afflict Africans, EFFs have helped politicize (Posel 2013)—or repoliticize— race at a time when ANC leaders seemed to have an almost essentialized approach to it. Within the UPM itself, many have been seduced by what Deborah Posel identifies as "racial populism" (2014, 32). Above all, I believe that the language of this party quite simply resonated with the familiar worlds of these activists, in particular those between twenty and thirty years old. The latter were, it is true, less exposed than their elders to the nonracialism embodied by Nelson Mandela and some of the figures of the early democratic years. On the other hand, just like their parents, they see every day that the intertwining of blackness and poverty has not loosened with the end of apartheid. The chances of successfully completing the course of study you have chosen or finding a job with a view to making plans still appear fragile, as do those of leaving the family home before your thirtieth birthday.

Reference to this politics of the near is not meant to lengthen the list of notions and neologisms built up by the social sciences. The label we give it is actually pretty unimportant. If I resort to such a phrase, it is not as a way of categorizing things but so as to emphasize that a *family resemblance* and, even more, a certain coherence link some of the actions and activities that characterize, on a daily basis, a poor people's movement such as the UPM. These actions and activities come together, as we have seen, on the basis of a certain proximity and autochthony, both of which are absolutely essential to the movement in its relation to its environment. They also attest to the existence among activists of a strong social conscience or, more precisely, the exacerbated awareness of a social belonging. This latter draws on registers that are not merely political, as we see from the regular use of a vocabulary of life ("My heart is with the UPM," "My blood is in the UPM," etc.) that underlines one's emotional bond with the movement. In addition, this sense of belonging lessens the differences that may exist within the group. The UPM is no more homogenous than any other movement. Some of its members are politicized, others not. Some even vote for an ANC that is spurned by the main leaders. Several live in shacks, others in houses that may be rather bare but are at least built of cement. Some manage to make an occasional profit from the "informal economy" while others depend on benefits to bring up their children. And yet everyone seems to be "in the same boat,"[3] as the title of a press communiqué released by a Cape Town poor people's movement in solidarity with their Grahamstown comrades puts it. In other words, these disparities do not undermine the conviction of sharing the same concrete, day-to-day experience of life in the township and the informal settlements. What the movement produces—the politics of the near—is rooted in this experience, gives it a voice, and draws nourishment exclusively from it. Indeed, this is what authorizes militants to attempt to discredit a "party politics" accused of being out of touch with life as they see it in the poor areas of the country.

The politics of the near therefore emerges from various material sources, both political and social, both cultural and emotional. Perhaps, then, this should be seen as an invitation to be less susceptible to the temptation of the great division that inevitably seems to be imposed on analyses of contemporary societies. Drawing a firm border between politics and the social, between institutionalized politics and popular politics, between politics, infrapolitics, and protopolitics, or between the public and private spheres, may not be so fundamental.

ACKNOWLEDGMENTS

It is certainly only fair to start by thanking the activists of the Unemployed People's Movement for accepting my presence at their side for six years. I am thinking in particular of Ayanda Kota, who has guided me so often through the township. There, I was also able to draw on the experience and knowledge of Sally Matthews, Pedro Tabenski, and Lindelwa Nxele.

A first version of this text benefited from remarks by Martine Kaluszynski, Élisabeth Claverie, Olivier Ihl, Jean-Philippe Heurtin, and Éric Agrikoliansky. Subsequently, Isabelle Génot, Milena Jaksic, Sarah Gensburger, Cris Beauchemin, and Marie-Claire Lavabre provided me with advice and support. Marie-Claire, in particular, read and commented on each of the pages of the manuscript.

My stays in South Africa and a large part of the translation of the manuscript were funded by my research center, the Institute for Social Sciences of the Political (affiliated with the CNRS, the French national center for scientific research). I also received a grant from the French Institute of South Africa (IFAS), whose scientific director at the time was Thomas Vernet.

Helping me throughout the process that transformed the manuscript into a book, Thomas Lay, of Fordham University Press, and Clara Han and Bhrigupati Singh, co-editors of the Thinking from Elsewhere series, have given me constant and benevolent support. Their contribution reminded me that the writing of a book can sometimes be a collective endeavor. So I know very well what this text owes them. I am also indebted to the two reviewers, one of whom, Fiona Ross, has agreed to reveal her identity to me. Their remarks have led to an undeniable improvement in the manuscript. I also thank Eric Newman (managing editor), Gregory McNamee (and his expert copyediting), and the many staff members at Fordham University Press for their assistance at various stages of the long process leading to the publication.

Andrew Brown translated this text from French to English. I am grateful to him both for the quality of his work and for the patience and availability he has shown on many occasions.

Prior versions of some of the material for this book appeared in the following articles: "Between Boredom, Protest, and Community: Ethnography of Young Activists in a South African Township," *Journal of Contemporary Ethnography* 49, no. 3 (June 2020); "'I am a full-time activist': Activism and Sense of Community in a South African Township," *Terrain*, December 2020; "Away from Demonstrations: South African Poor People's Movements and the 'Regime of the Near,'" *Social Analysis* 66, no. 1 (2022).

NOTES

INTRODUCTION

At the end of 2018, Grahamstown changed its name to Makhanda. To the extent that the research from which this book is derived was conducted between July 2012 and July 2018, however, I chose to continue to use the name "Grahamstown." This is obviously not a matter of taking up a position in the sometimes virulent debates that followed the official announcement, but merely for the sake of convenience.

The seasons referred to in the text are those of the Southern Hemisphere. The names of the people mentioned in this book have usually been changed to preserve their anonymity.

1. Townships are settlements created by the apartheid regime to house the non-white, that is, the Black, Indian, and Coloured populations. The last are the descendants of slaves from Southeast Asia or natives who had been living in the Cape region before the arrival of the whites.

2. "A Better Life for All" was the African National Congress (ANC) campaign slogan in the first general elections in 1994.

3. See Stats SA, "Bucket Toilets: An Update," September 7, 2015. Retrieved from http://www.statssa.gov.za/?p=5375 (accessed September 15, 2015).

4. The reader can also follow this link to access a webpage presenting various videos of UPM events, including the one that led to the occupation of the town hall by dozens of people in 2011: http://abahlali.org/node/7788/.

5. We could draw a parallel here with what Cymene Howe refers to as the "negative space" between one and another activist period—a space "where there is no action: when nonhappening, nil events, quiet, calm, and ostensibly little movement are, in fact, the most vivid" (2016, 163).

6. *The Politics of the Near* is based on intermittent fieldwork undertaken from July 2012 to July 2018. More than fifty interviews were conducted during this period, mainly with UPM activists, but also with some of their external supporters. In addition, there were various informal exchanges with residents of Black neighborhoods and members of NGOs working there. The first contact with the Unemployed People's Movement was made through an email sent about ten days before my arrival in town. I had found the movement's email address at the bottom of a press release. What followed fed into the pages of this book.

7. "Contentious politics means episodic, public, collective interaction among makers of claims and their objects when: (a) at least one government is a claimant, an object of claims, or a party to the claims, and (b) the claims would, if realized, affect the interests of at least one of the claimants or objects of claims" (Tarrow 2013).

8. A first attempt to set out such an approach, applied to several areas of fieldwork in South Africa, lies at the heart of Tournadre 2017.

9. This is the main point for which Bayat criticizes "many resistance writers." He says they too often "overestimate and read too much into the acts of the agents" or, worse, confuse "an awareness about oppression with acts of resistance against it" (Bayat 2000, 543–544).

I use the term "Global South" for convenience, while being aware that it is not actually satisfactory. As Étienne Balibar noted at the beginning of the twenty-first century, "the line of demarcation between 'North' and 'South,' between zones of prosperity and power and zones of 'development of underdevelopment,' is not actually drawn in a stable way. The North itself contains much 'South,' and the South has not given up on becoming part of the 'North.' Where would a country like China be situated? Or Brazil?" (2004, 14–15).

10. See the useful article that Kalyanakrishnan Sivaramakrishnan (2005) wrote about "some intellectual genealogies for the concept of everyday resistance."

11. By street politics, he means "a set of conflicts and the attendant implications between a collective populace and the authorities, shaped and expressed episodically in the physical and social space of the streets" (1998, 15).

12. Achille Mbembe, "Class, Race and the New Native," *Mail & Guardian*, September 25, 2014. Available at: https://mg.co.za/article/2014-09-25-class-race-and -the-new-native/ (accessed October 5, 2020).

13. Ayanda Kota, "Apartheid Petty and Grand, Old and New Is Evil," *Pambazuka News*, April 26, 2012. Available at: https://www.pambazuka.org/governance /apartheid-petty-and-grand-old-and-new-evil/ (accessed October 5, 2015).

14. Unemployed People's Movement, "The Rebellion of the Poor Comes to Grahamstown," press release, February 13, 2011.

15. The "rooted cosmopolitans" are people who are firmly embedded in a national context but are also capable of engaging in transnational networks. This

means they can get away temporarily from their countries while relying on domestic resources to carry out their work (Tarrow 2005, chapter 3).

16. Casual workers are defined in South African law as working no more than three days a week. The legislators sought to protect them, from the second half of the 1990s onward, by allowing those who work more than twenty-four hours a month to be entitled to the same rights and protections as other employees.

17. In certain articles in English, Laurent Thévenot decided to translate *"régime du proche"* as "regime of familiar engagement" (2015). Making very free use of his concept, I have opted for a literal translation—"regime of the near"—to emphasize the idea of familiarity as much as that of proximity.

18. On the developments to which South African masculinities have been subjected, see Morell 2001, and Hunter 2010.

19. Other authors have stated the need to revise the list of entrants. Haenfler, Johnson, and Jones have examined the points of intersection between social movements and engaging in alternative "lifestyles," those expressions of individuality that, like veganism or community life, question dominant social and cultural norms and thus become potential vectors of social change (2012). This broader interpretation of the category is also proposed by Van Dyke, Soule, and Taylor, who suggest that public protest may have other targets than the representations of political and administrative power (2004).

20. On the uses and criticisms addressed to a drastic separation of the public and private spheres, the domestic and the politico-jural, see in particular Collier and Yanagisako 1987.

21. In January 2015, Stats SA stated that nearly 54 percent of the population were living below the poverty line. "Extreme poverty" affected 21 percent of South Africans.

22. Soweto and Thembelihle lie in the Johannesburg conurbation, and Khayelitsha is one of Cape Town's major townships.

23. It often happens that the activists whom we will meet in these pages speak of "Grahamstown East" when referring to the township and the informal housing areas.

24. National statistics even report that between 2008 and 2017, more than four in five South Africans (85.3 percent) had experienced at least one period of poverty (Statistics South Africa 2019, 149).

25. Seeking to specify the nature of the "non-places" generated by "supermodernity" (airports, supermarkets, even hospitals), Marc Augé also defines their exact opposites, "anthropological places." These are "places of identity, of relationships and of history." This kind of place is also "a principle of meaning for the people who live in it, and also a principle of intelligibility for the person who observes it" (1995, 52).

26. A good example is the successful collaboration between anthropologist Philippe Bourgois and photographer Archie Schonberg (2009).

27. This is indeed what Walter Benjamin predicted, as João Biehl recalls (2005, 42).

1. A SOUTH AFRICAN CITY

1. In March 2015, a student protest movement, known as "Rhodes Must Fall," was intended to challenge the persistence of colonialism and white supremacy in South African society. Symbolically, the first protest actions and demands focused on representations of the colonial era in the public space, especially the statue of Cecil Rhodes erected on the campus of the University of Cape Town. This was finally removed a few weeks later. See Nyamnjoh 2016.

2. Pedro Tabenski, "Tales of a Divided City: What Are We Afraid Of?" *The Grocott's Mail*, July 29, 2013. Available at http://www.grocotts.co.za/2013/07/29/tales-of-a-divided-city-what-are-we-afraid-of (accessed September 13, 2014).

3. The Xhosa are an ethnic group that numbered nearly eight million people in the mid-2010s (out of a population of fifty-three million South Africans). Nelson Mandela, notably, was a Xhosa.

4. This "vision of things" justified the creation of the Bantustans—poor, land-locked territories with relative autonomy, of which Blacks were officially "citizens."

5. Used by the apartheid administration to designate Blacks and thus distinguish them from whites, Asians, and Coloureds, the term Africans (or "natives") is still today claimed or, at the very least, used by many Black South Africans to define themselves.

6. The Gini coefficient is a summary statistic of income inequality. It varies from 0 to 1. If the Gini coefficient is equal to zero, income is distributed in a perfectly equal manner. In contrast, if the Gini coefficient equals 1, income distribution is completely inequitable: one individual in the population is earning all the income.

7. By way of comparison, in 2015, the Organization for Economic Cooperation and Development (OECD) established the Gini coefficients of, among others, the United States of America at 0.39, United Kingdom at 0.36, France at 0.297, Germany at 0.289, and Iceland at 0.246.

8. The 2011 census established Makhana's total population at just over 82,000, with most (about 80 percent) living in Grahamstown, the city's major urban center. Nevertheless, it is likely that the population actually exceeds 100,000, as the occupation of informal settlements is sometimes underestimated by national statistics.

9. Makhanda, the Xhosa warrior and prophet who was defeated at eGazini, is also known as Makana and Nxele.

10. A "location" reserved for the Coloured population had been established a few years earlier.

11. In 2016, the municipality revealed that 45 percent of the population did not receive any income and 10.5 percent earned less than R801 per month (less than US

$70), which placed this part of the population below the poverty line. See Makana Municipality 2016, 73.

12. According to Ben Scully, "42% of South Africa's employed labor force can be identified as precarious" (2016, 302).

13. I will use quotation marks when I talk about the "informal economy." As several studies have clearly shown, the main effect of the wide division between formal and informal economies is to confine the latter, and those who depend on it, to illegality. This division also naturalizes the legitimacy of the "formal economy," while obviously keeping silent about what it owes to social and legal norms. (On this issue, see Goldstein 2016 and Millar 2017). Those who work in the so-called informal economy in Grahamstown do not use this term. They simply state their activity ("builder," "hairdresser," etc.) and sometimes present themselves as "self-employed."

14. As noted by some economists, however, "the most common way of finding a job" among the poor unemployed is through "waiting to hear from family and friends about jobs that become available, rather than through active job search methods" (such as registering at an employment agency). This strategy is not recognized, however, as "searching for work in official statistical surveys." From 2008 onward, StatsSA decided that discouraged work seekers and the nonsearching unemployed were "not economically active" and therefore not unemployed. See Dorrit Posel, Daniela Casale, and Claire Vermaak, "The Unemployed in South Africa: Why Are So Many Not Counted," Econ3x3, February 26, 2013. Available at: http://www.econ3x3.org/article/unemployed-south-africa-why-are-so-many-not-counted (accessed October 8, 2015).

15. This prohibition had been somewhat modified, however, over the years. After setting up thirty-year leases solely for those with permanent residence rights in urban areas, the authorities would create ninety-nine-year-long leases in 1977 before resolving to permanently open up access to real estate and land ownership to all social groups in 1986.

16. Between 1996 and 2007, more than 4,900 RDP houses were built in Grahamstown (Mukorombindo 2012, 63).

17. In 2016, 46 percent of households in the municipality lived in "very formal dwelling units," 41.5 percent in "formal dwelling units" (i.e., dwellings "built according to approved plans" but without running water or without a flush toilet within the dwelling), and just over 12 percent in informal or traditional dwelling units. See Eastern Cape Socio Economic Consultative Council 2017, 76.

18. The ward is the lowest level of political representation in local government.

19. Sandton is an affluent area in Johannesburg.

20. When a municipality fails to fulfil its obligations, the South African Constitution allows the provincial government to intervene. The municipality can then be put under administration for a limited time. An administrator will be appointed to manage and oversee the day-to-day running of the municipality.

21. Pierre Bourdieu used this term to describe a view that he thought was prominent in "critical social thought," based on "the fantasy of the conspiracy, the idea that an evil will is responsible for everything that happens in the social world" (Bourdieu and Wacquant 1992, 102).

22. A documentary made by students in journalism at Rhodes University perfectly captures this situation. Activate Independent Student News Source, "eThembeni Speaks: Enough of the Government of Lies," May 2012, https://www.youtube.com/watch?v=LqSku05af4c.

23. A twenty-five-year-old male resident of eThembeni, quoted in Pillay 2012.

24. Siyanda Centwa (with Pedro Tabenski), "Tales of a Divided City: Not a Place for Peasants," *The Gocott's Mail*, March 10, 2014. Available at: http://www.grocotts.co.za/2014/03/10/tales-of-a-divided-city-not-a-place-for-peasants (accessed September 8, 2014).

25. Pedro Tabenski and Learners from Ntsika Secondary School, "Tales of a Divided City: Tsotsis and Learners," *The Gocott's Mail*, November 6, 2013. Available at: http://www.grocotts.co.za/2013/11/06/tales-of-a-divided-city-tsotsis-and-learners (accessed September 8, 2014).

26. In 2016, it was estimated that 12 percent of Makhana's population had HIV (Eastern Cape Socio Economic Consultative Council 2017, 19).

27. Caroline Skinner, "Informal Sector Employment: Policy Reflections," REDI3X3 Conference, November 28, 2016.

2. THE SENSE OF COMMUNITY

1. I was not in Grahamstown in 2009. This description is based on what I have heard many times from activists. This event is also similar to most of those I have seen elsewhere in South Africa.

2. As I wrote in the first chapter, this figure is regularly brandished by the leaders of the Unemployed People's Movement.

3. In 2009, the reelection of an ANC majority to Parliament led logically to the election of Jacob Zuma as president of the republic. The election campaign saw the leader of the ANC relying on the "left" of the coalition, and so a number of commentators drew a direct link between this election and the proliferation of demonstrations, which were analyzed as a means for the poorest to remind Zuma of his commitments. The intelligence services also highlighted the importance of factionalism in these uprisings, since some of the ANC's local activists and cadres saw this protest as an instrument for destabilizing a municipality or provincial executive under the control of another faction within the party.

4. Created in 1983 and mainly led by the Black Archbishop Desmond Tutu and the Coloured pastor Allan Boesak (also the President of the World Alliance of Reformed Churches), the UDF brought together several hundreds of thousands of

individuals—Black, white, Coloured, and Indian—who wished to establish a "non-racial, non-sexist and democratic society." Influential on the national level, the UDF became really active on the local level only from autumn 1984. Its leaders then adopted as their own Oliver Tambo's call on Radio Freedom on January 1, 1985, to make the townships "ungovernable."

5. This comparison, quite common in international institutions such as the OECD, is due to the fact that Brazil and South Africa have long been rivals for the title of the most unequal country in the world.

6. It should be remembered that from the start of the twentieth century, in cities, Black populations had already been confined to certain spaces. The passing of the Native (Urban Areas) Act, in 1923, intensified this policy, in particular by imposing a regulation of flows between the rural and urban worlds.

7. During the 2010s, a debate took shape around "white poverty." Some associations, known to be close to the Afrikaner community, said that nearly 400,000 whites were affected by this phenomenon. The controversy then focused on the development of white squatter camps since the early 2000s. Various foreign media, including the BBC, echoed these claims. In 2016, the data made public by StatsSA, however, established at "only" 13,300 the number of white individuals living in these villages of caravans and encampments. More generally, 47,500 white South Africans (1 percent of the total white population) were considered poor. See https://africacheck.org/factsheets/factsheet-south-africas-official-poverty-numbers/ (accessed February 24, 2018).

8. Interview with an activist of the Soweto Electricity Crisis Committee (SECC), July 15, 2009, Johannesburg.

9. It may happen, admittedly in very particular circumstances, that these positions result in reprisals or isolation within the neighborhood. In Khutsong (Gauteng Province), for example, the call to boycott the local elections in 2006, following violent demonstrations, definitely lay behind an abstention rate close to 99 percent, making it easy to see who was actually turning out to vote. Voters were then cold-shouldered by the community, and the house of one of them was torched (Steyn Kotze 2006, 210).

10. The Indian and African communities do not share the same history, if only because of the differential treatment accorded them by the apartheid regime. After 1994, the Indians saw the disappearance of the "advantages" of the intermediate position they occupied in the racial hierarchy established by white power. These differences in treatment and consideration were emphasized by, among other things, the relationship to urban locations assigned to races by the state. We can thus conclude that there were two types of townships under apartheid. The first, reserved for Africans, was designed as a temporary housing area intended for populations naturally intended to live in rural areas, more precisely in the Bantustans (homelands). The second was reserved for "in-between groups": Coloureds and Indians.

Unlike Blacks, these two groups had the right to live in cities (in clearly defined and demarcated spaces).

11. This mistrust, produced by the end of the flow control set up under apartheid, transcends racial barriers. In the Indian township studied by Thomas Blom Hansen, it accompanies the conviction, within the ordinary working class, of a moral decay underlined by the way the younger generation of Indians is part of a supposed "African urban culture" (2012). This sense of intrusion is also found in the Black neighborhoods described by Dlamini. He mentions the parallel drawn by an eighty-four-year-old resident between violence and the fact that the township now has "too many outsiders" (2009, 4).

12. Achille Mbembe, "Blacks from Elsewhere and the Right to Abode," Ruth First Lecture, October 3, 2019, Johannesburg.

13. According to Jean and John Comaroff (2012, 635), the primacy granted to 'national autochthony' is not solely a "tactic" pursued by governments. It also resonates with "deeply felt populist fears—and with the proclivity of citizens of all stripes to deflect shared anxieties onto outsiders."

INTERLUDE 1: FOOTBALL, COMMUNITY, AND POLITICS

1. "Tales of a Divided City: Church of soccer," *Grocott's Mail*, September 24, 2014. Available online at: https://www.grocotts.co.za/2014/09/24/tales-of-a-divided-city -church-of-soccer (accessed September 9, 2015).

3. "WE ARE THE PEOPLE WHO STAY WITH THEM IN THE TOWNSHIP"

1. A large room was built in the QQ Section of the sprawling shanty town of Kayelitsha (Cape Town) to accommodate fifteen or so very young children every day under the supervision of two women paid by the "community" via Abahlali.

2. On this issue of "space of protest" or "space of social movements," see Mathieu 2021.

3. One morning in May 2016, while I was in the living room, a man left a packet of sugar on the doorstep. One of the leaders of the organization who was also there told me that neighbors and strangers regularly brought them tea and milk.

4. The car that I use significantly changes the daily rounds of my interlocutors. This vehicle seems a resource for individuals who are regularly forced to rely on outside help or on unreliable public transport when they need to get about. The fact I can give them a lift means they are able to do more things or, more simply, helps them to do what would normally be impossible when I'm not there: they can get to different points of the conurbation to notify people of an event scheduled for a few hours later (demonstration, community meeting, etc.), mix activist and personal

business (transporting loved ones, doing some shopping in the city center, etc.), or move material (banners, leaflets, food) from the office to a rallying point. Part of the equilibrium on which their activism is based is therefore changed during my stay. This situation inevitably influences what I am supposed to observe and therefore produces a certain contingency in my results. Nevertheless, as Mitchell Duneier notes, drawing on Howard Becker's reflections, "most social processes are so organized that the presence of a tape recorder (or white male) is not as influential as all the other pressures, obligations, and possible sanctions in the setting" (1999, 340). One needs merely to be aware of the existence of these possible discrepancies, in order to treat them as effects of the survey situation and not as immediate representations of reality. In other words, the researcher must always bear in mind that the impossibility of merging into the publics studied does not mean that he has no effect on his fieldwork.

5. See the presentation of the CWP on the dedicated government site: http://www.cogta.gov.za/?programmes=community-work-programme.

6. Mandela Park Backyarders, "Ayanda Kota: We Are All in the Same Boat. Solidarity Statement with the Unemployed People's Movement in Grahamstown," press release, January 13, 2012.

7. I was not in South Africa when Bheki was offered this job. According to one of the leaders, the movement had drawn up a list of about ten activists "who were struggling" and took it to one of the companies based in the city, which then agreed to hire some of them. It was impossible for me to know the terms of this potential transaction or, more simply, the reasons that had led the company to respond favorably to this request.

8. Pali Lehohla, *Methodological Report on Rebasing of National Poverty Lines and Development of Pilot Provincial Poverty Lines* (Pretoria: Statistics South Africa, 2015). Available at: http://beta2.statssa.gov.za/publications/Report-03-10-11/Report-03-10-11.pdf (accessed October 10, 2016).

9. Only above this threshold can these workers enjoy rights and protections similar to those of other employees.

10. Ayanda Kota interviewed by Sally Matthews, "'If you want to know what NGOs are all about follow the money and you will know': NGOs and Social Movements," July 2, 2014. Available at: http://thinkingafricangos.blogspot.fr/2014/07/if-you-want-to-know-what-ngos-are-all.html (accessed July 7, 2014).

11. Gladys Mpepho interviewed by Thembani Onceya, "Social Movements and NGOs," June 13, 2014. Available at: http://thinkingafricangos.blogspot.fr/2014/06/social-movements-and-ngos.html (accessed July 7, 2014).

4. "MY BLOOD IS STILL HERE, IN UPM"

1. Steve Biko was one of the main leaders in the fight against apartheid. He helped to set up a Black student union in the late 1970s, which merged with the

Black Consciousness Movement (BCM—see note 3) of which he became leader. Biko was murdered by the regime's police while undergoing interrogation in 1977. Neil Aggett was a figure of "white" resistance to apartheid. He was a doctor who moved in Black trade union circles; he died after seventy days in detention on February 5, 1982. In 1998, the work of the Truth and Reconciliation Commission revealed the extent of the violence suffered during the interrogations, though the police had claimed at the time that Aggett committed suicide on their premises.

2. The Congress of the People (COPE) was set up in November 2008 by former ANC leaders from Thabo Mbeki's circle. A few weeks previously, the latter had been forced to step down as president under pressure from Jacob Zuma's supporters.

3. The Black Consciousness Movement (BCM) emerged in the 1960s and led to the creation of the South African Students Organisation and the Black People's Convention in the following decade. Mainly embodied by Steve Biko, the BCM developed a thinking radically opposed to the "multiracialism" advocated by the ANC leaders. It was closer to pan-Africanism and the American Black Panther movement. Nurtured by the writings of Fanon, Césaire, and Du Bois, its leaders advocated the emancipation of Blacks on their own initiative and therefore maintained a mistrust of white liberals and progressives. In the 1970s, the movement succeeded in gaining popularity among young people who were encouraged to "think Black" and reject the oppressor's models. It thus promoted a "Black culture," blending the urban culture of the townships, theatre, poetry, and a music that combined traditional tunes, jazz, and soul. Its representatives also approached Black churches, student clubs and societies, and YMCA groups. The dissemination and reception of Black Consciousness were also facilitated by the demographic and sociological changes experienced by a country where more than one in two Black South Africans (55 percent) was under the age of twenty.

4. In the mid-2010s, the maximum amount of a retirement pension was R1,600 (1,620 for those over the age of seventy-five). It should be noted that in 2018 the government set the minimum wage at R3,500 per month.

5. Rocco Zizzamia et al., "Vulnerability and the Middle Class in South Africa," SALDRU Working Paper 188, Cape Town, 2016. Available at: http://www.opensaldru.uct.ac.za/bitstream/handle/11090/846/2016_188_Saldruwp.pdf?sequence=1 (accessed July 3, 2018).

6. Achille Mbembe, "Class, Race and the New Native," *Mail & Guardian*, September 25, 2014. Available at: https://mg.co.za/article/2014-09-25-class-race-and-the-new-native/.

7. Passed in 2003, the Broad-based Black Economic Empowerment Act was officially meant to enable historically disadvantaged people, and particularly Black people, women, the young, the disabled, and rural communities, to join the main trend of the South African economy.

8. On the scope of the concept of commitment, see the now classic article by Howard Becker (1960).

INTERLUDE 2: WHAT REALLY MATTERS

1. Paul is a white academic close to the UPM.

2. Black Liberation Theology appeared in the United States in the late 1960s. Its supporters proposed that racism and segregation should be combated on the basis of Christianity.

5. "IT IS MORAL TO REBEL"

1. Unemployed People's Movement, "The Rebellion of the Poor Comes to Grahamstown," press release, February 13, 2011.

2. Richard Pithouse, "The Service Delivery Myth," SACSIS, January 26, 2011. Available at: http://sacsis.org.za/site/article/610.1 (accessed October 20, 2015).

3. Ibid.

4. Quoted in Kayla Roux, "UPM Rallies to Secure Housing," *Grocott's Mail*, June 25, 2013. Available at: https://www.grocotts.co.za/2013/06/25/upm-rallies-to -secure-housing (accessed October 19, 2014).

5. On this question of "social status" and its recognition in society, see Fraser 2003.

6. Phiri is a poor neighborhood in Soweto.

7. UPM, "Rebellion of the Poor Comes to Grahamstown."

8. Activate—Independent Student News Source, "eThembeni Speaks: Enough of the Government of Lies," May 2012, https://www.youtube.com/watch?v=LqSkuo5af4c.

9. According to Sassen (2014), the idea of expulsion (from "professional livelihood, from living space, even from the very biosphere that makes life possible") is enough to encapsulate contemporary socioeconomic and environmental dislocations.

10. Journalists of *The Guardian* newspaper conducted an interesting investigation into the "red ants," security agents specialized in clearing out "illegal invaders." These agents often resort to a violence that was regularly denounced in the 2000s and 2010s. Available at: https://www.theguardian.com/world/ng-interactive/2018 /may/08/red-ants-mass-evictions (accessed May 8, 2018).

11. For the example of Mumbai, see Anand 2017.

12. Even if we should not systematically read the action of a political or social movement in the light of the writings of intellectuals who are close to it, we should not neglect the fact that some of their reflections can sometimes be taken up by the movement's leaders. As in most postapartheid protest organizations, activists from the Unemployed People's Movement have set up a small library over the years, relying on donations from sympathizers. The library follows them in their moves from one

premises to another. One morning in July 2012, while we were driving into the center of Grahamstown, Ayanda asked me if I had a "book to give to the organization."

"A book on Marxism?" I asked.

"No, no, not necessarily. A political book. We're a social movement and the comrades must be able to find out about different things, not just Marxism."

Whether in Durban, Soweto, Cape Town or Grahamstown, these libraries generally contain one or two books by Marx, biographies of revolutionaries such as Trotsky, books on colonization, brochures on socioeconomic rights in the "new" South Africa, and some of those essays that have been circulating in the international antiglobalization sphere since the end of the twentieth century (the books of Mike Davis, Naomi Klein, John Holloway, etc.). While these libraries must contribute to raising the awareness of the most curious activists, they are also used by leaders to add authority to the arguments they advance in their speeches. Indeed, when they take the floor at internal meetings, their speeches are often marked by a certain political sophistication which can contrast with the very practical aspect of the agendas. It is not uncommon for Lenin or Gramsci, among others, to be cited as a way of putting the movement's mission into perspective.

13. I am here using the definition given on the website of the Government Pensions Administration Agency: http://www.gpaa.gov.za/special.html.

14. André Brink, "Ténèbres à midi," *Libération* (Paris), July 24, 2008.

15. "For example, a recession that leads to unemployment may well be the planned result of an anti-inflationary monetary policy, but it may just as well be— and in most cases is—an unintended outcome of economic behavior" (Margalit 1996, 225).

6. "WE DO NOT DISCUSS POLITICS"

1. Mike Rogan, "Informal Economies Are Diverse: South Africa Policies Need to Recognise This," *The Conversation*, October 15, 2018. Available at: https://theconversation.com/informal-economies-are-diverse-south-african-policies-need-to-recognise-this-104586 (accessed 15 October 2018).

2. We need to add to this the fact that "between 1995 and 2005, the number of women in the labor force increased by 59 percent, whereas for men the increase was 35 percent" (Hunter 2010, 108).

3. On this epidemiological crisis and the political and scholarly issues it has raised in South Africa, see Fassin 2007.

4. The concerned residents committee is a very common form of association in South Africa, which most often comes into being in response to a problem (increased crime in the neighborhood, increased water cuts, etc.).

5. Quoted in Yeukai C. Mukorombindo, "Social Networks and the Developments of Sustainable Human Settlements," International Conference on Build-

ing Capacity for Sustainable Delivery, The Southern African Housing Foundation, Cape Town, September 16–18, 2012.

6. It is not uncommon for some of the residents to talk about the "real ANC" in this respect, something other researchers confirm in other cities. See Matlala and Bénit-Gbaffou 2012.

7. Local government is responsible for services such as sanitation. Housing, on the other hand, is a jurisdiction shared with the provincial government.

8. It is certainly the Durban squatter movement, Abahlali baseMjondolo, that has been the most regularly hit by this violence.

9. Led by a former leader of the ANC Youth League, the Economic Freedom Fighters (EFF) were founded in 2013. Their leaders initiated many actions aimed at distancing them from the rules of a liberal democracy too closely associated with political elites (marches protesting against the cost of living, insults targeting political opponents, violence in parliament, etc.). This UPM activist, who I interviewed in April 2014, was very involved in setting up the EFF in Grahamstown. He considered this party to be "a social movement in politics." In his view, its program resembled that promoted by the unemployed movement.

10. Nkandla is the name of the locality from which Jacob Zuma comes. He owns a residence there, which has been sumptuously furnished on the pretext of tightening its security.

11. This family of businessmen of Indian origin is accused of exploiting its closeness to Zuma so as to indulge in large-scale "state capture" ventures and directly influence the composition of governments so as to further its own economic and financial interests.

12. On April 26, the anniversary of the first democratic elections (1994), South Africa celebrates Freedom Day.

13. Anna Selmeczi, "Challenging Abandonment: The South African Shackdwellers' 'Living Politics' as a Counter-Conduct," Conference on Reading Foucault in the Post-Colonial Present, Bologna, Italy, March 3–4, 2011.

14. Civics are residents' associations that emerged in the 1970s. Present at the level of streets, neighborhoods, and townships, they embodied the internal front of anti-apartheid protest.

15. This was a way of increasing the representation of social interests by inviting the groups concerned to participate in policy development in the areas of housing, transport, health, and education. This "neocorporatism" was to "facilitate the production of specific agreements [binding] the parties present and [involving] them in the new political and social order" (Crouzel 1996, 25).

16. This definition and this example are taken directly from the official IDP presentation page: http://www.etu.org.za/toolbox/docs/localgov/webidp.html.

17. *Imbizo* means "gathering" in the Nguni and Zulu languages. See Kassner 2014, 112–114.

18. It was at this conference that Jacob Zuma defeated Thabo Mbeki in the race for the presidency of the party, which opened the way for the ANC candidate to stand for the presidency of the Republic of South Africa.

7. LEADERS IN THE COMMUNITIES

1. We can refer here to the abundant sociological and anthropological literature devoted to poor neighborhoods in Latin America and Asia. For contemporary accounts, see Lazar 2008; Anand 2017; Herzfeld 2016.

8. LOST IN TRANSITION?

1. The 1970s saw the torch being handed on from one generation to the next in the domestic resistance to apartheid. The demonstrations by young Blacks in 1976 were perhaps the best illustration of this.

2. Cress and Snow distinguish between three categories of actors in the ranks of the protest movement: "cadres" are those that "function as lieutenants on a relatively permanent basis," while the "leaders" provide "organisational leadership." "Captive audiences" are "the contributors and spectating populations assembled for recruitment and calls for resources" (1996, 1095). While these categories have the merit of simplicity and clarity, they do not always correspond to the population that in the final analysis oscillates between "cadres" and "captive audiences" without ever becoming confused with them.

3. Yeukai Mukorombindo and Gabriel Nahmias, "What Do the Matric Results Mean?" *GroundUp*, January 8, 2016. Available at: http://ww.groundup.org.za/article/what-do-matric_results-mean (accessed October 15, 2017).

4. Stats SA, *Quarterly Labour Force Survey*, June 2017. Available at: http://www.statssa.gov.za/?p=9960 (accessed November 13, 2017).

5. See Kate Wilkinson, "Checked: 80% of South African Schools Indeed 'Dysfunctional,'" *Mail & Guardian*, March 25, 2015. Available at: https://mg.co.za/article/2015-03-25-are-80-of-south-african-schools-dysfunctional (accessed August 7, 2017).

6. Stats SA, "Youth Unemployment Still High in Q1: 2018." Available at: http://www.statssa.gov.za/?p=11129 (accessed July 28, 2018).

7. Secretary general of the Communist Party and principal of the armed wing of the ANC, Chris Hani was murdered by a White far-right militant in 1993. Robert Sobukwe was one of the main leaders of the Pan Africanist Congress (PAC), which broke away from the ANC.

8. As part of a previous survey, I noted the same feeling in older activists. Tournadre 2018, 73–74.

9. The South African legislature legalized homosexual marriage in November 2006; the ANC had worked to get this right recognized from 1993. As for the

right to abortion, it is part of the 1996 constitution, as is the reference to gender identity.

9. THE COMMUNITY, THE MOVEMENT, AND THE "OUTSIDE WORLD"

1. I take this expression from the sociologists Ruth Lister and David Piachaud, who used it in a quite different context—that of the policy of British governments in the early twenty-first century.

2. Numerous foreign sources of funding have financed postapartheid protest, including the NGO Oxfam Canada, considered to be less cautious about the use of funds than its European counterparts (especially when it comes to paying bail for those arrested after illegal protest actions); the Rosa Luxemburg Foundation (Germany); which for a while paid the UPM's rent; the Oratorian Church (United States); and the Fences and Windows Foundation created by Canadian essayist Naomi Klein, among other groups.

3. Paper distributed at a first meeting between representatives of the research center and the Unemployed People's Movement, April 2016.

10. "YES, WE DO THE SAME THING"

1. Matuma Letsoalo, "ANC Seeks New Grass-Roots Leaders," *Mail & Guardian*, April 17, 2015.

2. Both quotations are in Thembeni Plaatjie, "Ward 10 Meet Their ANC Candidate," *Grocott's Mail*, April 14, 2011.

3. In 2000, the ANC controlled 163 of the 238 municipal councils in South Africa. In the 2006 and 2011 polls, this figure rose to 179.

4. The voting system consists of two components: one is based on a one-round majority vote at ward level; the other is a proportional distribution of votes at municipality level.

5. *National General Council 2005: Organisational Report by Secretary General Kgalema Motlanthe*, June 30, 2005. Available online: http://www.anc.org.za/content /national-general-council-2005-organisational-report-secretary-general-kgalema -motlanthe (accessed December 12, 2013).

6. *52nd National Conference: Organisational Report*, presented by ANC Secretary General Kgalema Motlanthe, December 17, 2007. Available online: http://www .anc.org.za/content/52nd-national-conference-organisational-report (accessed December 12, 2013).

7. *51st National Conference: Report of the Secretary General*, Stellenbosch, December 16, 2002. Available online: http://www.anc.org.za/content/51st-national -conference-report-secretary-general (accessed October 9, 2011).

8. Thembani Onceya, "ANC Members Protest against Party Leaders," *Grocott's Mail*, March 30, 2011.

9. The Pan Africanist Congress (PAC) was founded in 1959 by former ANC members opposed to the Freedom Charter adopted in 1955 by different organizations, committing them to struggle for a "multiracial" South Africa. Heavily involved in the struggle against apartheid, particularly through large-scale actions and the activities of its paramilitary branch, the PAC was not able to find its place on the electoral scene after 1994; it had five members of Parliament in the first democratic elections, and only one in 2014.

10. I have attempted in another book to highlight the processes that resulted from the opening up of the political field to Blacks and its powerful attraction for the different groups that had, before 1994, organized the world of protest. See Tournadre 2018, 28–36.

11. Anela Mjekula, "Job-Seekers Vow to Halt Festival," *Grocott's Mail*, June 29, 2015.

12. The Anti-Eviction Campaign was one of the leading postapartheid social movement organizations in the first decade of the twenty-first century.

13. David McGregor, "Wheelchair-Bound Activist Backs Peaceful March in Grahamstown," *The Herald* (Port Elizabeth), June 23, 2015.

EPILOGUE

1. The Congress of South African Unions (COSATU) and the South African Communist Party (SACP), together with the ANC, form the alliance in power since the beginning of the democratic era.

2. Operation Khanyisa is also the name given to the major campaign conducted by the SECC in the early 2000s to illegally reconnect the hundreds of households whose access to the network had been cut off due to unpaid bills.

3. Mandela Park Backyarders, "Ayanda Kota: We Are All in the Same Boat: Solidarity Statement with the Unemployed People's Movement in Grahamstown," press release, January 13, 2012.

WORKS CITED

Abbink, Jan. 2005. "Being Young in Africa: The Politics of Despair and Renewal."
    In *Vanguard or Vandals: Youth, Politics and Conflict in Africa*, edited by Jon
    Abbink and Ineke van Kessel, 1–33. Boston: Brill.

African Union. 2006. *Youth Charter*. Addis-Ababa: African Union.

Agier, Michel. 2016. *Borderlands: Towards an Anthropology of the Cosmopolitan
    Condition*. Translated by David Fernbach. Cambridge: Polity Press.

———. 1999. *L'invention de la ville*. Amsterdam: Overseas Publishers Association
    & Éditions des Archives Contemporaines.

Alexander, Peter. 2013. "Affordability and Action: Introduction and Overview."
    In *Class in Soweto*, edited by Peter Alexander, Claire Cerutti, Keke Motseke,
    Mosa Phadi, and Kim Wale, 1–34. Pietermaritzburg: University of KwaZulu-
    Natal Press.

Alexander, Peter, Luke Sinwell, Thapelo Lekgowa, Botasang Mmope, and Bongani
    Xezwi. 2012. *Marikana: A View From the Mountain and a Case to Answer*.
    London: Bookmarks.

Altman, Miriam. 2003. "The State of Employment and Unemployment in South
    Africa." In *The State of the Nation: South Africa 2003-2004*, edited by John
    Daniel, Adam Habib, and Roger Southall, 158–183. Cape Town: HRSC Press.

Aminzade, Ronald, and Doug McAdam. 2001. "Emotions and Contentious
    Politics." In *Silence and Voice in the Study of Contentious Politics*, edited by
    Ronald Aminzade, J. A. Goldstone, et al., 14–50. New York: Cambridge
    University Press.

Anand, Nikhil. 2017. *Hydraulic City: Water & the Infrastructures of Citizenship in
    Mumbai*. Durham, NC: Duke University Press.

Appadurai, Arjun. 2013. *The Future as Cultural Fact: Essays on the Global
    Condition*. New York: Verso.

———. 2003. "Illusion of Permanence (Interview)." *Perspecta* 34: 44–52.

Ashforth, Adam. 2005. *Witchcraft, Violence, and Democracy in South Africa*. Chicago: University of Chicago Press.

Augé, Marc. 1995. *Non-Places: Introduction to an Anthropology of Supermodernity*. London: Verso.

Auyero, Javier. 2003. *Contentious Lives: Two Argentine Women, Two Protests, and the Quest for Recognition*. Durham, NC: Duke University Press.

———. 2005. "L'espace des luttes: Topographie des mobilisations collectives." *Actes de la Recherche en Sciences Sociales* 160: 122–132.

———. 2012a. *Patients of the State: The Politics of Waiting in Argentina*. Durham, NC: Duke University Press.

———. 2012b. "Poor People's Lives and Politics: The Things a Political Ethnographer knows (and doesn't know) after 15 Years." *New Perspectives on Turkey* 46: 95–127.

———. 2021. "Taking Bourdieu to the Shantytown." *International Journal of Urban and regional Research* 45, no. 1: 176–185.

Averweg, Udo Richard, and Marcus Leaning, 2015. "The Use of 'Community' in South Africa's 2011 Local Government Elections." *Africa Spectrum* 50, no. 2: 101–111.

Bähre, Erik. 2007a. *Money and Violence: Financial Self-Help Groups in a South African Township*. Boston: Brill.

———. 2007b. "Reluctant Solidarity: Death, Urban Poverty and Neighbourly Assistance in South Africa." *Ethnography* 8, no. 1: 33–59.

Ballard, Richard, Adam Habib, and Imran Valodia, eds. 2006. *Voices of Protest: Social Movements in Post-Apartheid South Africa*. Durban: University of KwaZulu-Natal Press.

Bank, Leslie J. 2011. *Home Spaces, Street Styles: Contesting Power and Identity in a South African City*. London and Johannesburg: Pluto Press and Wits University Press.

Barchiesi, Franco. 2011. *Precarious Liberation: Workers, the State, and Contested Citizenship in Postapartheid South Africa*. Albany: State University of New York Press.

Bauman, Zygmunt. 2004. *Wasted Lives: Modernity and its Outcasts*. Cambridge: Polity Press.

Bayat, Asef. 2000. "From 'Dangerous Classes' to 'Quiet Rebels': Politics of the Urban Subaltern in the Global South." *International Sociology* 15, no. 3: 533–557.

———. 2010. *Life as Politics: How Ordinary People Change the Middle East*. Stanford, CA: Stanford University Press.

———. 1998. *Street Politics: Poor People's Movement in Iran*. New York: Columbia University Press.

Becker, Howard S. 1981. *Exploring Society Photographically*. Chicago: University of Chicago Press.

———. 1960. "Notes on the Concept of Commitment." *American Journal of Sociology* 66, no. 1: 32–40.

———. 1974. "Photography and Sociology." *Studies in the Anthropology of Visual Communication* 1, no. 1: 3–26.

Beinart, William, and Marcelle C. Dawson, eds. 2010. *Popular Politics and Resistance Movements in South Africa*. Johannesburg: Wits University Press.

Bénit-Gbaffou, Claire. 2011. "Party Politics, Civil Society and Local Democracy: Reflections from Johannesburg." *Geoforum* 43, no. 2: 178–189.

Bénit-Gbaffou, Claire, ed. 2015. *Popular Politics in South African Cities: Unpacking Community Participation*. Cape Town: HSRC Press.

Bhorat, Haroon, Karmen Naidoo, Morné Oosthuizen, and Kavisha Pillay. 2016. *Demographic, Employment, and Wage Trends in South Africa*. Cape Town: UNU-WIDER-Brookings Institution-DPRU.

Biehl, João. 2005. *Vita: Life in a Zone of Social Abandonment*. Berkeley: University of California Press.

Biko, Steve. 1987. *I Write What I Like: A Selection of His Writings*. Edited by Aelred Stubbs. London: Heinemann.

Boltanski, Luc. 2011. *On Critique: A Sociology of Emancipation*. Cambridge: Polity Press.

Bourdieu, Pierre. 2020. *Habitus and Field: General Sociology, Volume 2*. Translated by Peter Collier. Cambridge: Polity Press.

———. 1993a. *Language and Symbolic Power*. Cambridge: Polity Press.

———. 2000. *Pascalian Meditations*. Palo Alto, CA: Stanford University Press.

———. 1999. "Site Effects." In *The Weight of the World: Social Suffering in Contemporary Society*, edited by Pierre Bourdieu, 123–129. Cambridge: Polity Press.

———. 1993b. *Sociology in Question*. Translated by Richard Nice. London: Sage.

Bourdieu, Pierre, and Loïc Wacquant. 1992. *An Invitation to Reflexive Sociology*. Cambridge: Polity Press.

Bourgois, Philippe, and Archie Schonberg. 2009. *Righteous Dopefiend*. Berkeley: University of California Press.

Brown, Julian. 2015. *South Africa's Insurgent Citizens*. London: Zed Books.

Buhlungu, Sakhela. 2006. "COSATU and the First Ten Years of Democratic Transition in South Africa." In *Trade Unions and Democracy: COSATU Workers' Political Attitudes in South Africa*, edited by Sakhela Bulhungu, 1–19. Cape Town: HSRC Press.

———. 2008. "Gaining Influence but Losing Power? COSATU Members and the Democratic Transition of South Africa." *Social Movement Studies* 7, no. 1: 31–42.

Buijs, Gina. 1998. "Savings and Loan Clubs: Risky Ventures or Good Business Practice? A Study of the Importance of Rotating Savings and Credit Associations for Poor Women." *Development Southern Africa* 15, no. 1: 55–65.

Bundy, Colin. 2000. "Survival and Resistance: Townships Organisations and Nonviolent Direct Action in Twentieth Century." In *From Comrades to*

Citizens: The South African Civics Movement and the Transition to Democracy,
edited by Glen Adler and Jon Steinberg, pp. 26–51. London: Macmillan and
Albert Einstein Institute.

Burawoy, Michael. 2017. "Social Movements in the Neoliberal Age." In Marcel
Paret, Carin Runciman, and Luke Sinwell, *Southern Resistance in Critical
Perspective*, 21–35.

Butler, Judith. 2012. "Can One Lead a Good Life in a Bad Life? Adorno Prize
Lecture." *Radical Philosophy* 176: 9–18.

Buton, François, Patrick Lehingue, Nicolas Mariot, and Sabine Rozier, eds. 2016.
L'Ordinaire du Politique: Enquêtes sur les rapports profanes au politique. Lille:
Presses Universitaires du Septentrion.

Cefaï, Daniel. 2003. *L'enquête de terrain*. Paris: La Découverte.

———. 2011. "Vers une ethnographie (du) politique: Décrire des ordres
d'interaction, analyser des situations sociales." In *Du civil au politique:
Ethnographies du vivre-ensemble*, edited by Mathieu Berger, Daniel Cefaï, and
Carole Gayet-Viaud, 545–598. Bruxelles: Peter Lang.

Chance, Kerry. 2018. *Living Politics in South Africa's Urban Shacklands.* Chicago:
University of Chicago Press.

Chartier, Roger. 1987. *The Order of Books: Readers, Authors, and Libraries in
Europe between the Fourteenth and Eighteenth Centuries.* Translated by
Lydia G. Cochrane. Palo Alto, CA: Stanford University Press.

Chatterjee, Partha. 2008. "Democracy and Economic Transformation in India."
Economic and Political Weekly 43, no. 16: 53–63.

———. 2011. *Lineages of Political Society: Studies in Postcolonial Democracy.* New
York: Columbia University Press.

———. 2004. *The Politics of the Governed: Reflections on Popular Politics in Most
of the World.* New York: Columbia University Press.

Cherry, Janet, Kris Jones, and Jeremy Seekings. 2000. "Democratization and Politics
in South African Townships." *International Journal of Urban and Regional
Research* 24, no. 4: 889–905.

Cole, Josette. 1987. *Crossroads: The Politics of Reform and Repression, 1976–1986.*
Johannesburg: Raven Press.

Collier, Jane F., and Sylvia J. Yanagisako. 1987. "Toward a Unified Analysis of
Gender and Kinship." In *Gender and Kinship: Essays Toward a Unified
Analysis*, edited by Jane Fishburn Collier and Sylvia Junko Yanagisako, 14–52.
Stanford, CA: Stanford University Press.

Comaroff, Jean, and John L. Comaroff. 2003. "Ethnography on An Awkward
Scale: Postcolonial Anthropology and the Violence of Abstraction." *Ethnography* 4, no. 2: 147–179.

———. 2012. *Theory from the South: Or, How Euro-America Is Evolving toward
Africa.* Boulder, CO: Paradigm Publishers.

Comaroff, Jean, and John L. Comaroff, eds. 2001. *Millennial Capitalism and the Culture of Neoliberalism*. Durham, NC: Duke University Press.

Comaroff, John L., Jean Comaroff, and Deborah James. 2007. *Picturing a Colonial Past: The African Photographs of Isaac Schapera*. Chicago: University of Chicago Press.

Corbridge, Stuart, Glyn Williams, Manoj Srivastava, and René Véron, eds. 2005. *Seeing the State: Governance and Governmentality in India*. Cambridge: Cambridge University Press.

Cornwall, Andrea. 2002. *Making Spaces, Changing Spaces: Situating Participation in Development*. Brighton: Institute of Development Studies.

Crouzel, Ivan. 1996. "Le vote et la négociation: La démocratisation du régime Sud-Africain." *Hérodote* 82–83: 17–29.

Crush, Jonathan. 2000. "The Dark Side of Democracy: Migration, Xenophobia and Human Rights in South Africa." *International Migration* 38, no. 6, S1/2: 103–133.

Crush, Jonathan, Abel Chikanda, and Caroline Skinner. 2015. *Mean Streets: Migration, Xenophobia and Informality in South Africa*. Cape Town: SAMP & ACC & IDRC.

Das, Veena. 2014. "Action, Expression, and Everyday Life: Recounting Household Events." In *The Ground Between: Anthropologists Engage Philosophy*, edited by Veena Das, Michael D. Jackson, Arthur Kleinman, and Bhrigupati Singh, 279–306. Durham, NC: Duke University Press.

Das, Veena, and Arthur Kleinman. 2000. "Introduction." In *Violence and Subjectivity*, edited by Veena Das, Arthur Kleinman, Mamphela Ramphele, and Pamela Reynolds, 1–18. Berkeley: University of California Press.

Das, Veena, and Deborah Poole. 2004. *Anthropology in the Margins of the State*. Santa Fe, NM: School of American Research Press.

Das, Veena, and Shalini Randeria. 2015. "Politics of the Urban Poor: Aesthetics, Ethics, Volatility, Precarity." *Current Anthropology* 56 (Supplement 11): S3–S14.

Das, Veena, and Michael Walton. 2015. "Political Leadership and the Urban Poor: Local Histories." *Current Anthropology* 56 (Supplement 11): S44–S54.

Davis, Mike. 2006. *Planet of Slums*. London and New York: Verso.

Dawson, Hannah. 2014. "Youth Politics: Waiting and Envy in a South African Informal Settlement." *Journal of Southern African Studies* 40, no. 4: 861–882.

Dawson, Marcelle C., and Luke Sinwell. 2012. *Contesting Transformation: Popular Resistance in Twenty-First-Century South Africa*. London: Pluto Press.

Denning, Michael. 2010. "Wageless Life." *New Left Review* 66: 79–97.

Dhillon, Navtej, and Tarik M. Youssef. 2009. *Waiting: The Unfulfilled Promise of Young People in the Middle East*. Washington, DC: Brookings Institution Press.

Di Nunzio, Marco. 2015. "Embracing Uncertainty: Young People on the Move in Addis Ababa's Inner City." In *Ethnographies of Uncertainty in Africa*, edited by Elizabeth Cooper and David Pratten, 149–172. Basingstoke: Palgrave Macmillan.

Dlamini, Jacob. 2010. "2009 Annual Ruth First Memorial Lecture, University of the Witswatersrand: The Root of the Matter—Scenes from an ANC Branch." *African Studies* 69, no. 1: 187–203.

———. 2009. *Native Nostalgia*. Auckland Park: Jacana.

Douglas, Mary. 1986. *How Institutions Think*. Syracuse, NY: Syracuse University Press.

Driscoll, Adam. 2013. "NIMBY Movements." In *The Wiley-Blackwell Encyclopedia of Social and Political Movements*, edited by David Snow, Donatella della Porta, Bert Klandermans, and Doug McAdam, 852–855. Oxford: Blackwell.

Dubar, Claude. 1994. "Socialisation politique et identités partisanes: Pistes de recherche." In *L'identité politique*, edited by CURAPP, 227–236. Paris: Presses Universitaires de France.

Duriez, Bruno, and Frédéric Sawicki. 2003. "Réseaux de sociabilité et adhésion syndicale: Le cas de la CFDT." *Politix* 63: 17–57.

Du Toit, Andries, and David Neves. 2007. "In Search of South Africa's 'Second Economy': Chronic Poverty, Economic Marginalisation and Adverse Incorporation in Mt Frere and Khayelitsha." Working Paper 1, Programme for Land and Agrarian Studies (PLAAS), University of the Western Cape, South Africa.

Eastern Cape Socio Economic Consultative Council. 2017. "Makana Local Municipality Socio Economic Review and Outlook." East London: ECSEC.

Escobar, Arturo. 1992. "Culture, Practice and Politics: Anthropology and the Study of Social Movements." *Critique of Anthropology* 12, no. 4: 395–432.

———. 2008. *Territories of Difference: Place, Movements, Life*. Durham, NC: Duke University Press.

Evans, Sara M. 1979. *Personal Politics: The Roots of Women's Liberation in the Civil Rights Movement and the New Left*. New York: Vintage Books.

Fanon, Frantz. 1961. *The Wretched of the Earth*. Translated by Constance Farrington. New York: Grove Press.

Fassin, Didier. 2014. "The Ethical Turn in Anthropology: Promises and Uncertainties." *HAU: Journal of Ethnographic Theory* 4, no. 1: 429–435.

———. 2018. *Life: A Critical User's Manual*. Cambridge: Polity Press.

———. 2007. *When Bodies Remember: Experiences and Politics of AIDS in South Africa*. Translated by Amy Jacobs and Gabrielle Varro. Berkeley: University of California Press.

Fassin, Didier, Frédéric Le Marcis, and Todd Lethata. 2008. "Life & Times of Magda A: Telling a Story of Violence in South Africa." *Current Anthropology* 49, no. 2: 225–246.

Fassin, Didier, Matthew Wilhelm-Solomon, and Aurelia Segatti. 2017. "Asylum as a Form of Life: The Politics and Experience of Indeterminacy in South Africa." *Current Anthropology* 58, no. 2: 160–176.

Ferguson, James. 2015. *Give a Man a Fish: Reflections on the New Politics of Distribution*. Durham, NC: Duke University Press.

Ferguson, James, and Tania M. Li. 2018. "Beyond the 'Proper Job': Political-Economic Analysis after the Century of Labouring Man." Working Paper 51. PLAAS. Cape Town: UWC.

Fernandes, Sujatha. 2010. *Who Can Stop the Drums: Urban Social Movements in Chávez's Venezuela*. Durham, NC: Duke University Press.

Fill-Flynn, Maj. 2001. *The Electricity Crisis in Soweto*. Johannesburg: Municipal Services Project.

Fillieule, Olivier, and Érik Neveu. 2019. "Activists' Trajectories in Space and Time: An introduction." In *Activists Forever? Long-Term Impacts of Political Activism*, edited by Olivier Fillieule and Érik Neveu, 1–36. Cambridge: Cambridge University Press.

Fischer, Brodwyn, Bryan McCann, and Javier Auyero, eds. 2014. *Cities from Scratch: Poverty and Informality in Urban Latin America*. Durham, NC: Duke University Press.

Fourie, Frederick, ed. 2018. *The South African Informal Sector: Creating Jobs, Reducing Poverty*. Cape Town: HSRC Press.

Fraser, Nancy. 1997. *Justice Interruptus: Critical Reflections on the Postsocialist Condition*. New York: Routledge.

———. 2003. "Rethinking Recognition: Overcoming Displacement and Reification in Cultural Politics." In *Recognition Struggles and Social Movements: Contested Identities, Agency and Power*, edited by Barbara Hobson, 21–32. Cambridge: Cambridge University Press.

Friedman, Debra, and Douglas McAdam. 1992. "Collective Identity and Activism: Networks, Choices and the Life of the Social Movement." In *Frontiers in Social Movement Theory*, edited by Aldon D. Morris and Carol McClurg Mueller, 156–173. New Haven, CT: Yale University Press.

Friedman, Steve, and Robert van Niekerk. 2016. "Social Policy Post 1994 in South Africa." *Transformation* 91: 1–18.

Galland, Olivier. 2009. *Les jeunes*. Paris: La Découverte.

Gamson, William, and Emilie Schmeidler. 1984. "Organizing the Poor." *Theory and Society* 13, no. 4: 567–584.

Gaxie, Daniel. 1977. "Économie des partis et rétributions du militantisme." *Revue Française de Science Politique* 27, no. 1: 123–154.

Gecas, Viktor. 2000. "Value Identities, Self-Motives, and Social Movements." In *Self, Identity, and Social Movements*, edited by Sheldon Stryker, Timothy J. Owens, and Robert W. White, 93–109. Minneapolis and London: University of Minnesota Press.

Geertz, Clifford. 1973. *The Interpretation of Cultures: Selected Essays*. New York: Basic Books.

Gervais-Lambony, Philippe. 2001a. "Petite histoire d'espace et d'identité dans une ville Sud-Africaine." *Champ psychosomatique*, no. 21: 119–131.

———. 2001b. *Territoires citadins: Quatre villes africaines*. Paris: Belin.

Gibson, Nigel C. 2011. *Fanonian Practices in South Africa: From Steve Biko to Abahlali baseMjondolo*. Scottsville: University of KwaZulu-Natal Press.

Ginzburg, Carlo. 1992. *The Cheese and the Worms: The Cosmos of a Sixteenth-Century Miller*. Translated by John Tedeschi and Anne Tedeschi. Baltimore, MD: Johns Hopkins University Press.

Giugni, Marco, and Maria T. Grasso. 2016. "The Biographical Impact of Participation in Social Movements Activities: Beyond Highly New Left Activism." In *The Consequences of Social Movements*, edited by Lorenzo Bosi, Marco Giugni, and Katrin Uba, 85–105. Cambridge: Cambridge University Press.

Glaser, Daryl. 2011. "The New Black/African Racial Nationalism in SA: Towards a Liberal-Egalitarian Critique." *Transformation* 76: 67–94.

Goldblatt, David. 2005. *Intersections*. New York: Prestel.

Goldstein, Daniel M. 2016. *Owners of the Sidewalk: Security and Survival in the Informal City*. Durham, NC: Duke University Press.

Gould, Roger V. 1995. *Insurgent Identities: Class, Community, and Protest in Paris from 1848 to the Commune*. Chicago: University of Chicago Press.

Haegel, Florence, and Marie-Claire Lavabre. 2010. *Destins ordinaires: Identité singulière et mémoire partagée*. Paris: Les Presses de Sciences Po.

Haenfler, Ross, Brett Johnson, and Ellis Jones. 2012. "Lifestyle Movements: Exploring the Intersection of Lifestyle and Social Movements." *Social Movements Studies* 11, no. 1: 1–20.

Halbwachs, Maurice. 1913. *La classe ouvrière et les niveaux de vie: Recherches sur la hiérarchie des besoins dans les sociétés industrielles contemporaines*. Paris: Félix Alcan.

Hall, Stuart. 1980. "Race, Articulation and Societies Structured in Dominance." In *Sociological Theories: Race and Colonialism*, edited by Marion O'Callaghan, 305–345. Paris: UNESCO.

Han, Hahrie. 2014. *How Organizations Develop Activists: Civic Associations and Leadership in the 21st Century*. New York: Oxford University Press.

Hansen, Thomas Blom. 2005. "Melancholia of Freedom: Humour and Nostalgia among Indians in South Africa." *Modern Drama* 48, no. 2: 297–315.

———. 2012. *Melancholia of Freedom: Social Life in an Indian Township in South Africa*, Princeton, NJ: Princeton University Press.

Harper, Douglas. 2003. "Framing Photographic Ethnography: A Case Study." *Ethnography* 4, no. 2: 241–266.

———. 1982. *Good Company: A Tramp Life*. Chicago: University of Chicago Press.

Hart, Gillian. 2002. *Disabling Globalization: Places of Power in Post-Apartheid South Africa*. Berkeley: University of California Press.

———. 2013. *Rethinking the South African Crisis*. Athens: University of Georgia Press.

Harvey, David. 2008. "The Right to the City." *New Left Review* 53: 23–40.

Hayem, Judith. 2014. "Marikana: Répression étatique d'une mobilisation ouvrière indépendante." *Politique Africaine* 133: 111–130.

Herzfeld, Michael. 2016. *Siege of the Spirits: Community and Polity in Bangkok*. Chicago: University of Chicago Press.

Hickel, Jason. 2014. "'Xenophobia' in South Africa: Order, Chaos, and the Moral Economy of Witchcraft." *Cultural Anthropology* 29, no. 1: 103–127.

Hirschman, Albert O. 1982. *Shifting Involvements: Private Interest and Public Action*. Princeton, NJ: Princeton University Press.

Hobson, Barbara. 2003. "Introduction." In *Recognition Struggles and Social Movements: Contested Identities, Agency and Power*, edited by Barbara Hobson, 1–20. Cambridge: Cambridge University Press.

Holston, James. 1991. "Autoconstruction in Working-Class Brazil." *Cultural Anthropology* 6, no. 4: 447–465.

———. 2007. *Insurgent Citizenship: Disjunctions of Democracy and Modernity in Brazil*. Princeton, NJ: Princeton University Press.

———. 2019. "Metropolitan Rebellions and the Politics of Commoning the City." *Anthropological Theory* 19, no. 1: 120–142.

Holzner, Claudio. 2004. "The End of Clientelism? Strong and Weak Networks in a Mexican Squatter Movement." *Mobilization: An International Quarterly* 9, no. 3: 223–240.

Honneth, Axel. 2007. *Disrespect: The Normative Foundations of Critical Theory*. Cambridge: Polity Press.

———. 1995. *The Struggle for Recognition: The Moral Grammar of Social Conflicts*. Translated by Joel Anderson. Cambridge, MA: MIT Press.

Honwana, Alcinda. 2014. "'Waithood': Youth Transitions and Social Change." In *Development and Equity: An Interdisciplinary Exploration by Ten Scholars from Africa, Asia and Latin America*, edited by Dick Foeken, Ton Dietz, Leo Haan, and Amanda Johnson, 28–40. Boston: Brill.

Howe, Cymene. 2014. "Negative Space: Unmovement and the Study of Activism When There Is No Action." In *Impulse to Act: A New Anthropology of Resistance and Social Justice*, edited by Othon Alexandrakis, 161–182. Bloomington: Indiana University Press.

Hunter, Mark. 2011. "Beneath the 'Zunami': Jacob Zuma and the Gendered Politics of Social Reproduction in South Africa." *Antipode* 43, no. 4: 1102–1126.

———. 2010. *Love in the Time of Aids: Inequality, Gender, and Rights in South Africa*. Bloomington: Indiana University Press.

Hyden, Göran. 1983. *No Shortcuts to Progress*. London: Heinemann Educational.

Ihl, Olivier. 2016. *La barricade renversée: Histoire d'une photographie*. Bellecombes-en-Bauges: Le Croquant.

Jackson, Michael D. 1995. *At Home in the World*. Durham, NC: Duke University Press.

Jasper, James M. 1997. *The Art of Moral Protest: Culture, Biography, and Creativity in Social Movements.* Chicago: University of Chicago Press.

Jeffrey, Craig. 2010. *Timepass: Youth, Class, and the Politics of Waiting in India.* Palo Alto, CA: Stanford University Press.

Jensen, Steffen. 2004. "Claiming Community: Local Politics on the Cape Flats, South Africa." *Critique of Anthropology* 24, no. 2: 179–207.

———. 2008. *Gangs, Politics & Dignity in Cape Town.* Chicago: University of Chicago Press.

Kassner, Malte. 2014. *The Influence of the Type of Dominant Party in Democracy: A Comparison between South Africa and Malaysia.* Wiesbaden: Springer VS.

Katsaura, Obvious. 2012. "Community Governance in Urban South Africa: Spaces of Political Contestation and Coalition." *Urban Forum* 23, no. 3: 319–42.

Kehler, Johanna. 2001. "Woman and Poverty: The South African Experience." *Journal of International Women's Studies* 3, no. 1: 41–53.

Kielcot, K. Jill. 2000. "Self-Change in Social Movements." In *Self, Identity, and Social Movements,* edited by Sheldon Stryker, Timothy J. Owens, and Robert W. White, 110–131. Minneapolis: University of Minnesota Press.

Klandermans, Bert, Marlene Roefs, and Johan Olivier. 2001. *The State of the People: Citizens, Civil Society and Governance in South Africa, 1994–2000.* Pretoria: Human Science Research Council.

Kleinman, Arthur. 2006. *What Really Matters: Living a Moral Life amidst Uncertainty and Danger.* Oxford: Oxford University Press.

Koster, Martijn. 2012. "Mediating and Getting 'Burnt' in the Gap: Politics and Brokerage in a Recife Slum, Brazil." *Critique of Anthropology* 32, no. 4: 479–497.

Koster, Martijn, and Pieter A. de Vries. 2012. "Slum Politics: Community Leaders, Everyday Needs, and Utopian Aspirations in Recife, Brazil." *Focaal: Journal of Global and Historical Anthropology* 62: 83–89.

Laclau, Ernesto. 2005. *On Populist Reason.* New York: Verso.

Lagroye, Jacques. 1997. "On ne subit pas son rôle." *Politix* 38: 7–17.

Landau, Paul S. 2010. *Popular Politics in the History of South Africa, 1400–1948.* Cambridge: Cambridge University Press.

Langford, Malcom, Ben Cousins, Jackie Dugard, and Tshepo Madingozi. 2014. *Socioeconomic Rights in South Africa: Symbols or Substance?* Cambridge: Cambridge University Press.

Lazar, Sian. 2008. *El Alto, Rebel City: Self and Citizenship in Andean Bolivia.* Durham, NC: Duke University Press.

———. 2017. *The Social Life of Politics: Ethics, Kinship, and Union Activism in Argentina.* Stanford, CA: Stanford University Press.

Lazzeri, Christian. 2009. "Conflits de reconnaissance et mobilisation collective." *Politique et Sociétés* 28, no. 3: 117–160.

Lee, Rebekah. 2009. *African Women and Apartheid: Migration and Settlement in Urban South Africa*. New York: I. B. Tauris.

Lehohla, Pali. 2015. "Methodological Report on Rebasing of National Poverty Lines and Development of Pilot Provincial Poverty Lines." Pretoria: Statistics South Africa. Retrieved from http://beta2.statssa.gov.za/publications/Report-03-10-11/Report-03-10-11.pdf. Accessed October 10, 2016.

Levi, Giovanni. 1988. *Inheriting Power: The Story of an Exorcist*. Translated by Lydia G. Cochrane. Chicago: University of Chicago Press.

Lewicka, Maria. 2011. "Place Attachment: How Far Have We Come in the Last 40 Years?" *Journal of Environmental Psychology* 31, no. 3: 207–230.

Li, Tania Murray. 2010. "To Make Live or Let Die? Rural Dispossession and the Protection of Surplus Population." *Antipode* 41, S1: 66–93.

Lodge, Tom. 2006. "The Future of South Africa's Party System." *Journal of Democracy* 17, no. 3: 152–166.

Mabasa, Khwezi. 2019. "Democratic Marxism and the National Question: Race and Class in Post-Apartheid South Africa." In *Racism after Apartheid: Challenges for Marxism and Anti-Racism*, edited by Vishwas Satgar, 173–193. Johannesburg: Wits University Press.

MacDonald, Michael. 2004. "The Political Economy of Identity Politics." *South Atlantic Quarterly* 103, no. 4: 629–656.

Mains, Daniel. 2012. *Hope Is Cut: Youth, Unemployment, and the Future in Urban Ethiopia*. Philadelphia: Temple University Press.

———. 2007. "Neoliberal Times: Progress, Boredom, and Shame among Young Men in Urban Ethiopia." *American Ethnologist* 34, no. 4: 659–673.

Makana Municipality. 2009. *Local Economic Development (LED) Strategy Part I: Situation Analysis*. Port Elizabeth: Urban-Econ Development Economists.

———. 2016. *Final Makana Municipality Integrated Development Plan 2017–2022*. Makana: Makana Municipality.

Makhulu, Anne-Maria. 2015. *Making Freedom: Apartheid, Squatter Politics, and the Struggle for Home*. Durham, NC: Duke University Press.

Mandela, Nelson. 1994. *A Long Walk to Freedom*. Boston: Little, Brown.

Manona, Cecil Wele. 1994. "The Impact of Political Conflict and Violence on the Youth in Grahamstown." In *Youth in the New South Africa: Towards Policy Formulation*, edited by Frederik van Zyl Slabbert, Charles Malan, Hendrik Marais, Johan L. Olivier, and Rory Riordan, 357–362. Pretoria: HSRC.

Mansbridge, Jane. 2001a. "Complicating Oppositional Consciousness." In *Oppositional Consciousness: The Subjective Roots of Social Protest*, edited by Jane Mansbridge and Aldon Morris, 238–264. Chicago: University of Chicago Press.

———. 2013. "Everyday Activism." In *Blackwell Encyclopedia of Social and Political Movements*, edited by David Snow, Donatella della Porta, Bert Klandermans, and Doug McAdam, 337–339. Malden, MA: Wiley.

———. 2001b. "The Making of Oppositional Consciousness." In Mansbridge and Morris, *Oppositional Consciousness*, 1–19.

Mansbridge, Jane, and Aldon Morris, eds. 2001. *Oppositional Consciousness: The Subjective Roots of Social Protest*. Chicago: University of Chicago Press.

Margalit, Avishai. 1996. *The Decent Society*. Translated by Naomi Goldblum. Cambridge, MA: Harvard University Press.

Mariot, Nicolas. 2011. "Does Acclamation Equal Agreement? Rethinking Collective Effervescence through the Case of the Presidential 'Tour de France' during the 20th Century." *Theory & Society* 40, no. 2: 191–221.

———. 2012. "L'habitus du dehors: Questions sans réponse et présence des institutions." *Politix* 100: 189–200.

Marshall, Thomas H. 1992. "Citizenship and Social Class." In *Citizenship and Social Class*, edited by Thomas H. Marshall and Tom Bottomore, 8–17. London: Pluto Press.

Masquelier, Adeline. 2013. "Teatime: Boredom and the Temporalities of Young Men in Niger." *Africa* 83, no. 3: 470–491.

Mathieu, Lilian. 2021. "The Space of Social Movements." *Social Movement Studies* 20, no. 2: 193–207.

Matlala, Boitumelo, and Claire Bénit-Gbaffou. 2012. "Local Activists and the Management of Contradicting Political Loyalties: The Case of Phiri, Johannesburg." *Geoforum* 43: 207–218.

Matonti, Frédérique, and Franck Poupeau. 2004. "Le capital militant: Essai de définition." *Actes de la Recherche en Sciences Sociales* 155: 5–11.

Mattes, Robert. 2012. "The 'Born Frees': The Prospects for Generational Change in Post-Apartheid South Africa." *Australian Journal of Political Science* 47, no. 1: 133–153.

Matthews, Sally. 2015. "Privilege, Solidarity and Social Justice Struggles in South Africa: A View from Grahamstown." *Transformation* 88, no. 1: 1–24.

Mayekiso, Mzwanele. 1996. *Township Politics: Civic Struggles for a New South Africa*. New York: Monthly Review Press.

Mbembe, Achille, Nsizwa Dlamini, and Grace Khunou. 2008. "Soweto Now." In *Johannesburg: The Elusive Metropolis*, edited by Sarah Nuttall and Achille Mbembe, 239–247. Durham, NC: Duke University Press.

McAdam, Doug. 2003. "Beyond Structural Analysis: Toward a More Dynamic Understanding of Social Movements." In *Social Movements and Networks: Relational Approaches to Collective Action*, edited by Mario Diani and Doug McAdam, 281–298. Oxford: Oxford University Press.

———. 1986. "Recruitment to High-Risk Activism: The Case of Freedom Summer." *American Journal of Sociology* 92, no. 1: 64–90.

McIness, Peter. 2006. "Making the Kettle Boil: Rights Talk and Political Mobilisation around Electricity and Water Services in Soweto." Master's thesis, University of the Witwatersrand.

McKinley, Dale, and Ahmed Veriava. 2005. *Arresting Dissents: State Repression and Post-Apartheid Social Movements.* Johannesburg and Cape Town: Center for the Study of Violence and Reconciliation.

Melucci, Alberto. 1996. *Challenging Codes: Collective Action in the Information Age.* Cambridge: Cambridge University Press.

———. 1995. "The Process of Collective Identity." In *Social Movements and Culture*, edited by Hank Johnston and Bert Klandermans, 41–63. Minneapolis: University of Minnesota Press.

Meth, Paula. 2013. "Committees, Witchdoctors and the 'Mother-Body': Everyday Politics in The Township of Cato Manor, South Africa." *Habitat International* 39: 269–277.

Misago, Jean Pierre, Tamlyn Monson, Tara Polzer, and Loren Landau. 2010. *May 2008 Violence Against Foreign Nationals in South Africa: Understanding Causes and Evaluating Responses.* Johannesburg: Forced Migration Studies Program.

Mischi, Julian. 2016. *Le bourg et l'atelier: Sociologie du combat syndical.* Marseille: Agone.

Morrell, Robert, ed. 2001. *Changing Men in Southern Africa.* New York: Zed Books.

Morris, Aldon, and Naomi Braine. 2001. "Social Movements and Oppositional Consciousness." In Mansbridge and Morris, *Oppositional Consciousness*, 20–37.

Mosoetsa, Sarah. 2005. "Compromised Communities and Re-Emerging Civic Engagement in Mpumalanga Township, Durban, KwaZulu-Natal." *Journal of Southern African Studies* 31, no. 4: 868–869.

———. 2011. *Eating from One Pot: The Dynamics of Survival in Poor South African Households.* Johannesburg: Wits University Press.

Mostert, Noël. 1992. *Frontiers: The Epic of South Africa's Creation and the Tragedy of the Xhosa People.* New York: Knopf.

Mukorombindo, Yeukai Chido. 2012. "Social Networks in Recently Established Settlements in Grahamstown East-Rhini, South Africa." Master's thesis, Rhodes University.

Muyeba, Singumbe, and Jeremy Seekings. 2012. "Homeownership, Privacy and Neighbourly Relations in Poor Urban Neighbourhoods in Cape Town, South Africa." *South African Review of Sociology* 43, no. 3: 41–63.

Naepels, Michel. 2011. *Ethnographie, pragmatique, histoire.* Paris: Publications de la Sorbonne.

Naong, M. N. 2007. "Stokvels: A Possible Panacea for Fostering a Savings Culture." *Journal for New Generation Sciences* 7, no. 2: 248–266.

Neal, Sarah, and Karim Murji. 2015. "Sociologies of Everyday Life: Editors' Introduction to the Special Issue." *Sociology* 49, no. 5: 811–819.

Neocosmos, Michael. 2006. *From "Foreign Natives" to "Native Foreigners": Explaining Xenophobia in Postapartheid South Africa: Citizenship and Nationalism, Identity and Politics.* Dakar: CODESRIA.

Nyamnjoh, Francis B. 2016. *#RhodesMustFall: Nibbling at Resilient Colonialism in South Africa*. Bamenda: Langaa RPCIG.

O'Meara, Emily, and Duncan Greaves. 1995. *Grahamstown Reflected*. Grahamstown: Albany Museum.

Oberschall, Anthony. 1973. *Social Conflict and Social Movements*. Englewood Cliffs, NJ: Prentice Hall.

Ortner, Sherry B. 2016. "Dark Anthropology and Its Others: Theory since the Eighties." *HAU: Journal of Ethnographic Theory* 6, no. 1: 47–73.

———. 2005. "Subjectivity and Cultural Critique." *Anthropological Theory* 5, no. 1: 31–52.

Osterweil, Michal. 2014. "Social Movements." In *A Companion to Urban Anthropology*, edited by Donald N. Nonini, 470–485. Oxford: Wiley-Blackwell.

Oxhorn, Philip. 1995. *Organizing Civil Society: The Popular Sectors and the Struggle for Democracy in Chile*. University Park: Pennsylvania State University Press.

———. 2011. *Sustaining Civil Society: Economic Change, Democracy and the Social Construction of Citizenship in Latin America*. University Park: Pennsylvania State University Press.

Palmer, Ian, Nishendra Moodley, and Susan Parnell. 2017. *Building a Capable State: Service Delivery in Post-Apartheid South Africa*. London: Zed Books.

Paret, Marcel. 2018. "Critical Nostalgias in Democratic South Africa." *Sociological Quarterly* 59, no. 4: 678–696.

———. 2017. "Postcolonial Politics: Theorizing Protest from Spaces of Exclusion." In *Southern Resistance in Critical Perspective: The Politics of Protest in South Africa's Contentious Democracy*, edited by Marcel Paret, Carin Runciman, and Luke Sinwell, 55–70. London: Routledge.

Paret, Marcel, Carin Runciman, and Luke Sinwell, eds. 2017. *Southern Resistance in Critical Perspective: The Politics of Protest in South Africa's Contentious Democracy*. London: Routledge.

Passy, Florence. 2005. "Interactions sociales et imbrications des sphères de vie." In *Le désengagement militant*, edited by Olivier Fillieule, 111–130. Paris: Belin.

Pillay, Sarita. 2012. "Spatial Reorganisation, Decentralisation and Dignity: Applying a Fanonian Lens to a Grahamstown Shack Settlement." Retrieved from http://abahlali.org/files/Sarita%20Pillay.pdf. Accessed October 8, 2014.

Piper, Laurence. 2015. "From Party-State to Party-Society in South Africa: SANCO and the Informal Politics of Community Representation in Imizamo Yethu, Hout Bay, Cape Town." In *Popular Politics in South African Cities: Unpacking Community Participation*, edited by Claire Bénit-Gbaffou, 21–41. Cape Town: HSRC Press.

Piper, Laurence, and Fiona Anciano. 2015. "Party over Outsiders, Centre over Branch: How ANC Dominance Works at the Community Level in South Africa." *Transformation* 87: 72–94.

Piper, Laurence, and Claire Bénit-Gbaffou. 2014. "Mediation and the Contradictions of Representing the Urban Poor in South Africa: The Case of SANCO Leaders in Imizamo Yethu in Cape Town, South Africa." In *Mediated Citizenship: The Informal Politics of Speaking for Citizens in the Global South*, edited by Laurence Piper and Bettina von Lieres, 25–42. Basingstoke: Palgrave.

Piper, Laurence, and Bettina von Lieres. 2016. "The Limits of Participatory Democracy and the Rise of the Informal Politics of Mediated Representation in South Africa." *Journal of Civil Society* 12, no. 3: 314–327.

Pithouse, Richard. 2013. "Conjunctural Remarks on the Political Significance of 'the Local.'" *Thesis Eleven* 115, no. 1: 95–111.

———. 2006. "Struggle Is a School: The Rise of a Shack Dwellers' Movement in Durban, South Africa." *Monthly Review* 57, no. 9: 30–51.

Piven, Frances F., and Richard Cloward. 1977. *Poor People's Movements: Why They Succeed, How They Fail*. New York: Vintage Books.

Pointer, Rebecca. 2004. "Questioning the Representation of South Africa's 'New Social Movements': A Case Study of the Mandela Park Anti-Eviction Campaign." *Journal of Asian and African Studies* 39, no. 4: 271–294.

Poole, Deborah. 2005. "An Excess of Description: Ethnography, Race, and Visual Technologies." *Annual Review of Anthropology* 34: 159–179.

Posel, Deborah. 2013. "The ANC Youth League and the Politicization of Race." *Thesis Eleven*, 115, no. 1: 58–76

———. 2014. "Julius Malema and the Postapartheid Public Sphere." *Acta Academica*, 46, no. 1: 32–54.

———. 2010. "Races to Consume: Revisiting South Africa's History of Race, Consumption and the Struggle for Freedom." *Ethnic and Racial Studies* 33, no. 2: 157–175.

———. 2015. "Whither 'Non-Racialism': The 'New' South Africa Turns Twenty-One." *Ethnic and Racial Studies*, 38, no. 13: 2167–2174.

Posel, Dorrit, and Michael Rogan. 2014. *Measured as Poor versus Feeling Poor: Comparing Objective and Subjective Poverty Rates in South Africa*. Helsinki: World Institute for Development Economics Research.

Poupeau, Franck. 2008. *Carnets boliviens 1999–2007: Un goût de poussière*. Montreuil: Aux lieux d'être.

Powell, Derek. 2012. "Imperfect Transition—Local Government Reform in South Africa 1004–2011." In *Local Elections in South Africa: Parties, People, Politics*, edited by Susan Booysen, 11–30. Stellenbosch: SUN Press.

Ramphele, Mamphela. 2002. *Steering by the Stars: Being Young in South Africa*. Cape Town: Tafelberg Publishers.

Reed, Amber R. 2016. "Nostalgia in the Post-Apartheid State." *Anthropology Southern Africa* 39, no. 2: 97–109.

Retière, Jean-Noël. 2003. "Autour de l'autochtonie: Réflexions sur la notion de capital social populaire." *Politix* 63: 121–143.

Revel, Jacques. 1996. *Jeux d'échelles: La micro-analyse à l'expérience*. Paris: Le Seuil & Gallimard.

Rex, John. 1973. *Race, Colonialism and the City*. London: Routledge & Kegan Paul.

Reynolds, Pamela. 2013. *War in Worcester: Youth and the Apartheid State*. New York: Fordham University Press.

Robbins, Joel. 2013. "Beyond the Suffering Subject: Toward an Anthropology of the Good." *Journal of the Royal Anthropological Institute* 19, no. 3: 447–462.

Rogan, Michael, and John Reynolds. 2015. *The Working Poor in South Africa, 1997–2012*. ISER Working Paper. Grahamstown: Institute of Social and Economic Research, Rhodes University.

Ross, Fiona C. 2010. *Raw Life, New Hope: Decency, Housing and Everyday Life in a Post-Apartheid Community*. Cape Town: University of Cape Town Press.

Roy, Arundhati. 2004. *Public Power in the Age of Empire*. New York: Seven Stories.

Runciman, Carin. 2015. "The Decline of the Anti-Privatisation Forum in the Midst of South Africa's 'Rebellion of the Poor.'" *Current Sociology* 63, no. 7: 961–979.

———. 2017. "South African Social Movements in the Neoliberal Age." In Marcel Paret, Carin Runciman, and Luke Sinwell, *Southern Resistance in Critical Perspective*, 37–52.

Ryan, James R. 1997. *Picturing Empire: Photography and the Visualization of the British Empire*. Chicago: University of Chicago Press.

Salman, Ton, and Willem Assies. 2017. "Anthropology and the Study of Social Movements." In *Handbook of Social Movements across Disciplines*, 2nd edition, edited by Conny Roggeband and Bert Klandermans, 57–101. Berlin: Springer.

Sarrat, Austin, and Stuart Scheingold, eds. 1998. *Cause Lawyering: Political Commitments and Professional Responsibilities*. Oxford: Oxford University Press.

Sassen, Saskia. 2014. *Expulsions: Brutality and Complexity in the Global Economy*. Cambridge, MA: Harvard University Press.

Scannell, Leila, and Robert Gifford. 2010. "Defining Place Attachment: A Tripartite Organizing Framework." *Journal of Environmental Psychology* 30, no. 1: 1–10.

Schoeman, Karel. 1991. *Another Country*. London: Sinclair-Stevenson.

Scott, James C. 2008. "Dans le dos du pouvoir." *Vacarme* 42: 4–12.

———. 1990. *Domination and the Arts of Resistance: Hidden Transcripts*. New Haven, CT: Yale University Press.

———. 1985. *Weapons of the Weak: Everyday Forms of Peasant Resistance*. New Haven, CT: Yale University Press.

Scully, Ben. 2016. "From the Shop Floor to the Kitchen Table: The Shifting Centre of Precarious Workers' Politics in South Africa." *Review of African Political Economy* 148: 295–311.

Seekings, Jeremy. 2008. *Beyond "Fluidity": Kinship and Households as Social Projects*. Working Paper 237, Centre for Social Science Research, University of Cape Town.

———. 1996. "The Decline of South Africa's Civic Organizations, 1990–1996." *Critical Sociology* 22, no. 3: 135–157.

———. 2014. "Taking Disadvantage Seriously: The 'Underclass' in Post-Apartheid South Africa." *Africa* 84, no. 1: 135–141.

Seekings, Jeremy, and Nicoli Nattrass. 2005. *Class, Race, and Inequality in South Africa.* New Haven, CT : Yale University Press.

———. 2015. *Policy, Politics and Poverty in South Africa.* Basingstoke: Palgrave.

Sewell, William H. 2001. "Space in Contentious Politics." In *Silence and Voice in the Study of Contentious Politics,* edited by Ronald R. Aminzade et al., 51–88. Cambridge: Cambridge University Press.

Shah, Alpa. 2013. "The Intimacy of Insurgency: Beyond Coercion, Greed or Grievance in Maoist India." *Economy and Society* 42, no. 3: 480–506.

Shefner, Jon. 2008. *The Illusion of Civil Society: Democratization and Community Mobilization in Low-Income Mexico.* University Park: Pennsylvania State University Press.

Sinwell, Luke. 2010. "The Alexandra Development Forum: The Tyranny of Invited Participatory Spaces?" *Transformation* 74: 23–46.

———. 2016. *The Spirit of Marikana: The Rise of Insurgent Trade Unionism in South Africa.* London: Pluto Press.

Sivaramakrishnan, Kalyanakrishnan. 2005. "Some Intellectual Genealogies for the Concept of Everyday Resistance." *American Anthropologist* 107, no. 3: 346–355.

Skinner, Caroline, and Vanessa Watson. 2018. "The Informal Economy in Cities of the Global South: Challenges to the Planning Lexicon." In *The Routledge Companion to Planning in the Global South,* edited by Gautam Bhan, Smita Srinivas, and Vanessa Watson, 140–152. Oxford: Routledge.

Smith, Gavin A. 1989. *Livelihood and Resistance: Peasants and the Politics of Land in Peru.* Berkeley: University of California Press.

———. 2011. "Selective Hegemony and Beyond-Populations with 'No Productive Function': A Framework for Enquiry." *Identities* 18, no. 1: 2–38.

Snow, David A. 2004. "Social Movements as Challenges to Authority: Resistance to an Emerging Conceptual Hegemony." In *Authority in Contention: Research in Social Movements, Conflict, and Change,* edited by Daniel J. Meyers and Daniel M. Cress, 3–25. New York: Elsevier.

Snow, David A., and Doug McAdam. 2000. "Identity Work Processes in the Context of Social Movements: Clarifying the Identity/Movement Nexus." In *Self, Identity, and Social Movements,* edited by Sheldon Stryker, Timothy J. Owens, and Robert W. White, 41–67. Minneapolis: University of Minnesota Press.

Southall, Roger. 2016. *The New Black Middle Class in South Africa.* Johannesburg: Jacana Media.

Spiegel, Andrew D., and Heike Becker. "South Africa: Anthropology or Anthropologies." *American Anthropologist* 117, no. 4: 754–760.

Staggenborg, Suzanne. 1998. *Gender, Family, and Social Movements*. Thousand Oaks, CA: Pine Forge Press.

Statistics South Africa. 2019. *Inequality Trends in South Africa: A Multidimensional Diagnostic of Inequality*. Pretoria: StatsSA.

———. 2017. *Poverty Trends in South Africa: An Examination of absolute poverty between 2006 and 2015*. Pretoria: StatsSA.

———. 2002. *Quarterly Labour Force Survey* 1.

Steyn Kotze, Joleen. 2006. "Service Delivery and Voting Behaviour: A Comparative Overview of the 2004 General Election and 2006 Municipal Elections in South Africa." *Politeia* 25, no. 3: 207–218.

Swartz, Sharlene. 2010. *Ikasi: The Moral Ecology of South Africa's Township Youth*. Johannesburg: Wits University Press.

Swartz, Sharlene, James Hamilton Harding, and Ariane De Lannoy. 2013. "*Ikasi Style* and the Quiet Violence of Dreams: A Critique of Youth Belonging in Post-Apartheid South Africa." In *Youth Citizenship and the Politics of Belonging*, edited by Sharlene Swartz and Madeleine Arnot, 27–40. New York: Routledge.

Tarrow, Sidney. 2013. "Contentious Politics." In *The Wiley-Blackwell Encyclopedia of Social and Political Movements*, edited by David Snow et al., 266–270. Malden, MA: Wiley-Blackwell.

———. 2005. *The New Transnational Activism*. Cambridge: Cambridge University Press.

Terreblanche, Sampie J. 2002. *A History of Inequality in South Africa, 1652 to 2002*. Pietermaritzburg: University of Natal Press.

Theron, Jan. 2010. "Informalization from Above, Informalization from Below: The Options for Organization." *African Studies Quarterly* 11, no. 2/3: 87–105.

Thévenot, Laurent. 2006. *L'action au pluriel: Sociologie des régimes d'engagement*. Paris: La Découverte.

———. 2015. "Making Commonality in the Plural on the Basis of Binding Engagements." In *Social Bonds as Freedom: Revisiting the Dichotomy of the Universal and the Particular*, edited by Paul Dumouchel and Reiko Gotoh, 82–108. New York: Berghahn.

Thompson, Edward P. 1971. "The Moral Economy of the English Crowd in the 18th Century." *Past & Present* 50: 76–136.

———. 1975. *Whigs and Hunters: The Origin of the Black Act*. New York: Pantheon Books.

Thornton, Robert, and Mamphela Ramphele. 1988. "The Quest for Community." In *South African Keywords: The Uses and Abuses of Political Concepts*, edited by Emile Boonzaier and John Sharp, 29–39. Cape Town: David Philip.

Tilly, Charles. 1986. *The Contentious France*. Cambridge, MA: Harvard University Press.

———. 1995. "Contentious Repertoires in Great Britain, 1758–1834." In *Repertoires & Cycles of Collective Action*, edited by Mark Traugott, 15–42. Durham, NC: Duke University Press.

———. 2000. "Spaces of Contention." *Mobilizations* 5, no. 2: 135–159.

Tournadre, Jérôme. 2017. "'Because We Are the Only Ones in the Community!': Protest, Daily Life and Poor Neighborhoods in South Africa." *Focaal: Journal of Global and Historical Anthropology* 78: 52–64.

———. 2018. *A Turbulent South Africa: Post-Apartheid Social Protest*. Albany: State University of New York Press.

Turner, Ralph H. 1987. "Articulating Self and Social Structure." In *Self and Identity: Psychosocial Perspectives*, edited by Krysia Yardley and Terry Honess, 119–132. New York: Wiley.

Valodia, Imraan, and Richard Devey. 2010. "Formal-Informal Economy Linkages: What Implications for Poverty in South Africa." *Law, Democracy & Development* 14: 118–143.

Van Dyke, Nella, Sarah A. Soule, and Verta Taylor. 2004. "The Targets of Social Movements: Beyond a Focus on the State." In *Authority in Contention*, edited by Daniel J. Myers and Daniel M. Cress, 27–51. Bingley, UK: Emerald Group.

van Heusden, Peter, and Rebecca Pointer. 2006. *Subjectivity, Politics and Neo-Liberalism in Post-Apartheid Cape Town*. Durban: Centre for Civil Society.

Varma, Rashmi. 2012. *The Postcolonial City and Its Subjects: London, Nairobi, Bombay*. New York: Routledge.

Veblen, Thorstein. 2000. *The Theory of the Leisure Class*. New Brunswick, NJ: Transaction Publishers.

von Schnitzler, Antina. 2016. *Democracy's Infrastructure: Techno-Politics & Protest after Apartheid*. Princeton, NJ: Princeton University Press.

———. 2014. "Performing Dignity: Human Rights, Citizenship, and the Techno-Politics of Law in South Africa." *American Ethnologist* 41, no. 2: 336–350.

Wacquant, Loïc. 2004. *Body and Soul: Notebooks of an Apprentice Boxer*. New York: Oxford University Press.

———. 2007. *Urban Outcasts: A Comparative Sociology of Advanced Marginality*. Cambridge: Polity Press.

Walker, Sherryl. 1982. *Women and Resistance in South Africa*. London: Onyx Press.

Wells, Julia C. 2003. "From Grahamstown to Egazini: Using Art and History to Construct Post Colonial Identity and Healing in the New South Africa." *African Studies* 62, no. 1: 79–98.

Wesemüller, Ellen. 2005. *African Nationalism from Apartheid to Post-Apartheid South Africa: A Critical Analysis of ANC Party Political Discourse*. Stuttgart: Ibidem-Verlag.

Withley, Meredith, Laura A. Hayden, and Daniel Gould. 2013. "Growing Up in the Kayamandi Township: The Role of Sport in Helping Young People Overcome Challenges Within Their Community." *Qualitative Research in Sport, Exercise and Health* 5, no. 3: 373–397.

World Bank. 2018. *Overcoming Poverty and Inequality in South Africa: An Assessment of Drivers, Constraints and Opportunities.* Washington, DC: International Bank for Reconstruction and Development/The World Bank.

Yeoh, Brenda S. A. 2001. "Postcolonial Cities." *Progress in Human Geography* 25, no. 3: 456–468.

Young, Michael. 1998. *Malinowski's Kirwina: Fieldwork Photography 1915–1918.* Chicago: University of Chicago Press.

Zorn, Annika. 2013. "Poor People's Movements." In *The Wiley-Blackwell Encyclopedia of Social and Political Movements,* edited by David Snow, Donatella della Porta, Bert Klandermans, and Doug McAdam, 983–986. Oxford: Blackwell.

Zuern, Elke. 2011. *The Politics of Necessity: Community Organizing and Democracy in South Africa.* Madison: University of Wisconsin Press.

INDEX

civil society, 167–169, 172, 192, 230, 232. *See also* Chatterjee, Partha
clientelism, 43, 144, 179
Cloward, Richard, 11, 156
commitment(s), 15, 18, 19–21, 39, 50, 51, 58, 62, 63, 66, 68, 70, 72, 74, 95, 96, 104, 106–114, 120, 121, 124, 127–129, 132, 140, 142, 144, 147, 160, 164, 175, 177, 178, 189–200, 202, 212–217, 219, 225–227, 235, 237, 256, 260, 265, 266, 276, 281
community: caring community, 52, 224; community-based organization(s), 14, 50, 67, 81, 87, 163, 164, 232, 244, 248; community leader(s), 2, 16, 154, 163, 171, 172, 176–183, 185, 186, 191, 192, 193, 217, 222, 231, 234, 236, 253, 260, 265; community meeting(s), 57, 59, 69, 79, 82, 87, 113, 124, 149, 154–156, 158, 162, 165, 166, 185, 190, 197, 199, 209, 214, 234, 254, 265, 278; Community Work Programme (CWP), 88–90, 279n5; moral economy and, 59, 179; sense of, 46, 50, 54, 59–61, 69, 70, 78, 195; values of, 59, 60, 62, 63, 165, 172, 214, 266
Congress of South African Students (COSAS), 182
Congress of South African Trade Unions (COSATU), 83, 84, 155, 127, 248, 263, 286n1
contentious politics, 4, 6, 18, 272n7
corruption, 3, 36, 101, 124, 156, 159, 172, 192, 210, 235, 241

daily life, 7, 17, 21, 23, 25, 26, 49, 71, 147, 159, 175, 204, 206, 225, 226, 246, 254, 260, 267
Das, Veena, 7, 11, 20, 266
Davis, Mike, 31, 282
de Vries, Pieter, 176, 177
Democratic Alliance (DA), 50, 126, 155, 182, 246, 256, 263, 264
désoeuvrement, 206, 211. *See also* waithood
Di Nunzio, Marco, 208
dignity; 13, 89, 109, 122, 130, 135, 138, 139, 145, 147, 150, 166
Dlamini, Jacob, 59, 65, 157, 179, 255, 278

Economic Freedom Fighters (EFF), 158, 217, 224, 256, 267, 283n9
ethnography, 18, 21, 22, 25, 42, 59, 162
Escobar, Arturo, 9, 14
everyday, 7, 8, 9, 13, 14, 16–18, 38, 42, 46, 51, 54, 68, 78, 80, 84, 85, 104, 139, 149, 180, 224, 239, 260, 266, 272n10. *See also* daily life; ordinary

Fanon, Frantz, 41, 102, 103, 125, 280
Fassin, Didier, 101, 123, 166, 267, 282n3

feminism, 79, 200, 221, 223, 224. *See also* gender; LGBT
Ferguson, James, 34, 39, 89, 135, 152, 231
football, 29, 58, 62, 64, 71–74, 104, 115, 121, 124, 127, 187, 188, 265

gender, 16–18, 78, 170, 222, 225, 266, 285n9. *See also* feminism; LGBT
Gini coefficient, 31, 145, 274n6, 274n7. *See also* poverty
Goldblatt, David, 228
Gould, Roger, 6, 114, 161
Group Areas Act, 54, 65

Halbwachs, Maurice, 25, 57
Hani, Chris, 209, 284n7
Hart, Gillian, 251, 252
Hart, Michael, 122
Harvey, David, 140
Holston, James, 43, 90, 146

identity, 2, 54, 68, 106, 122, 141, 193, 217, 273n25; collective, 65, 87, 88, 93; subordinate, 132
imbizo(s), 171, 283n17
informal economy, 11, 32, 33, 43, 83, 88, 96, 111, 123, 150, 151, 233, 268, 275n13
informal settlement(s), 3, 13, 33, 34, 39, 42, 75, 124, 139, 154, 155, 161, 191, 206, 268, 274n8
Integrated Development Plan (IDP), 47, 48, 170, 234, 235, 283n16
intimacy, 10, 16, 17, 19, 41, 54, 65, 79, 95, 107, 139, 188, 224, 267; "intimacy of insurgency," 10
invented spaces, 170. *See also* invited spaces
invited spaces, 170. *See also* invented spaces

Jasper, James, 62, 63, 134
Jeffrey, Craig, 206, 207
Jubilee South Africa, 46

Klein, Naomi, 12, 282n12, 285n2
Koster, Martijn, 176, 177

Laclau, Ernesto, 69, 93
Landless People's Movement (LPM), 3, 46
Lazar, Sian, 10, 226, 284n1
Lee, Rebekah, 54, 64
LGBT, 13, 79, 222; pride march, 200. *See also* feminism
Li, Tania Murray, 39, 152
liberal democracy, 3, 12, 30, 168, 169, 233, 255, 267, 283n9
lived experience, 18, 145, 266

Jérôme Tournadre is a research fellow at the French National Center for Scientific Research (CNRS). He is the author of *A Turbulent South Africa: Post-Apartheid Social Protest*.

www.ingramcontent.com/pod-product-compliance
Lightning Source LLC
Chambersburg PA
CBHW022138020426
42334CB00015B/949